## WORDS EDITION

D0313059

**KINGSWAY MUSIC**
**EASTBOURNE**

The words of most of the songs in this publication
are covered by the Christian Copyright Licence

United Kingdom
CCL UK Ltd, P.O. Box 1339, Eastbourne, East Sussex, BN21 4YF

United States
CCL Inc., 6130 NE 78th Court, Suite C11, Portland, Oregon 97218

Australasia
CCL Asia Pacific Ltd, P.O. Box 1254, Castle Hill, NSW 2154


ISBN 0 86065 936 4
Music edition ISBN 0 86065 935 6
Large Print Words edition ISBN 0 86065 937 2

Produced by Bookprint Creative Services
P.O. Box 827, BN21 3YJ, England for
KINGSWAY MUSIC LTD
Lottbridge Drove, Eastbourne, E. Sussex BN23 6NT
Printed in Great Britain

**1**

**ABBA FATHER,** let me be
Yours and Yours alone.
May my will for ever be
Evermore Your own.
Never let my heart grow cold,
Never let me go.
Abba Father, let me be
Yours and Yours alone.

**2**
W. H. Monk.

**ABIDE WITH ME,** fast falls the eventide;
The darkness deepens, Lord, with me abide;
When other helpers fail and comforts flee,
Help of the helpless, O abide with me.

Swift to its close ebbs out life's little day;
Earth's joys grow dim, its glories pass away;
Change and decay in all around I see;
O Thou who changest not, abide with me.

I need Thy presence every passing hour;
What but Thy grace can foil the tempter's
     power?
Who like Thyself my guide and stay can be?
Through cloud and sunshine, O abide with me.

I fear no foe, with Thee at hand to bless;
Ills have no weight, and tears no bitterness.
Where is death's sting? Where, grave, thy
     victory?
I triumph still, if Thou abide with me.

Reveal Thyself before my closing eyes;
Shine through the gloom, and point me to the
     skies,
Heaven's morning breaks, and earth's vain
     shadows flee;
In life, in death, O Lord, abide with me.

**3**

**AH LORD GOD,** Thou hast made the heavens,
And the earth by Thy great power.
Ah Lord God, Thou hast made the heavens,
And the earth by Thine outstretched arm.

Nothing is too difficult for Thee,
Nothing is too difficult for Thee.
O great and mighty God,
Great in counsel and mighty in deed,
Nothing, nothing, absolutely nothing,
Nothing is too difficult for Thee.

**4**

**ALLELUIA,** alleluia,
Alleluia, alleluia,
Alleluia, alleluia,
Alleluia, alleluia.

He's my Saviour…

He is worthy…

I will praise Him…

**5**

**ALLELUIA! ALLELUIA!**
*Opening our hearts to Him,*
*Singing alleluia! alleluia!*
*Jesus is our King!*

Create in us, O God,
A humble heart that sets us free
To proclaim the wondrous majesty,
Of our Father in heaven.

We bear the name of Christ,
Justified, we meet with Him.
His words and presence calm our fear,
Revealing God our Father here.

Let kindred voices join,
Honouring the Lamb of God,
Who teaches us by bread and wine
The mystery of His body.

Pour out Your Spirit on us,
Empowering us to live as one,
To carry Your redeeming love
To a world enslaved by sin.

**6**

**ALLELUIA, ALLELUIA,**
*Give thanks to the risen Lord,*
*Alleluia, Alleluia, give praise to His name.*

Jesus is Lord of all the earth,
He is the King of creation.

Spread the good news o'er all the earth,
Jesus has died and has risen.

We have been crucified with Christ,
Now we shall live for ever.

God has proclaimed the just reward,
Life for all men, Alleluia!

Come let us praise the living God,
Joyfully sing to our Saviour.

**7**

**ALL HAIL KING JESUS!** All hail Emmanuel!
King of kings, Lord of lords,
Bright morning star.
And throughout eternity I'll sing Your praises,
And I'll reign with You throughout eternity.

**8**

**ALL HAIL THE LAMB,** enthroned on high;
His praise shall be our battle cry.
He reigns victorious, forever glorious,
His name is Jesus, He is the Lord.

**9**

**ALL HAIL THE POWER OF JESUS' NAME!**
Let angels prostrate fall;
Bring forth the royal diadem,
And crown Him Lord of all.

Crown Him, ye martyrs of your God,
Who from His altar call;
Extol Him in whose path ye trod,
And crown Him Lord of all.

Ye seed of Israel's chosen race,
Ye ransomed of the fall,
Hail Him who saves you by His grace,
And crown Him Lord of all.

Sinners, whose love can ne'er forget
The wormwood and the gall,
Go, spread your trophies at His feet,
And crown Him Lord of all.

Let every kindred, every tribe
On this terrestrial ball,
To Him all majesty ascribe,
And crown Him Lord of all.

O that, with yonder sacred throng,
We at His feet may fall,
Join in the everlasting song,
And crown Him Lord of all!

**10**

**ALL HEAVEN DECLARES**
The glory of the risen Lord.
Who can compare
With the beauty of the Lord?
Forever He will be
The Lamb upon the throne.
I gladly bow the knee
And worship Him alone.

I will proclaim
The glory of the risen Lord,
Who once was slain
To reconcile man to God.
Forever You will be
The Lamb upon the throne.
I gladly bow the knee
And worship You alone.

**11**

**ALL HEAVEN WAITS** with bated breath,
For saints on earth to pray.
Majestic angels ready stand
With swords of fiery blade.
Astounding power awaits a word
From God's resplendent throne.
But God awaits our prayer of faith
That cries 'Your will be done.'

Awake, O church, arise and pray;
Complaining words discard.
The Spirit comes to fill your mouth
With truth, His mighty sword.
Go place your feet on Satan's ground
And there proclaim Christ's name,
In step with heaven's armies march
To conquer and to reign!

Now in our hearts and on our lips
The word of faith is near,
Let heaven's will on earth be done,
Let heaven flow from here.
Come blend your prayers with Jesus' own
Before the Father's throne,
And as the incense clouds ascend
God's holy fire rains down.

Soon comes the day when with a shout
King Jesus shall appear,
And with Him all the church,
From every age, shall fill the air.
The brightness of His coming shall
Consume the lawless one,
As with a word the breath of God
Tears down his rebel throne.

One body here, by heaven inspired,
We seek prophetic power;
In Christ agreed, one heart and voice,
To speak this day, this hour,
In every place where chaos rules
And evil forces brood;
Let Jesus' voice speak like the roar
Of a great multitude.

**12**

Roy Turner.
Copyright © Kingsway's
Thankyou Music 1984.

## ALL OVER THE WORLD THE SPIRIT IS MOVING,

All over the world as the prophet said it would
  be;
All over the world there's a mighty revelation
Of the glory of the Lord, as the waters cover
  the sea.

All over His church God's Spirit is moving,
All over His church as the prophet said it would
  be;
All over His church there's a mighty revelation
Of the glory of the Lord, as the waters cover
  the sea.

Right here in this place the Spirit is moving,
Right here in this place as the prophet said it
  would be;
Right here in this place there's a mighty
  revelation
Of the glory of the Lord, as the waters cover
  the sea.

**13**   William Kethe.

## ALL PEOPLE THAT ON EARTH DO DWELL,

Sing to the Lord with cheerful voice;
Him serve with mirth, His praise forthtell,
Come ye before Him and rejoice.

Know that the Lord is God indeed,
Without our aid He did us make:
We are His flock, He doth us feed,
And for His sheep He doth us take.

O enter then His gates with praise,
Approach with joy His courts unto:
Praise, laud, and bless His name always,
For it is seemly so to do.

For why, the Lord our God is good;
His mercy is for ever sure;
His truth at all times firmly stood,
And shall from age to age endure.

Praise God from whom all blessings flow,
Praise Him all creatures here below,
Praise Him above, ye heavenly hosts;
Praise Father, Son and Holy Ghost.

**14**   Cecil F. Alexander.

## ALL THINGS BRIGHT AND BEAUTIFUL,
*All creatures great and small,*
*All things wise and wonderful,*
*The Lord God made them all.*

Each little flower that opens,
Each little bird that sings,
He made their glowing colours,
He made their tiny wings.

The purple-headed mountain,
The river running by,
The sunset, and the morning
That brightens up the sky;

The cold wind in the winter,
The pleasant summer sun,
The ripe fruits in the garden,
He made them every one.

He gave us eyes to see them,
And lips that we might tell
How great is God Almighty,
Who has made all things well.

**15**   Marc Nelson.
Copyright © Mercy Publishing/
Kingsway's Thankyou Music 1989.

## ALL YOU ANGELS ROUND HIS THRONE,
  praise Him!
All you people on earth below, praise Him!
Mountains high and oceans wide, praise Him!
Beasts of the field and birds of the sky, praise
  Him!

  *Give Him praise, give Him praise,*
  *Give Him praise from your hearts.*
  *Give Him praise, give Him praise,*
  *Give Him praise for He is God.*

All the angels round Your throne praise You!
All the people on earth below praise You!
Mountains high and oceans wide praise you!
Beasts of the field and birds of the sky praise
  You!

  *We give You praise, we give You praise,*
  *We give You praise from our hearts.*
  *We give You praise, we give You praise,*
  *We give You praise for You are God.*

**16**   Austin Martin.
Copyright © Kingsway's
Thankyou Music 1983.

## ALMIGHTY GOD, we bring You praise
For Your Son, the Word of God,
By whose power the world was made,
By whose blood we are redeemed.
Morning star, the Father's glory,
We now worship and adore You,
In our hearts Your light has risen,
Jesus, Lord, we worship You.

**17**

**ALMIGHTY GOD, OUR HEAVENLY FATHER,**
We have sinned against You,
And against our fellow men,
In thought and word and deed,
Through negligence, through weakness,
Through our own deliberate fault.
We are truly sorry
And repent of all our sins.
For the sake of Your Son Jesus Christ,
Who died for us,
Who died for us,
Who died for us,
Forgive us all that is past;
And grant that we may serve You
In newness of life.
To the glory of Your name, *(Men)*
To the glory of Your name, *(Women)*
To the glory of Your name, *(Men)*
To the glory of Your name, *(Women)*
To the glory of Your name. *(All)*
Amen, amen.

**18**

**ALMIGHTY SOVEREIGN LORD,** Creator God,
You made the heavens and the earth.
You've spoken to the world,
Yourself the living Word,
You give us eyes to see Your kingdom.

*So stretch out Your hand, O God,*
*In signs and wonders,*
*We rest our faith on Your almighty power.*
*Stretch out Your hand, O God,*
*To heal and deliver. We declare,*
*We declare Your kingdom is here.*

Stir up Your people like a mighty wind,
Come shake us, wake us from our sleep.
Give us compassion, Lord,
Love for Your holy word,
Give us the courage of Your kingdom.

Why do so many stand against You now,
Bringing dishonour to Your name?
Consider how they mock,
But we will never stop
Speaking with boldness of Your kingdom.

**19**

**AMAZING GRACE!** how sweet the sound
That saved a wretch like me;
I once was lost, but now am found,
Was blind, but now I see.

'Twas grace that taught my heart to fear,
And grace my fears relieved;
How precious did that grace appear,
The hour I first believed!

Through many dangers, toils and snares
I have already come;
'Tis grace that brought me safe thus far,
And grace will lead me home.

The Lord has promised good to me,
His word my hope secures;
He will my shield and portion be
As long as life endures.

Yes, when this heart and flesh shall fail,
And mortal life shall cease,
I shall possess within the veil
A life of joy and peace.

When we've been there a thousand years,
Bright shining as the sun,
We've no less days to sing God's praise
Than when we first begun.

**20**

**AN ARMY OF ORDINARY PEOPLE,**
A kingdom where love is the key,
A city, a light to the nations,
Heirs to the promise are we.
A people whose life is in Jesus,
A nation together we stand.
Only through grace are we worthy,
Inheritors of the land.

*A new day is dawning,*
*A new age to come,*
*When the children of promise*
*Shall flow together as one.*
*A truth long neglected,*
*But the time has now come*
*When the children of promise*
*Shall flow together as one.*

A people without recognition,
But with Him a destiny sealed,
Called to a heavenly vision,
His purpose shall be fulfilled.
Come, let us stand strong together,
Abandon ourselves to the King,
His love shall be ours for ever,
This victory song we shall sing.

**21**

**AND CAN IT BE** that I should gain
An interest in the Saviour's blood?
Died He for me, who caused His pain?
For me, who Him to death pursued?
Amazing love! how can it be
That Thou, my God, shouldst die for me?

'Tis mystery all! The Immortal dies:
Who can explore His strange design?
In vain the first-born seraph tries
To sound the depths of love divine!
'Tis mercy all! let earth adore,
Let angel minds inquire no more.

He left His Father's throne above,
So free, so infinite His grace;
Emptied Himself of all but love,
And bled for Adam's helpless race.
'Tis mercy all, immense and free;
For, O my God, it found out me.

Long my imprisoned spirit lay
Fast bound in sin and nature's night;
Thine eye diffused a quickening ray,
I woke, the dungeon flamed with light;
My chains fell off, my heart was free;
I rose, went forth, and followed Thee.

No condemnation now I dread;
Jesus, and all in Him, is mine!
Alive in Him, my living Head,
And clothed in righteousness divine,
Bold I approach the eternal throne,
And claim the crown, through Christ my own.


## 22   Author unknown.

### A NEW COMMANDMENT
I give unto you,
That you love one another
As I have loved you,
That you love one another
As I have loved you.
By this shall all men know
That you are My disciples,
If you have love one for another.
By this shall all men know
That you are My disciples,
If you have love one for another.


## 23   James Montgomery.

### ANGELS FROM THE REALMS OF GLORY,
Wing your flight o'er all the earth;
Ye who sang creation's story,
Now proclaim Messiah's birth:

*Come and worship*
*Christ, the new-born King.*
*Come and worship*
*Christ, the new-born King.*

Shepherds, in the field abiding,
Watching o'er your flocks by night,
God with man is now residing,
Yonder shines the infant-light:

Sages, leave your contemplations,
Brighter visions beam afar;
Seek the great desire of nations,
Ye have seen His natal star:

Saints, before the altar bending,
Watching long in hope and fear,
Suddenly the Lord descending
In His temple shall appear:


## 24    Francis Pott.

### ANGEL VOICES EVER SINGING
Round Thy throne of light,
Angel harps for ever ringing,
Rest not day nor night;
Thousands only live to bless Thee,
And confess Thee
Lord of might.

Thou who art beyond the farthest
Mortal eye can scan,
Can it be that Thou regardest
Songs of sinful man?
Can we know that Thou art near us
And wilt hear us?
Yes, we can.

Yes, we know that Thou rejoicest
O'er each work of Thine;
Thou didst ears and hands and voices
For Thy praise design;
Craftsman's art and music's measure
For Thy pleasure
All combine.

In Thy house, great God, we offer
Of Thine own to Thee,
And for Thine acceptance proffer,
All unworthily,
Hearts and minds and hands and voices
In our choicest
Psalmody.

Honour, glory, might, and merit
Thine shall ever be,
Father, Son, and Holy Spirit,
Blessèd Trinity.
Of the best that Thou hast given
Earth and heaven
Render Thee.


## 25   Martin Luther.
Tr. Thomas Carlyle.

### A SAFE STRONGHOLD OUR GOD IS STILL,
A trusty shield and weapon;
He'll help us clear from all the ill
That hath us now o'ertaken.
The ancient prince of hell
Hath risen with purpose fell;
Strong mail of craft and power
He weareth in this hour;
On earth is not His fellow.

With force of arms we nothing can,
Full soon were we down-ridden;
But for us fights the proper Man,
Whom God Himself hath bidden.
Ask ye: Who is this same?
Christ Jesus is His name,
The Lord Sabaoth's Son;
He, and no other one,
Shall conquer in the battle.

And were this world all devils o'er,
And watching to devour us,
We lay it not to heart so sore;
Not they can overpower us.
And let the prince of ill
Look grim as e'er he will,
He harms us not a whit;
For why? his doom is writ;
A word shall quickly slay him.

God's word, for all their craft and force,
One moment will not linger,
But, spite of hell, shall have its course;
'Tis written by His finger.
And though they take our life,
Goods, honour, children, wife,
Yet is their profit small:
These things shall vanish all;
The city of God remaineth.

**26**  Mary Lou Locke and Mary Kirkbride.
Copyright © Peter West/
Integrity's Hosanna! Music.
Adm. Kingsway's Thankyou Music 1979.

**ASCRIBE GREATNESS** to our God, the Rock,
His work is perfect and all His ways are just.
Ascribe greatness to our God, the Rock,
His work is perfect and all His ways are just.
A God of faithfulness and without injustice,
Good and upright is He;
A God of faithfulness and without injustice,
Good and upright is He.

**27**  Martin Nystrom.
Copyright © Restoration Music Ltd/
Sovereign Lifestyle Music Ltd 1983.

**AS THE DEER** pants for the water,
So my soul longs after You.
You alone are my heart's desire
And I long to worship You.

*You alone are my strength, my shield,*
*To You alone may my spirit yield.*
*You alone are my heart's desire*
*And I long to worship You.*

I want You more than gold or silver,
Only You can satisfy.
You alone are the real joy-giver
And the apple of my eye.

You're my Friend and You are my Brother,
Even though You are a King.
I love You more than any other,
So much more than anything.

**28**  John Daniels.
Copyright © Springtide/
Word Music (UK)/CopyCare Ltd 1979.

**AS WE ARE GATHERED** Jesus is here;
One with each other, Jesus is here.
Joined by the Spirit, washed in the blood,
Part of the body, the church of God.
As we are gathered Jesus is here,
One with each other, Jesus is here.

**29**  Dale Garratt.
Copyright © Scripture in Song/
CopyCare Ltd 1982.

**AS WE COME WITH PRAISE** *before His*
  *majesty,*
*We will celebrate with joy and victory,*
*For the Lord has come and set His people*
  *free,*
*We are marching on with Him,*
*He's our deliverer.*
  *(Repeat)*

The two-edgèd sword is sharpened in our
  hand.
We come with vengeance to possess our land.
We bind the kings because of God's right hand
And carry out the sentence that our God has
  planned.

  *(Last time)*
*As we come with praise before His majesty*
*We will celebrate with joy and victory,*
*For the Lord has come and set His people*
  *free,*
*We are marching on with Him,*
*He's our deliverer,*
*He's our deliverer,*
*He's our deliverer,*
*He's our deliverer.*

**30**  Dave Bilbrough.
Copyright © Kingsway's
Thankyou Music 1990.

**AS WE SEEK YOUR FACE,**
May we know Your heart,
Feel Your presence, acceptance,
As we seek Your face.

Move among us now,
Come reveal Your power,
Show Your presence, acceptance,
Move among us now.

At Your feet we fall,
Sovereign Lord,
We cry 'Holy, holy'
At Your feet we fall.

**31**  W. C. Dix.

**AS WITH GLADNESS** men of old
Did the guiding star behold;
As with joy they hailed its light,
Leading onward, beaming bright,
So, most gracious God, may we
Evermore be led by Thee.

As with joyful steps they sped,
Saviour, to Thy lowly bed,
There to bend the knee before
Thee whom heaven and earth adore,
So may we with willing feet
Ever seek Thy mercy-seat.

As they offered gifts most rare
At Thy cradle rude and bare,
So may we with holy joy,
Pure, and free from sin's alloy,
All our costliest treasures bring,
Christ, to Thee, our heavenly King.

Holy Jesus, every day
Keep us in the narrow way;
And, when earthly things are past,
Bring our ransomed souls at last
Where they need no star to guide,
Where no clouds Thy glory hide.

In the heavenly country bright
Need they no created light;
Thou its light, its joy, its crown,
Thou its sun, which goes not down.
There for ever may we sing
Hallelujahs to our King.

**32**   Caroline Maria Noel.

## AT THE NAME OF JESUS
Every knee shall bow,
Every tongue confess Him
King of glory now;
'Tis the Father's pleasure
We should call Him Lord,
Who from the beginning
Was the mighty Word.

Humbled for a season,
To receive a name
From the lips of sinners
Unto whom He came;
Faithfully He bore it
Spotless to the last,
Brought it back victorious,
When from death He passed.

Bore it up triumphant
With its human light,
Through all ranks of creatures
To the central height,
To the throne of Godhead,
To the Father's breast,
Filled it with the glory
Of that perfect rest.

In your hearts enthrone Him;
There let Him subdue
All that is not holy,
All that is not true;
Crown Him as your captain
In temptation's hour,
Let His will enfold you
In its light and power.

Brothers, this Lord Jesus
Shall return again,
With His Father's glory,
With His angel-train;
For all wreaths of empire
Meet upon His brow,
And our hearts confess Him
King of glory now.

**33**   Graham Kendrick.
Copyright © Make Way Music 1988.

### AT THIS TIME OF GIVING,
*Gladly now we bring*
*Gifts of goodness and mercy*
*From a heavenly King.*

Earth could not contain the treasures
Heaven holds for you,
Perfect joy and lasting pleasures,
Love so strong and true.

May His tender love surround you
At this Christmastime;
May you see His smiling face
That in the darkness shines.

But the many gifts He gives
Are all poured out from one;
Come receive the greatest gift,
The gift of God's own Son.

Lai, lai, lai... (etc.)

**34**   David Fellingham.
Copyright © Kingsway's
Thankyou Music 1982.

### AT YOUR FEET WE FALL, mighty risen Lord,
As we come before Your throne to worship
      You.
By Your Spirit's power You now draw our
      hearts,
And we hear Your voice in triumph ringing
      clear.

> *I am He that liveth, that liveth and was dead,*
> *Behold I am alive for evermore.*

There we see You stand, mighty risen Lord,
Clothed in garments pure and holy shining
      bright.
Eyes of flashing fire, feet like burnished bronze,
And the sound of many waters is Your voice.

Like the shining sun in its noonday strength,
We now see the glory of Your wondrous face.
Once that face was marred, but now You're
      glorified,
And Your words like a two-edged sword have
      mighty power.

**35**
David J. Hadden.
Copyright © Springtide/
Word Music (UK)/CopyCare Ltd 1982.

**AWAKE, AWAKE, O ZION,**
*Come clothe yourself with strength.*
*Awake, awake, O Zion,*
*Come clothe yourself with strength.*

Put on your garments of splendour,
O Jerusalem.
Come sing your songs of joy and triumph,
See that your God reigns.

Burst into songs of joy together,
O Jerusalem.
The Lord has comforted His people,
The redeemed Jerusalem.

**36**
Verses 1 & 2 unknown.
Verse 3 J. T. McFarland.

**AWAY IN A MANGER,** no crib for a bed,
The little Lord Jesus laid down His sweet head;
The stars in the bright sky looked down where
    He lay;
The little Lord Jesus asleep on the hay.

The cattle are lowing, the Baby awakes,
But little Lord Jesus, no crying He makes:
I love You, Lord Jesus! Look down from the sky
And stay by my side until morning is nigh.

Be near me, Lord Jesus: I ask You to stay
Close by me for ever and love me, I pray;
Bless all the dear children in Your tender care,
And fit us for heaven to live with You there.

**37**
Morris Chapman.
Copyright © Word Music USA/
Word Music (UK)/CopyCare Ltd 1983.

**BE BOLD, BE STRONG,**
For the Lord your God is with you.
Be bold, be strong,
For the Lord your God is with you.
I am not afraid,
I am not dismayed,
Because I'm walking in faith and victory,
Come on and walk in faith and victory,
For the Lord your God is with you.

**38**
Eric Glass.
Copyright © Gordon V. Thompson Music.

**BEHOLD THE DARKNESS** shall cover the earth,
And gross darkness the people,
But the Lord shall arise upon thee
And His glory shall be seen upon thee.

*So arise, shine, for thy light is come*
*And the glory of the Lord is risen;*
*So arise, shine, for thy light is come*
*And the glory of the Lord is upon thee.*

The Gentiles shall come to thy light,
And kings to the brightness of thy rising,
And they shall call thee the city of the Lord,
The Zion of the Holy One of Israel.

Lift up thine eyes round about and see,
They gather themselves together;
And they shall come, thy sons from afar,
And thy daughters shall be nursed at thy side.

Then shalt thou see and flow together,
And thy heart shall be enlarged.
The abundance of the sea is converted unto
    thee,
And the nations shall come unto thee.

The sun shall no more go down,
Neither shall the moon withdraw itself,
But the Lord shall be thine everlasting light,
And the days of thy mourning shall be ended.

**39**
Elizabeth C. Clephane.

**BENEATH THE CROSS OF JESUS**
I fain would take my stand,
The shadow of a mighty rock
Within a weary land;
A home within the wilderness,
A rest upon the way,
From the burning of the noontide heat,
And the burden of the day.

O safe and happy shelter!
O refuge tried and sweet!
O trysting place where heaven's love
And heaven's justice meet!
As to the holy patriarch
That wondrous dream was given,
So seems my Saviour's cross to me
A ladder up to heaven.

There lies, beneath its shadow,
But on the farther side,
The darkness of an awful grave
That gapes both deep and wide;
And there between us stands the cross,
Two arms outstretched to save;
Like a watchman set to guard the way
From that eternal grave.

Upon that cross of Jesus
Mine eye at times can see
The very dying form of One
Who suffered there for me;
And from my smitten heart, with tears,
Two wonders I confess—
The wonders of His glorious love,
And my own worthlessness.

I take, O cross, thy shadow,
For my abiding place;
I ask no other sunshine than
The sunshine of His face;
Content to let the world go by,
To know no gain nor loss
My sinful self my only shame,
My glory all the cross.

**40**  
David J. Evans.
Copyright © Kingsway's
Thankyou Music 1986.

**BE STILL,** for the presence of the Lord, the Holy
    One is here;
Come bow before Him now with reverence and
    fear.
In Him no sin is found, we stand on holy
    ground;
Be still, for the presence of the Lord, the Holy
    One is here.

Be still, for the glory of the Lord is shining all
    around;
He burns with holy fire, with splendour He is
    crowned.
How awesome is the sight, our radiant King of
    light;
Be still, for the glory of the Lord is shining all
    around.

Be still, for the power of the Lord is moving in
    this place;
He comes to cleanse and heal, to minister His
    grace.
No work too hard for Him, in faith receive from
    Him;
Be still, for the power of the Lord is moving in
    this place.

**41**  
Author unknown.

**BE STILL AND KNOW** that I am God,
Be still and know that I am God,
Be still and know that I am God.

I am the Lord that healeth thee... *(etc.)*

In Thee, O Lord, do I put my trust... *(etc.)*

**42**  
Tr. Mary E. Byrne & Eleanor H. Hull.

**BE THOU MY VISION,** O Lord of my heart,
Be all else but naught to me, save that Thou
    art;
Be Thou my best thought in the day and the
    night,
Both waking and sleeping, Thy presence my
    light.

Be Thou my wisdom, be Thou my true word,
Be Thou ever with me, and I with Thee, Lord;
Be Thou my great Father, and I Thy true son;
Be Thou in me dwelling, and I with Thee one.

Be Thou my breastplate, my sword for the
    fight;
Be Thou my whole armour, be Thou my true
    might;
Be Thou my soul's shelter, be Thou my strong
    tower:
O raise Thou me heavenward, great Power of
    my power.

Riches I need not, nor man's empty praise:
Be Thou mine inheritance now and always;
Be Thou and Thou only the first in my heart:
O Sovereign of heaven, my treasure Thou art.

High King of heaven, Thou heaven's bright
    Sun,
O grant me its joys after victory is won;
Great Heart of my own heart, whatever befall,
Still be Thou my vision, O Ruler of all.

**43**   
Bob Gillman.
Copyright © Kingsway's
Thankyou Music 1977.

**BIND US TOGETHER,** *Lord,*
*Bind us together*
*With cords that cannot be broken.*
*Bind us together, Lord,*
*Bind us together,*
*Bind us together with love.*

There is only one God,
There is only one King,
There is only one Body,
That is why we sing:

Made for the glory of God,
Purchased by His precious Son.
Born with the right to be clean,
For Jesus the victory has won.

You are the family of God,
You are the promise divine,
You are God's chosen desire,
You are the glorious new wine.

**44**  
Fanny J. Crosby.

**BLESSÈD ASSURANCE,** Jesus is mine:
O what a foretaste of glory divine!
Heir of salvation, purchase of God;
Born of His Spirit, washed in His blood.

> *This is my story, this is my song,*
> *Praising my Saviour all the day long.*
> *This is my story, this is my song,*
> *Praising my Saviour all the day long.*

Perfect submission, perfect delight,
Visions of rapture burst on my sight;
Angels descending bring from above
Echoes of mercy, whispers of love.

Perfect submission, all is at rest,
I in my Saviour am happy and blessed;
Watching and waiting, looking above,
Filled with His goodness, lost in His love.

**45** David Fellingham.
Copyright © Kingsway's
Thankyou Music 1983.

**BLESSÈD BE** the God and Father
Of our Lord Jesus Christ,
Who has blessed us with every spiritual
　　blessing
In heavenly places in Christ.
And He has chosen us
Before the world was formed
To be holy and blameless before Him,
In His love He has predestined us
To be adopted as sons
Through Jesus Christ to Himself.

**46** Kevin Prosch & Danny Daniels.
Copyright © Mercy Publishing/
Kingsway's Thankyou Music 1989.

**BLESSED BE THE NAME OF THE LORD.**
Blessed be the name of the Lord.
Blessed be the name of the Lord.
Blessed be the name of the Lord.
For He is our Rock, for He is our Rock,
He is the Lord.
For He is our Rock, for He is our Rock,
He is the Lord.

Jesus reigns on high in all the earth.
Jesus reigns on high in all the earth.
Jesus reigns on high in all the earth.
Jesus reigns on high in all the earth.
The universe is in the hands
Of the Lord.
The universe is in the hands
Of the Lord.

**47** Phil Rogers.
Copyright © Kingsway's
Thankyou Music 1989.

**BLESS THE LORD O MY SOUL,**
And let all that is within me bless His name.
O Lord my God, You are so great,
For You are clothed with splendour and with
　　majesty.

How can I forget all Your benefits to me?
You forgive my sin in its entirety.
You heal me when I'm sick, from the pit You
　　set me free!
You crown my life with Your love.

**48** Author unknown.

　**BLESS THE LORD, O MY SOUL,**
　*Bless the Lord, O my soul,*
　*And all that is within me*
　*Bless His holy name.*
　*Bless the Lord, O my soul,*
　*Bless the Lord, O my soul,*
　*And all that is within me*
　*Bless His holy name.*

King of kings, (for ever and ever,)
Lord of lords, (for ever and ever,)
King of kings, (for ever and ever,)
King of kings and Lord of lords.

 **49** John Fawcett.

**BLEST BE THE TIE** that binds
Our hearts in Christian love;
The fellowship of kindred minds
Is like to that above.

Before our Father's throne,
We pour our ardent prayers;
Our fears, our hopes, our aims are one,
Our comforts and our cares.

We share our mutual woes,
Our mutual burdens bear,
And often for each other flows
The sympathising tear.

When for a while we part,
This thought will soothe our pain,
That we shall still be joined in heart,
And hope to meet again.

This glorious hope revives
Our courage by the way,
While each in expectation lives,
And longs to see the day.

From sorrow, toil and pain,
And sin we shall be free;
And perfect love and friendship reign
Through all eternity.

 **50** Verses 1 & 4 Mary A. Lathbury.
Verses 2 & 3 Alexander Groves.

**BREAK THOU THE BREAD OF LIFE,**
Dear Lord, to me,
As Thou didst break the bread
Beside the sea;
Beyond the sacred page
I seek Thee, Lord,
My spirit longs for Thee,
Thou Living Word.

Thou art the Bread of Life,
O Lord, to me,
Thy holy Word the truth
That saveth me;
Give me to eat and live
With Thee above,
Teach me to love Thy truth,
For Thou art love.

send Thy Spirit, Lord,
ow unto me,
hat He may touch my eyes
nd make me see;
how me the truth concealed
Vithin Thy Word,
nd in Thy Book revealed,
see Thee, O Lord.

less Thou the Bread of Life
o me, to me,
s Thou didst bless the loaves
y Galilee;
hen shall all bondage cease,
ll fetters fall,
nd I shall find my peace,
My all in all.

1    Edwin Hatch.

REATHE ON ME, BREATH OF GOD,
ill me with life anew;
hat I may love what Thou dost love
nd do what Thou wouldst do.

reathe on me, Breath of God,
Until my heart is pure;
Until my will is one with Thine
o do and to endure.

reathe on me, Breath of God,
ill I am wholly Thine;
Until this earthly part of me
ilows with Thy fire divine.

reathe on me, Breath of God,
o shall I never die,
ut live with Thee the perfect life
Of Thine eternity.

52    Brent Chambers.
Copyright © Scripture in Song/
CopyCare Ltd 1979.

BRING A PSALM to the Lord,
From the Spirit and from His word,
Lift your voice and rejoice,
For our God is a mighty King,
So come and clap your hands,
Raise a shout, as we stand before the Lord,
For the Lord is He who has the power to free,
Who by His mighty arm gives strength and
        victory,
So as we hail the King
Then let His praises ring,
And bring a psalm of joy before the Lord.

53    Janet Lunt.
Copyright © Mustard Seed Music/
Sovereign Lifestyle Music 1978.

BROKEN FOR ME, *broken for you,*
*The body of Jesus, broken for you.*

He offered His body, He poured out His soul;
Jesus was broken, that we might be whole:

Come to My table and with Me dine;
Eat of My bread and drink of My wine.

This is My body given for you;
Eat it remembering I died for you.

This is My blood I shed for you;
For your forgiveness, making you new.

54    Richard Gillard.
Copyright © Scripture in Song/
CopyCare Ltd 1977.

BROTHER, LET ME BE YOUR SERVANT,
Let me be as Christ to you;
Pray that I may have the grace
To let you be my servant, too.

We are pilgrims on a journey,
We are brothers on the road;
We are here to help each other
Walk the mile and bear the load.

I will hold the Christlight for you
In the night-time of your fear;
I will hold my hand out to you,
Speak the peace you long to hear.

I will weep when you are weeping,
When you laugh I'll laugh with you;
I will share your joy and sorrow
Till we've seen this journey through.

When we sing to God in heaven
We shall find such harmony,
Born of all we've known together
Of Christ's love and agony.

Brother, let me be your servant,
Let me be as Christ to you;
Pray that I may have the grace
To let you be my servant, too.

55    Noel & Tricia Richards.
Copyright © Kingsway's
Thankyou Music 1989.

BY YOUR SIDE I would stay;
In Your arms I would lay.
Jesus, lover of my soul,
Nothing from You would I withhold.

*Lord, I love You, and adore You;*
*What more can I say?*
*You cause my love to grow stronger*
*With every passing day.*
(Repeat)

**56**
R. Edward Miller.
Copyright © Maranatha! Music/
CopyCare Ltd 1974.

**CAUSE ME TO COME** to Thy river, O Lord,
Cause me to come to Thy river, O Lord,
Cause me to come to Thy river, O Lord,
Cause me to come,
Cause me to drink,
Cause me to live.

Cause me to drink from Thy river, O Lord,
Cause me to drink from Thy river, O Lord,
Cause me to drink from Thy river, O Lord,
Cause me to come,
Cause me to drink,
Cause me to live.

Cause me to live by Thy river, O Lord,
Cause me to live by Thy river, O Lord,
Cause me to live by Thy river, O Lord,
Cause me to come,
Cause me to drink,
Cause me to live.

**57**
Gary Oliver.
Copyright © Integrity's Hosanna! Music
Adm. Kingsway's Thankyou Music 1988.

**CELEBRATE JESUS,** celebrate!
Celebrate Jesus, celebrate!
Celebrate Jesus, celebrate!
Celebrate Jesus, celebrate!

He is risen, He is risen,
And He lives for ever more.
He is risen, He is risen,
Come on and celebrate
The resurrection of our Lord.

**58**
Eddie Espinosa.
Copyright © Mercy Publishing/
Kingsway's Thankyou Music 1982.

**CHANGE MY HEART, O GOD,**
*Make it ever true,*
*Change my heart, O God,*
*May I be like You.*

You are the potter,
I am the clay,
Mould me and make me,
This is what I pray.

**59** J. Byrom altd.

**CHRISTIANS AWAKE!** Salute the happy morn,
Whereon the Saviour of mankind was born;
Rise to adore the mystery of love
Which hosts of angels chanted from above;
With them the joyful tidings first begun
Of God Incarnate and the Virgin's Son.

Then to the watchful shepherds it was told,
Who heard the angelic herald's voice 'Behold,
I bring good tidings of a Saviour's birth
To you and all the nations upon earth:
This day hath God fulfilled His promised word,
This day is born a Saviour, Christ the Lord.'

He spake; and straightway the celestial choir,
In hymns of joy unknown before conspire;
High praise of God's redeeming love they sang
And heaven's whole orb with hallelujahs rang;
God's highest glory was their anthem still,
'On earth be peace, and unto men goodwill.'

O may we keep and ponder in our mind
God's wondrous love in saving lost mankind;
Trace we the Babe who hath retrieved our loss
From His poor manger to His bitter cross;
Tread in His steps, assisted by His grace,
Till man's first heavenly state again takes place.

Then may we hope, the angelic hosts among,
To sing, redeemed, a glad triumphant song:
He that was born upon this joyful day
Around us all His glory shall display;
Saved by His love, incessant we shall sing
Eternal praise to heaven's almighty King.

**60**
Chris Rolinson.
Copyright © Kingsway's
Thankyou Music 1989.

**CHRIST IS RISEN!**
*Hallelujah, hallelujah!*
*Christ is risen!*
*Risen indeed, hallelujah!*

Love's work is done,
The battle is won.
Where now, O death, is your sting?
He rose again
To rule and to reign,
Jesus our conquering King.

Lord over sin,
Lord over death,
At His feet Satan must fall!
Every knee bow,
All will confess
Jesus is Lord over all!

Tell it abroad
'Jesus is Lord!'
Shout it and let your praise ring!
Gladly we raise
Our songs of praise,
Worship is our offering.

**61** Charles Wesley.

**CHRIST THE LORD IS RISEN TODAY:**
    Hallelujah!
Sons of men and angels say: Hallelujah!
Raise your joys and triumphs high: Hallelujah!
Sing, ye heavens, and earth reply: Hallelujah!

ove's redeeming work is done: Hallelujah!
ought the fight, the battle won: Hallelujah!
ain the stone, the watch, the seal: Hallelujah!
hrist hath burst the gates of hell: Hallelujah!

ives again our glorious King: Hallelujah!
Vhere, O death, is now thy sting? Hallelujah!
ince He died, our souls to save: Hallelujah!
Vhere thy victory, O grave? Hallelujah!

oar we now where Christ hath led: Hallelujah!
ollowing our exalted Head: Hallelujah!
Made like Him, like Him we rise: Hallelujah!
Ours the cross, the grave, the skies: Hallelujah!

ail the Lord of earth and heaven: Hallelujah!
'raise to Thee by both be given: Hallelujah!
hee we greet, in triumph sing: Hallelujah!
ail our resurrected King: Hallelujah!

 Michael Saward.
Copyright © Michael Saward/Jubilee Hymns.

CHRIST TRIUMPHANT, ever reigning,
aviour, Master, King,
ord of heaven, our lives sustaining,
lear us we sing:

*Yours the glory and the crown,*
*The high renown, the eternal name.*

Vord incarnate, truth revealing,
ion of Man on earth!
'ower and majesty concealing
By your humble birth:

iuffering servant, scorned, ill-treated,
'ictim crucified!
Death is through the cross defeated,
Sinners justified:

'riestly King, enthroned for ever
High in heaven above!
iin and death and hell shall never
itifle hymns of love:

io, our hearts and voices raising
Through the ages long,
Ceaselessly upon you gazing,
This shall be our song:

 Graham Kendrick.
Copyright © Make Way Music 1988.

CLEAR THE ROAD, make wide the way.    *(echo)*
Velcome now the God who saves.    *(echo)*
ill the streets with shouts of joy.    *(echo)*
*Cheers, etc.)*

*Prepare the way of the Lord!*    *(echo)*
*Prepare the way of the Lord!*    *(echo)*

Raise your voice and join the song,    *(echo)*
iod made flesh to us has come.    *(echo)*
Velcome Him, your banners wave.    *(echo)*
*Cheers, shouts, wave banners, etc.)*

For all sin the price is paid,    *(echo)*
All our sins on Jesus laid.    *(echo)*
By His blood we are made clean.    *(echo)*
*(Cheers, shouts of thanksgiving)*

At His feet come humbly bow,    *(echo)*
In your lives enthrone Him now.    *(echo)*
See, your great Deliverer comes.    *(echo)*
*(Cheers, shouts welcoming Jesus)*

**64** Sue McClellan, John Pac, Keith Ryecroft.
Copyright © Kingsway's Thankyou Music 1974.

COLOURS OF DAY dawn into the mind,
The sun has come up, the night is behind.
Go down in the city, into the street,
And let's give the message to the people we
    meet.

*So light up the fire and let the flame burn,*
*Open the door, let Jesus return.*
*Take seeds of His Spirit, let the fruit grow,*
*Tell the people of Jesus, let His love show.*

Go through the park, on into the town;
The sun still shines on, it never goes down.
The light of the world is risen again;
The people of darkness are needing a friend.

Open your eyes, look into the sky,
The darkness has come, the sun came to die.
The evening draws on, the sun disappears,
But Jesus is living, His Spirit is near.

**65** Andy Carter.
Copyright © Kingsway's
Thankyou Music 1977.

COME AND PRAISE HIM, ROYAL PRIESTHOOD,
Come and worship, holy nation,
Worship Jesus, our Redeemer,
He is precious, King of glory.

**66** Mike Kerry.
Copyright © Kingsway's
Thankyou Music 1982.

COME AND PRAISE THE LIVING GOD,
*Come and worship, come and worship.*
*He has made you priest and king,*
*Come and worship the living God.*

We come not to a mountain of fire and smoke,
Not to gloom and darkness or trumpet sound.
We come to the new Jerusalem,
The holy city of God.

By His voice He shakes the earth,
His judgements known throughout the world.
But we have a city that for ever stands,
The holy city of God.

**67** Graham Kendrick.
Copyright © Make Way Music 1989.

**COME AND SEE,** come and see,
Come and see the King of love;
See the purple robe and crown of thorns He
  wears.
Soldiers mock, rulers sneer,
As He lifts the cruel cross;
Lone and friendless now He climbs towards the
  hill.

*We worship at Your feet,*
*Where wrath and mercy meet,*
*And a guilty world is washed*
*By love's pure stream.*
*For us He was made sin.*
*Oh, help me take it in.*
*Deep wounds of love cry out*
*'Father, forgive'.*
*I worship, I worship,*
*The Lamb who was slain.*

Come and weep, come and mourn
For your sin that pierced Him there;
So much deeper than the wounds of thorn and
  nail.
All our pride, all our greed,
All our fallenness and shame;
And the Lord has laid the punishment on Him.

Man of heaven, born to earth
To restore us to Your heaven,
Here we bow in awe beneath Your searching
  eyes.
From Your tears comes our joy,
From Your death our life shall spring;
By Your resurrection power we shall rise.

**68** Author unknown.

**COME BLESS THE LORD,**
All ye servants of the Lord,
Who stand by night in the house of the Lord.
Lift up your hands in the holy place,
Come bless the Lord,
Come bless the Lord.

**69** John Sellers.
Copyright © Integrity's Hosanna! Music.
Adm. Kingsway's Thankyou Music 1984.

**COME INTO THE HOLY OF HOLIES,**
Enter by the blood of the Lamb;
Come into His presence with singing,
Worship at the throne of God.
*(Repeat)*

Lifting holy hands
To the King of kings,
Worship Jesus.

**70** Isaac Watts.

**COME, LET US JOIN OUR CHEERFUL SONGS**
With angels round the throne;
Ten thousand thousand are their tongues,
But all their joys are one.

'Worthy the Lamb that died,' they cry,
'To be exalted thus.'
'Worthy the Lamb,' our lips reply,
'For He was slain for us.'

Jesus is worthy to receive
Honour and power divine:
And blessings, more than we can give,
Be, Lord, for ever Thine.

Let all that dwell above the sky,
And air, and earth and seas,
Conspire to lift Thy glories high,
And speak Thine endless praise.

The whole creation join in one
To bless the sacred name
Of Him that sits upon the throne
And to adore the Lamb.

**71** Brent Chambers.
Copyright © Scripture in Song/
CopyCare Ltd 1985.

**COME, LET US SING** for joy to the Lord,
Come let us sing for joy to the Lord,
Come let us sing for joy to the Lord,
Come let us sing for joy to the Lord!

*Come let us sing for joy to the Lord,*
*Let us shout aloud to the Rock of our*
*  salvation!*
(Repeat)

Let us come before Him with thanksgiving,
And extol Him with music and song;
For the Lord, our Lord, is a great God,
The great King above all gods.

Let us bow before Him in our worship,
Let us kneel before God, our great King;
For He is our God, and we are His people,
That's why we shout and sing!

**72** Robert Walmsley.

**COME, LET US SING OF A WONDERFUL LOVE,**
Tender and true;
Out of the heart of the Father above,
Streaming to me and to you:
Wonderful love
Dwells in the heart of the Father above.

Jesus, the Saviour, this gospel to tell,
Joyfully came;
Came with the helpless and hopeless to dwell,
Sharing their sorrow and shame;
Seeking the lost,
Saving, redeeming at measureless cost.

Jesus is seeking the wanderers yet;
Why do they roam?
Love only waits to forgive and forget;
Home, weary wanderer, home!
Wonderful love
Dwells in the heart of the Father above.

Come to my heart, O Thou wonderful love,
Come and abide,
Lifting my life, till it rises above
Envy and falsehood and pride,
Seeking to be
Lowly and humble, a learner of Thee.

**73**
Patricia Morgan & Dave Bankhead.
Copyright © Kingsway's
Thankyou Music 1984.

## COME ON AND CELEBRATE

His gift of love, we will celebrate
The Son of God who loved us
And gave us life.
We'll shout Your praise, O King,
You give us joy nothing else can bring,
We'll give to You our offering
In celebration praise.

Come on and celebrate,
Celebrate,
Celebrate and sing,
Celebrate and sing to the King.
Come on and celebrate,
Celebrate,
Celebrate and sing,
Celebrate and sing to the King.

**74**
Graham Kendrick.
Copyright © Kingsway's
Thankyou Music 1985.

## COME SEE THE BEAUTY OF THE LORD,

Come see the beauty of His face.
See the Lamb that once was slain,
See on His palms is carv'd your name.
See how our pain has pierc'd His heart,
And on His brow He bears our pride;
A crown of thorns.
Come see the beauty of the Lord,
Come see the beauty of His face.

But only love pours from His heart
As silently He takes the blame.
He has my name upon His lips,
My condemnation falls on Him.
This love is marvellous to me,
His sacrifice has set me free
And now I live.

**75**
Henry Alford.

## COME, YE THANKFUL PEOPLE, COME,

Raise the song of harvest home!
All is safely gathered in
Ere the winter storms begin;
God, our Maker, doth provide
For our needs to be supplied;
Come to God's own temple, come,
Raise the song of harvest-home.

All the world is God's own field,
Fruit unto His praise to yield;
Wheat and tares together sown,
Unto joy or sorrow grown;
First the blade, and then the ear,
Then the full corn shall appear:
Lord of harvest, grant that we
Wholesome grain and pure may be.

For the Lord our God shall come
And shall take His harvest home,
From His field shall in that day
All offences purge away,
Give His angels charge at last
In the fire the tares to cast,
But the fruitful ears to store
In His garner evermore.

Even so, Lord, quickly come,
Bring Thy final harvest home;
Gather Thou Thy people in,
Free from sorrow, free from sin;
There, for ever purified,
In Thy garner to abide:
Come, with all Thine angels, come,
Raise the glorious harvest-home.

**76**
David Fellingham.
Copyright © Kingsway's
Thankyou Music 1983.

## CREATE IN ME a clean heart, O God,

And renew a right spirit in me.
Create in me a clean heart, O God,
And renew a right spirit in me.
Wash me, cleanse me, purify me,
Make my heart as white as snow.
Create in me a clean heart, O God,
And renew a right spirit in me.

**77** Matthew Bridges & Godfrey Thring.

## CROWN HIM WITH MANY CROWNS,

The Lamb upon His throne;
Hark, how the heavenly anthem drowns
All music but its own!
Awake, my soul, and sing,
Of Him who died for thee,
And hail Him as thy matchless King
Through all eternity.

Crown Him the Lord of life,
Who triumphed o'er the grave
And rose victorious in the strife
For those He came to save:
His glories now we sing,
Who died and rose on high,
Who died eternal life to bring
And lives that death may die.

Crown Him the Lord of love;
Behold His hands and side,
Those wounds yet visible above
In beauty glorified:
No angel in the sky
Can fully bear that sight,
But downward bends His burning eye
At mysteries so bright.

Crown Him the Lord of peace,
Whose power a sceptre sways
From pole to pole, that wars may cease,
And all be prayer and praise:
His reign shall know no end,
And round His piercèd feet
Fair flowers of paradise extend
Their fragrance ever sweet.

Crown Him the Lord of years,
The Potentate of time,
Creator of the rolling spheres,
Ineffably sublime!
All hail, Redeemer, hail!
For Thou hast died for me;
Thy praise shall never, never fail
Throughout eternity.

**78** Graham Kendrick.
Copyright © Kingsway's
Thankyou Music 1985.

DARKNESS LIKE A SHROUD covers the earth;
Evil like a cloud covers the people.
But the Lord will rise upon you,
And His glory will appear on you—
Nations will come to your light.

*Arise, shine, your light has come,*
*The glory of the Lord has risen on you!*
*Arise, shine, your light has come,*
*Jesus the Light of the world has come.*
   (instead, last time)
*Jesus the Light of the world,*   (twice)
*Jesus the Light of the world has come.*
*Your light has come!*   (Men)
*Your light has come!*   (Women) } (twice)
*Your light has come!*   (All)

Children of the light, be clean and pure.
Rise, you sleepers, Christ will shine on you.
Take the Spirit's flashing two-edged sword
And with faith declare God's mighty word;
Stand up and in His strength be strong

Here among us now, Christ the light
Kindles brighter flames in our trembling
      hearts!
Living Word, our Lamp, come guide our feet
As we walk as one in light and peace,
Till justice and truth shine like the sun.

Like a city bright so let us blaze;
Lights in every street turning night to day.
And the darkness shall not overcome
Till the fullness of Christ's kingdom comes,
Dawning to God's eternal day.

**79**    John G. Whittier.

DEAR LORD AND FATHER OF MANKIND,
Forgive our foolish ways;
Reclothe us in our rightful mind;
In purer lives Thy service find,
In deeper reverence, praise,
In deeper reverence, praise.

In simple trust like theirs who heard,
Beside the Syrian sea,
The gracious calling of the Lord,
Let us, like them, without a word
Rise up and follow Thee,
Rise up and follow Thee.

O sabbath rest by Galilee!
O calm of hills above,
Where Jesus knelt to share with Thee
The silence of eternity,
Interpreted by love,
Interpreted by love.

With that deep hush subduing all
Our words and works that drown
The tender whisper of Thy call,
As noiseless let Thy blessing fall
As fell Thy manna down,
As fell Thy manna down.

Drop Thy still dews of quietness,
Till all our strivings cease;
Take from our souls the strain and stress,
And let our ordered lives confess
The beauty of Thy peace,
The beauty of Thy peace.

Breathe through the heats of our desire
Thy coolness and Thy balm;
Let sense be dumb, let flesh retire;
Speak through the earthquake, wind and fire,
O still small voice of calm,
O still small voice of calm!

**80** Chris Bowater.
Copyright © Sovereign Lifestyle Music Ltd 1986.

DO SOMETHING NEW, LORD,
*In my heart, make a start;*
*Do something new, Lord,*
*Do something new.*

I open up my heart,
As much as can be known;
I open up my will
To conform to Yours alone.

I lay before Your feet
All my hopes and desires;
Unreservedly submit
To what Your Spirit may require.

I only want to live
For Your pleasure now;
I long to please You, Father—
Will You show me how?

**81**

DRAW ME CLOSER, Lord,
Draw me closer, dear Lord,
So that I might touch You,
So that I might touch You,
Lord I want to touch You.

Touch my eyes, Lord,
Touch my eyes, dear Lord,
So that I might see You,
So that I might see You,
Lord I want to see You.

*Your glory, Your love,*
*Your glory, Your love,*
*Your glory, Your love,*
*And Your majesty.*

**82**

*EL-SHADDAI, El-Shaddai,*
*El-Elyon na Adonai,*
*Age to age You're still the same*
*By the power of the name.*
*El-Shaddai, El-Shaddai,*
*Erkamka na Adonai,*
*We will praise and lift You high.*
*El-Shaddai.*

Through Your love and through the ram
You saved the son of Abraham;
Through the power of Your hand,
Turned the sea into dry land.
To the outcast on her knees
You were the God who really sees,
And by Your might You set Your children free.

Through the years You made it clear
That the time of Christ was near;
Though the people couldn't see
What Messiah ought to be.
Though Your word contained the plan,
They just could not understand
Your most awesome work was done
Through the frailty of Your Son.

**83**

EMMANUEL, Emmanuel,
We call Your name, Emmanuel.
God with us, revealed in us,
We call Your name, Emmanuel.

**84**

ENTER IN to His great love,
Kneel before His throne;
For His blood has washed away your sin,
So enter in and worship Him.

**85**

ETERNAL GOD, we come to You,
We come before Your throne;
We enter by a new and living way,
With confidence we come.
We declare Your faithfulness,
Your promises are true,
We will now draw near to worship You.

*(Men)*
O holy God, we come to You,
O holy God, we see Your faithfulness and love,
Your mighty power, Your majesty,
Are now revealed to us in Jesus who has died,
Jesus who was raised,
Jesus now exalted on high.

*(Women)*
O holy God, full of justice,
Wisdom and righteousness, faithfulness and
    love,
Your mighty power and Your majesty
Are now revealed to us in Jesus who has died
    for our sin,
Jesus who was raised from the dead,
Jesus now exalted on high.

**86**

EXALTED, YOU ARE EXALTED,
Lord of heaven and the earth.
Exalted, You are exalted,
Ruler of the universe.
For at the name of Jesus
Every knee shall bow,
Honour and praise to Jesus,
We give You glory now.
Lord, we come before You,
Worship and adore You.

**87**

EXALT THE LORD OUR GOD,
Exalt the Lord our God,
And worship at His footstool,
Worship at His footstool,
Holy is He, holy is He.

**88**

FACING A TASK UNFINISHED,
That drives us to our knees,
A need that, undiminished,
Rebukes our slothful ease,
We, who rejoice to know Thee,
Renew before Thy throne
The solemn pledge we owe Thee
To go and make Thee known.

Where other lords beside Thee
Hold their unhindered sway,
Where forces that defied Thee
Defy Thee still today;
With none to heed their crying
For life, and love, and light,
Unnumbered souls are dying,
And pass into the night.

We bear the torch that flaming
Fell from the hands of those
Who gave their lives proclaiming
That Jesus died and rose.
Ours is the same commission,
The same glad message ours,
Fired by the same ambition,
To Thee we yield our powers.

O Father who sustained them,
O Spirit who inspired,
Saviour, whose love constrained them
To toil with zeal untired,
From cowardice defend us,
From lethargy awake!
Forth on Thine errands send us
To labour for Thy sake.

**89** Brian Doerksen.
Copyright © Mercy Publishing/
Kingsway's Thankyou Music 1989.

FAITHFUL ONE, so unchanging,
Ageless One, You're my rock of peace.
Lord of all I depend on You,
I call out to You again and again.
I call out to You again and again.
You are my rock in times of trouble.
You lift me up when I fall down.
All through the storm Your love is the anchor,
My hope is in You alone.

**90** Danny Daniels.
Copyright © Mercy Publishing/
Kingsway's Thankyou Music 1989.

FATHER, I can call You Father,
For I am Your child today,
Tomorrow and always,
You are my Father.

Father, how I love You, Father,
I will sing Your praise today,
Tomorrow and always,
For You're my Father.
Father, Father,
Father to me.
Father, holy Father,
Father to me.

**91** Jack Hayford.
Copyright © Rocksmith Music/
Leosong Copyright Service 1981.

FATHER GOD,
I give all thanks and praise to Thee,
Father God,
My hands I humbly raise to Thee;
For Your mighty power and love
Amazes me, amazes me
And I stand in awe and worship, Father God.

**92** Ian Smale.
Copyright © Kingsway's
Thankyou Music 1984.

FATHER GOD I WONDER how I managed to
 exist
Without the knowledge of Your parenthood
 and Your loving care.
But now I am Your son, I am adopted in Your
 family
And I can never be alone,
'Cause Father God You're there beside me.

I will sing Your praises,
I will sing Your praises,
I will sing Your praises,
For evermore.
I will sing Your praises,
I will sing Your praises,
I will sing Your praises,
For evermore.

**93** Graham Kendrick.
Copyright © Kingsway's
Thankyou Music 1981.

FATHER GOD, we worship You,
Make us part of all You do.
As You move among us now
We worship You.

Jesus King, we worship You,
Help us listen now to You.
As You move among us now
We worship You.

Spirit pure, we worship You,
With Your fire our zeal renew.
As You move among us now
We worship You.

**94** Danny Daniels.
Copyright © Mercy Publishing/
Kingsway's Thankyou Music 1990.

FATHER HERE I AM again,
In need of mercy, hurt from sin,
So by the blood and Jesus' love,
Let forgiveness flow.

To me, from me,
So my heart will know;
Fully and sweetly,
Let forgiveness flow.

In my heart and in my mind,
In word and deed, I've been so blind,
So by the blood and Jesus' love,
Let forgiveness flow.

**95** Dave Bilbrough.
Copyright © Kingsway's
Thankyou Music 1985.

**FATHER IN HEAVEN,**
Our voices we raise,
Receive our devotion,
Receive now our praise;
As we sing of the glory
Of all that You've done,
The greatest love story
That's ever been sung.

> *And we will crown You Lord of all,*
> *Yes, we will crown You Lord of all,*
> *For You have won the victory,*
> *Yes, we will crown You Lord of all.*

Father in heaven,
Our lives are Your own;
We've been caught by a vision
Of Jesus alone,
Who came as a servant
To free us from sin,
Father in heaven,
Our worship we bring:

We will sing 'Hallelujah',
We will sing to the King,
To our Mighty Deliverer
Our hallelujahs will ring.
Yes, our praise is resounding
To the Lamb on the throne,
He alone is exalted
Through the love He has shown.

**96** Bob Fitts.
Copyright © Scripture in Song/
CopyCare Ltd 1985.

**FATHER IN HEAVEN HOW WE LOVE YOU,**
We lift Your name in all the earth,
May Your kingdom be established in our
  praises
As Your people declare Your mighty works.
Blessèd be the Lord God Almighty,
Who was and is and is to come;
Blessèd be the Lord God Almighty,
Who reigns for evermore.

**97** Jenny Hewer.
Copyright © Kingsway's
Thankyou Music 1975.

**FATHER, I PLACE INTO YOUR HANDS**
The things I cannot do.
Father, I place into Your hands
The things that I've been through.
Father, I place into Your hands
The way that I should go,
For I know I always can trust You.

Father, I place into Your hands
My friends and family.
Father, I place into Your hands
The things that trouble me.
Father, I place into Your hands
The person I would be,
For I know I always can trust You.

Father, we love to see Your face,
We love to hear Your voice.
Father, we love to sing Your praise
And in Your name rejoice.
Father, we love to walk with You
And in Your presence rest,
For we know we always can trust You.

Father, I want to be with You
And do the things You do.
Father, I want to speak the words
That You are speaking too.
Father, I want to love the ones
That You will draw to You,
For I know that I am one with You.

**98** Rick Ridings.
Copyright © Scripture in Song/
CopyCare Ltd 1976, 1983.

**FATHER MAKE US ONE,**
Father make us one,
That the world may know
Thou hast sent the Son,
Father make us one.

Behold how pleasant and how good it is
For brethren to dwell in unity,
For there the Lord commands the blessing,
Life for evermore.

Father make us one,
Father make us one,
That the world may know
Thou hast sent the Son,
Father make us one.

**99** Terrye Coelho.
Copyright © Maranatha! Music USA/
CopyCare Ltd 1972.

**FATHER, WE ADORE YOU,**
Lay our lives before You,
How we love You.

Jesus, we adore You... *(etc.)*

Spirit, we adore You... *(etc.)*

**100** Philip Lawson Johnston.
Copyright © Kingsway's
Thankyou Music 1989.

**FATHER, WE ADORE YOU,**
We are Your children gathered here;
To be with You is our delight,
A feast beyond compare.

Father, in Your presence
There is such freedom to enjoy.
We find in You a lasting peace
That nothing can destroy.

*You are the Fountain of life,*
*You are the Fountain of life,*
*And as we drink, we are more than satisfied*
*By You, O Fountain of life.*

**101**

**FATHER, WE ADORE YOU,**
You've drawn us to this place.
We bow down before You,
Humbly on our face.

*All the earth shall worship*
*At the throne of the King.*
*Of His great and awesome power,*
*We shall sing!*
*All the earth shall worship*
*At the throne of the King.*
*Of His great and awesome power,*
*We shall sing!*

Jesus we love You,
Because You first loved us,
You reached out and healed us
With Your mighty touch.

Spirit we need You,
To lift us from this mire,
Consume and empower us
With Your holy fire.

**102**

**FATHER, WE LOVE YOU,**
We worship and adore You,
Glorify Your name in all the earth.
Glorify Your name,
Glorify Your name,
Glorify Your name in all the earth.

Jesus, we love You... *(etc.)*

Spirit, we love You... *(etc.)*

 **103**

**FATHER, YOU ARE MY PORTION** in this life,
And You are my hope and my delight,
And I love You, yes, I love You,
Lord, I love You, my delight.

Jesus, You are my treasure in this life,
And You are so pure and so kind,
And I love You, yes, I love You,
Lord, I love You, my delight.

**104**

**FATHER, YOUR LOVE IS PRECIOUS** beyond all
loves,
Father, Your love overwhelms me.
Father, Your love is precious beyond all loves,
Father, Your love overwhelms me.
So I lift up my hands, an expression of my love
And I give you my heart in joyful obedience.
Father, Your love is precious beyond all loves,
Father, Your love overwhelms me.

**105**

**FEAR NOT,** for I am with you,
Fear not, for I am with you,
Fear not, for I am with you,
Says the Lord.
(Repeat)

I have redeemed you,
I've called you by name,
Child, you are Mine.
When you walk through the waters,
I will be there,
And through the flame.
You'll not be drowned,
You'll not be burned,
For I am with you.

**106**

**FEAR NOT, REJOICE AND BE GLAD,**
*The Lord hath done great thing;*
*Hath poured out His Spirit on all mankind,*
*On those who confess His name.*

The fig tree is budding, the vine beareth fruit,
The wheat fields are golden with grain.
Thrust in the sickle, the harvest is ripe,
The Lord has given us rain.

Ye shall eat in plenty and be satisfied,
The mountains will drip with sweet wine.
My children shall drink of the fountain of life,
My children will know they are mine.

My children shall dwell in a Body of love,
A light to the world they will be.
Life shall come forth from the Father above,
My Body will set mankind free.

**107**

**FIGHT THE GOOD FIGHT** with all thy might,
Christ is thy strength, and Christ thy right;
Lay hold on life, and it shall be
Thy joy and crown eternally.

Run the straight race through God's good
  grace,
Lift up thine eyes and seek His face;
Life with its way before thee lies,
Christ is the path, and Christ the prize.

Cast care aside, lean on thy Guide;
His boundless mercy will provide;
Lean, and the trusting soul shall prove
Christ is its life, and Christ its love.

Faint not, nor fear, His arms are near,
He changeth not, and thou art dear;
Only believe, and thou shalt see
That Christ is all in all to thee.


## 108 Horatius Bonar.

FILL THOU MY LIFE, O Lord my God,
In every part with praise,
That my whole being may proclaim
Thy being and Thy ways.

Not for the lip of praise alone
Nor e'en the praising heart,
  ask, but for a life made up
Of praise in every part:

Praise in the common things of life,
Its goings out and in;
Praise in each duty and each deed,
However small and mean.

Fill every part of me with praise;
Let all my being speak
Of Thee and of Thy love, O Lord,
Poor though I be and weak.

So shall Thou, gracious Lord, from me
Receive the glory due;
And so shall I begin on earth
The song for ever new.

So shall no part of day or night
From sacredness be free;
But all my life, in every step,
Be fellowship with Thee.


## 109 W. W. How.

FOR ALL THE SAINTS, who from their labours
  rest,
Who Thee by faith before the world confessed,
Thy name, O Jesus, be for ever blest.
Hallelujah! Hallelujah!

Thou wast their Rock, their fortress, and their
  might;
Thou, Lord, their Captain in the well-fought
  fight;
Thou in the darkness drear their one true light.
Hallelujah! Hallelujah!

O may Thy soldiers, faithful, true and bold,
Fight as the saints who nobly fought of old,
And win, with them, the victor's crown of gold!
Hallelujah! Hallelujah!

O blest communion, fellowship divine!
We feebly struggle, they in glory shine;
Yet all are one in Thee, for all are Thine.
Hallelujah! Hallelujah!

And when the strife is fierce, the warfare long,
Steals on the ear the distant triumph song,
And hearts are brave again, and arms are
  strong.
Hallelujah! Hallelujah!

The golden evening brightens in the west;
Soon, soon to faithful warriors cometh rest;
Sweet is the calm of paradise the blest.
Hallelujah! Hallelujah!

But lo! there breaks a yet more glorious day;
The saints triumphant rise in bright array;
The King of glory passes on His way.
Hallelujah! Hallelujah!

From earth's wide bounds, from ocean's
  farthest coast,
Through gates of pearl streams in the
  countless host,
Singing to Father, Son and Holy Ghost.
Hallelujah! Hallelujah!


## 110 Dale Garratt.

FOR HIS NAME IS EXALTED,
His glory above heaven and earth,
Holy is the Lord God Almighty,
Who was and who is and who is to come.
For His name is exalted,
His glory above heaven and earth,
Holy is the Lord God Almighty,
Who sitteth on the throne
And who lives for evermore.


## 111 Dave Richards.

FOR I'M BUILDING A PEOPLE OF POWER
And I'm making a people of praise,
That will move through this land by My Spirit,
And will glorify My precious Name.

Build Your Church, Lord,
Make us strong, Lord,
Join our hearts, Lord, through Your Son.
Make us one, Lord,
In Your Body,
In the Kingdom of Your Son.

## 112

Folliot S. Pierpoint.

**FOR THE BEAUTY OF THE EARTH,**
For the beauty of the skies,
For the love which from our birth
Over and around us lies;
Father, unto Thee we raise
This our sacrifice of praise.

For the beauty of each hour
Of the day and of the night,
Hill and vale, and tree and flower,
Sun and moon, and stars of light:
Father, unto Thee we raise
This our sacrifice of praise.

For the joy of human love,
Brother, sister, parent, child,
Friends on earth, and friends above;
For all gentle thoughts and mild:
Father, unto Thee we raise
This our sacrifice of praise.

For each perfect gift of Thine
To our race so freely given,
Graces, human and divine,
Flowers of earth, and buds of heaven:
Father, unto Thee we raise
This our sacrifice of praise.

## 113

Bonnie Low.
Copyright © Scripture in Song/
CopyCare Ltd 1977, 1982.

**FOR THE LORD IS MARCHING ON,**
And His army is ever strong;
And His glory shall be seen upon our land.
Raise the anthem, sing the victor's song.
Praise the Lord for the battle's won.
No weapon formed against us shall stand.

*For the Captain of the host is Jesus.*
*We're following in His footsteps,*
*No foe can stand against us in the fray.*
(Repeat)

We are marching in Messiah's band,
The keys of victory in His mighty hand.
Let us march on to take our promised land.
For the Lord is marching on,
And His army is ever strong;
And His glory shall be seen upon our land.

## 114

Graham Kendrick.
Copyright © Kingsway's
Thankyou Music 1985.

**FOR THIS PURPOSE** Christ was revealed,
To destroy all the works
Of the Evil One.
Christ in us has overcome,
So with gladness we sing
And welcome His kingdom in.

(Men)
*Over sin He has conquered,*
(Women)
*Hallelujah, He has conquered.*
(Men)
*Over death victorious,*
(Women)
*Hallelujah, victorious.*
(Men)
*Over sickness He has triumphed,*
(Women)
*Hallelujah, He has triumphed.*
(Together)
*Jesus reigns over all!*

In the name of Jesus we stand,
By the power of His blood
We now claim this ground.
Satan has no authority here,
Powers of darkness must flee,
For Christ has the victory.

## 115

Pete Sanchez Jnr.
Copyright © Pete Sanchez Jnr 1977.

**FOR THOU O LORD ART HIGH** above all the
earth,
Thou art exalted far above all gods.
For Thou O Lord art high above all the earth,
Thou art exalted far above all gods.

I exalt Thee, I exalt Thee,
I exalt Thee, O Lord.
I exalt Thee, I exalt Thee,
I exalt Thee, O Lord.

## 116

Author unknown.

**FOR UNTO US A CHILD IS BORN,**
Unto us a Son is given.
And the government shall be upon His
shoulder,
And His name shall be called
Wonderful Counsellor, the Mighty God,
The Everlasting Father,
And the Prince of Peace is He.

## 117

Sue Hutchinson.
Copyright © Springtide/
Word Music (UK)/CopyCare Ltd 1979.

**FOR WE SEE JESUS** enthroned on high,
Clothed in His righteousness we worship Him.
Glory and honour we give unto You,
We see You in Your holiness
And bow before Your throne;
You are the Lord,
Your name endures for ever,
Jesus the name high over all.

**118** David J. Hadden.
Copyright © Restoration Music Ltd/
Sovereign Lifestyle Music Ltd 1990.

**FOR YOUR WONDERFUL DEEDS** we give You
    thanks, Lord,
For Your marvellous acts on behalf of the
    people You love.
We honour You, we honour You,
For Your wonderful deeds we honour You.

For Your bountiful grace we give You thanks,
    Lord,
For the peace and the joy You bestow on the
    people You love.
We honour You, we honour You,
For Your bountiful grace we honour You.

**119** Isaac Watts.

**FROM ALL THAT DWELL BELOW THE SKIES**
Let the Creator's praise arise:
Alleluia! Alleluia!
Let the Redeemer's name be sung,
Through every land, by every tongue.

    *Alleluia! Alleluia!*
    *Alleluia! Alleluia!*
    *Alleluia!*

Eternal are Thy mercies, Lord;
Eternal truth attends Thy word:
Alleluia! Alleluia!
Thy praise shall sound from shore to shore,
Till suns shall rise and set no more.

Your lofty themes, ye mortals, bring
In songs of praise divinely sing:
Alleluia! Alleluia!
The great salvation loud proclaim,
And shout for joy the Saviour's name.

In every land begin the song;
To every land the strains belong.
Alleluia! Alleluia!
In cheerful sounds all voices raise,
And fill the world with loudest praise.

**120** Graham Kendrick.
Copyright © Kingsway's
Thankyou Music 1983.

**FROM HEAVEN YOU CAME,**
Helpless babe,
Entered our world,
Your glory veiled;
Not to be served
But to serve,
And give Your life
That we might live.

*This is our God,*
*The Servant King,*
*He calls us now*
*To follow Him,*
*To bring our lives*
*As a daily offering*
*Of worship to*
*The Servant King.*

There in the garden
Of tears,
My heavy load
He chose to bear;
His heart with sorrow
Was torn,
'Yet not My will
But Yours' He said.

Come see His hands
And His feet,
The scars that speak
Of sacrifice,
Hands that flung stars
Into space
To cruel nails
Surrendered.

So let us learn
How to serve,
And in our lives
Enthrone Him;
Each other's needs
To prefer,
For it is Christ
We're serving.

**121** Paul S. Deming.
Copyright © Integrity's Hosanna! Music.
Adm. Kingsway's Thankyou Music 1976.

**FROM THE RISING OF THE SUN**
To the going down of the same,
The Lord's name
Is to be praised.
From the rising of the sun
To the going down of the same
The Lord's name
Is to be praised.

Praise ye the Lord,
Praise Him all ye servants of the Lord,
Praise the name of the Lord.
Blessed be the name of the Lord
From this time forth and for evermore.

 Graham Kendrick.
Copyright © Make Way Music 1987.

**FROM THE SUN'S RISING**
Unto the sun's setting,
Jesus our Lord
Shall be great in the earth;
And all earth's kingdoms
Shall be His dominion,
All of creation
Shall sing of His worth.

Let every heart, every voice,
Every tongue join with spirits ablaze;
One in His love, we will circle the world
With the song of His praise.
Oh, let all His people rejoice,
And let all the earth hear His voice!

To every tongue, tribe
And nation He sends us,
To make disciples
To teach and baptise.
For all authority
To Him is given;
Now as His witnesses
We shall arise.

Come let us join with
The church from all nations,
Cross every border,
Throw wide every door;
Workers with Him
As He gathers His harvest,
Till earth's far corners
Our Saviour adore.

**123** Danny Daniels.
Copyright © Mercy Publishing/
Kingsway's Thankyou Music 1987.

GIVE ME LIFE, HOLY SPIRIT,
Guide my steps in Your sight;
Help me always give You pleasure,
Keep me walking in Your light.
Give me life, Holy Spirit,
Fill me now, make us one;
I will dwell with You for ever,
In the Father and the Son.

*I will dwell with You,*
*I will dwell with You.*
*I will dwell with You*
*In the Father and the Son.*

 Henry Smith.
Copyright © Integrity's Hosanna! Music.
Adm. Kingsway's Thankyou Music 1978.

GIVE THANKS with a grateful heart.
Give thanks to the Holy One.
Give thanks because He's given
Jesus Christ, His Son.
(Repeat)

And now let the weak say 'I am strong',
Let the poor say 'I am rich',
Because of what the Lord has done for us.
(Repeat)

(Last time)
Give thanks.

**125** Kevin Gould.
Copyright © Coronation/
Kingsway's Thankyou Music 1988.

GIVE THANKS TO THE LORD,
Call upon His name,
Make known among the nations
What He has done.
(Repeat)

Sing to Him,
Sing praise to Him,
Tell of all His wonderful acts.
Glory in His holy name,
Let the hearts of those
Who seek the Lord rejoice.

**126** Danny Reed.
Copyright © Kingsway's
Thankyou Music 1987.

GLORIOUS FATHER, we exalt You,
We worship, honour and adore You.
We delight to be in Your presence, O Lord,
We magnify Your holy name.

*And we sing, 'Come, Lord Jesus,*
*Glorify Your name.'*
*And we sing, 'Come, Lord Jesus,*
*Glorify Your name.'*

**127** John Newton.

GLORIOUS THINGS OF THEE ARE SPOKEN,
Zion, city of our God!
He whose word cannot be broken,
Formed thee for His own abode.
On the Rock of Ages founded,
What can shake thy sure repose?
With salvation's walls surrounded,
Thou mayest smile at all thy foes.

See! The streams of living waters,
Springing from eternal love,
Well supply thy sons and daughters,
And all fear of want remove;
Who can faint, whilst such a river
Ever flows their thirst to assuage?
Grace which, like the Lord, the Giver,
Never fails from age to age.

Round each habitation hovering,
See the cloud and fire appear!
For a glory and a covering,
Showing that the Lord is near.
He who gives them daily manna,
He who listens when they cry:
Let Him hear the loud hosanna
Rising to His throne on high.

Saviour, if of Zion's city
I, through grace, a member am,
Let the world deride or pity,
I will glory in Thy name.
Fading is the worldlings pleasure,
All his boasted pomp and show,
Solid joys and lasting treasure
None but Zion's children know.

**128**
Danny Daniels.
Copyright © Mercy Publishing/
Kingsway's Thankyou Music 1987.

GLORY, glory in the highest;
Glory, to the Almighty;
Glory to the Lamb of God,
And glory to the living Word;
Glory to the Lamb!

I give glory, (glory)
Glory, (glory)
Glory, glory to the Lamb!
I give glory, (glory)
Glory, (glory)
Glory, glory to the Lamb!
I give glory to the Lamb!

**129**
Carol Owens.
Copyright © Lexicon Music Inc/
U.N. Music Publishing Ltd/
CopyCare Ltd 1972.

GOD FORGAVE MY SIN in Jesus' name,
I've been born again in Jesus' name;
And in Jesus' name I come to you
To share His love as He told me to.

> He said: 'Freely, freely, you have received,
> Freely, freely give;
> Go in My name and because you believe
> Others will know that I live.'

All power is given in Jesus' name,
In earth and heaven in Jesus' name;
And in Jesus' name I come to you
To share His power as He told me to.

**130**
Austin Martin.
Copyright © Kingsway's
Thankyou Music 1984.

GOD HAS EXALTED HIM
*To the highest place,*
*Given Him the name*
*That is above every name.*

And every knee shall bow
And every tongue confess
That Jesus Christ is Lord
To the glory of God the Father.

**131**
Stuart Baugh.
Copyright © Restoration Music Ltd/
Sovereign Lifestyle Music 1982.

GOD HAS SPOKEN TO HIS PEOPLE,
Through His prophets long ago,
Of the days in which we're living
And the things His church should know.
Listen then you sons of Zion,
Lend your ears to what God says,
Then respond in full obedience,
Gladly walk in all His ways.

These are times of great refreshing
Coming from the throne in heaven,
Times of building and of shaking
When God rids His church of leaven.
Not a patching up of wineskins
Or of garments that are old,
But a glorious restoration
Just exactly as foretold.

Reign on, O God victorious,
Fulfil Your promises.
Seed of Abraham remember
You will see all nations blessed.
Powers of darkness, we remind you
Of Christ's victory on the cross.
Hear the truth we are declaring,
Jesus won and you have lost.

**132**
Graham Kendrick.
Copyright © Kingsway's
Thankyou Music 1985.

GOD IS GOOD, *we sing and shout it,*
*God is good, we celebrate.*
*God is good, no more we doubt it,*
*God is good, we know it's true.*

And when I think of His love for me,
My heart fills with praise
And I feel like dancing.
For in His heart there is room for me
And I run with arms open wide.

> (Last time)
> *We know it's true.*
> *Hey!*

**133**
Ian Smale.
Copyright © Kingsway's Thankyou Music 1987.

GOD IS HERE, GOD IS PRESENT,
God is moving by His Spirit,
Can you hear what He is saying,
Are you willing to respond?
God is here, God is present,
God is moving by His Spirit,
Lord, I open up my life to You,
Please do just what You will.

Lord, I won't stop loving You,
You mean more to me than anything else.
Lord, I won't stop loving You,
You mean more to me than life itself.

**134**
Alex Simons & Freda Kimmey.
Copyright © Celebration/
Kingsway's Thankyou Music 1977.

GOD IS OUR FATHER,
For He has made us His own,
Made Jesus our brother
And hand in hand we'll grow together as one.
Sing praise to the Lord with the tambourine,
Sing praise to the Lord with clapping hands,
Sing praise to the Lord with dancing feet,
Sing praise to the Lord with our voice.

La-la-la... (etc.)

## 135

Arthur C. Ainger.

**GOD IS WORKING HIS PURPOSE OUT,**
As year succeeds to year;
God is working His purpose out,
And the time is drawing near;
Nearer and nearer draws the time,
The time that shall surely be,
When the earth shall be filled
With the glory of God,
As the waters cover the sea.

From utmost East to utmost West,
Where'er man's foot hath trod,
By the mouth of many messengers
Goes forth the voice of God;
Give ear to Me, ye continents,
Ye isles, give ear to Me,
That the earth may be filled
With the glory of God,
As the waters cover the sea.

March we forth in the strength of God
With the banner of Christ unfurled,
That the light of the glorious gospel of truth
May shine throughout the world:
Fight we the fight with sorrow and sin,
To set their captives free,
That the earth may be filled
With the glory of God,
As the waters cover the sea.

All we can do is nothing worth,
Unless God blesses the deed;
Vainly we hope for the harvest-tide
Till God gives life to the seed;
Yet nearer and nearer draws the time,
The time that shall surely be,
When the earth shall be filled
With the glory of God,
As the waters cover the sea.

## 136

John Wimber.
Copyright © Mercy Publishing/
Kingsway's Thankyou Music 1988.

**GOD OF ALL COMFORT,**
God of all grace,
We have come to seek You,
We have come to seek Your face.

Because You have called us,
We're gathered in this place,
Oh, we have come to seek You,
We have come to seek Your face.

## 137

David Fellingham.
Copyright © Kingsway's
Thankyou Music 1982.

**GOD OF GLORY,** we exalt Your name,
You who reign in majesty,
We lift our hearts to You
And we will worship, praise and magnify
Your holy name.

In power resplendent
You reign in glory,
Eternal King, You reign for ever.
Your word is mighty,
Releasing captives,
Your love is gracious,
You are my God.

## 138

Chris Bowater.
Copyright © Sovereign Lifestyle Music Ltd 1990.

**GOD OF GRACE,** I turn my face
To you, I cannot hide;
My nakedness, my shame, my guilt,
Are all before Your eyes.

Strivings and all anguished dreams
In rags lie at my feet,
And only grace provides the way
For me to stand complete.

And Your grace clothes me in righteousness,
And Your mercy covers me in love.
Your life adorns and beautifies,
I stand complete in You.

## 139

H. E. Fosdick.

**GOD OF GRACE AND GOD OF GLORY,**
On Thy people pour Thy power;
Crown Thine ancient Church's story;
Bring her bud to glorious flower.
Grant us wisdom,
Grant us courage,
For the facing of this hour.

Lo! the host of evil round us
Scorn Thy Christ, assail His ways!
Fears and doubts too long have bound us;
Free our hearts to work and praise.
Grant us wisdom,
Grant us courage,
For the living of these days.

Heal Thy children's warring madness;
Bend our pride to Thy control;
Shame our wanton, selfish gladness,
Rich in things and poor in soul.
Grant us wisdom,
Grant us courage,
Lest we miss Thy kingdom's goal.

Set our feet on lofty places;
Gird our lives that they may be
Armoured with all Christlike graces
In the fight to set men free.
Grant us wisdom,
Grant us courage,
That we fail not man nor Thee.

Save us from weak resignation
To the evils we deplore;
Let the search for Thy salvation
Be our glory evermore.
Grant us wisdom,
Grant us courage,
Serving Thee whom we adore.

**140** John Mason Neale altd.

## GOOD CHRISTIAN MEN, REJOICE

With heart and soul and voice;
Give ye heed to what we say,
Jesus Christ is born today;
Ox and ass before Him bow,
And He is in the manger now.
Christ is born today;
Christ is born today!

Good Christian men, rejoice
With heart and soul and voice;
Now ye hear of endless bliss,
Jesus Christ was born for this:
He hath opened heaven's door
And man is blessed for ever more.
Christ was born for this;
Christ was born for this!

Good Christian men, rejoice
With heart and soul and voice;
Now ye need not fear the grave,
Jesus Christ was born to save;
Calls you one and calls you all
To gain His everlasting hall.
Christ was born to save;
Christ was born to save!

**141** Bob Pitcher.
Copyright © Kingsway's
Thankyou Music 1980.

## GREAT AND MARVELLOUS are Thy works,

O Lord God the Almighty,
Righteous and true are Thy ways,
O Thou King of the nations.
Who will not fear, O Lord,
And glorify Thy name?
For Thou alone art holy
And all the nations will come before Thee
And worship, worship, worship before Thee,
And worship, worship, worship before Thee.

**142** Kevin Prosch.
Copyright © Mercy Publishing/
Kingsway's Thankyou Music 1987.

## GREAT AND MARVELLOUS ARE THY WORKS

Lord God Almighty;
Just and true are Thy ways O Lord,
For you are the King of saints.

Who shall not fear Thee,
Who shall not glorify Thy name, O Lord?
For only Thou art holy.
All the nations shall come and worship before
Thee,
For Thy judgements are made manifest.
For Thy judgements are made manifest.

Hallelujah, (hallelujah)
Hallelujah to the King of saints.
Glory hallelujah, (glory hallelujah)
Glory hallelujah to the King of saints.

**143** Stuart Dauermann.
Copyright © Lillenas Publishing Co/
Kingsway's Thankyou Music 1972.

## GREAT AND WONDERFUL are Thy wondrous
deeds,
O Lord God the Almighty,
Just and true are all Thy ways, O Lord,
King of the ages art Thou.
Who shall not fear and glorify
Thy name, O Lord?
For Thou alone art holy,
Thou alone.
All the nations shall come and worship Thee,
For Thy glory shall be revealed,
Hallelujah, Hallelujah, Hallelujah, Amen.

Lai-lai-lai... *(etc.)*

**144** Author unknown.

## GREAT IS THE LORD and greatly to be praised,

In the city of our God,
In the mountain of His holiness.
Beautiful for situation, the joy of the whole
earth
Is Mount Zion on the sides of the north,
The city of the great King,
Is Mount Zion on the sides of the north,
The city of the great King.

One body, one Spirit, one faith, one Lord,
One people, one nation, praise ye the Lord.

**145** Steve McEwan.
Copyright © Body Songs/
CopyCare Ltd 1985.

## GREAT IS THE LORD and most worthy of
praise,
The city of our God, the holy place,
The joy of the whole earth.
Great is the Lord in whom we have the victory,
He aids us against the enemy,
We bow down on our knees.

*And Lord, we want to lift Your name on
high,
And Lord, we want to thank You,
For the works You've done in our lives;
And Lord, we trust in Your unfailing love,
For You alone are God eternal,
Throughout earth and heaven above.*

**146** Dale Garratt.
Copyright © Scripture in Song/
CopyCare Ltd 1980.

## GREAT IS THE LORD AND MIGHTY IN POWER,

His understanding has no limit;
The Lord delights in those who fear Him,
Who put their hope in His unfailing love.

He strengthens the bars of your gates,
He grants you peace in your borders,
He reveals His word to His people,
He has done this for no other nation.

Great is the Lord and mighty in power,
His understanding has no limit;
Extol the Lord, O Jerusalem,
Praise your God, O people of Zion.


**147**  Thomas O. Chisholm.
Copyright © Hope Publishing Co. 1923, 1951.

**GREAT IS THY FAITHFULNESS,** O God my
Father,
There is no shadow of turning with Thee;
Thou changest not, Thy compassions, they fail
not;
As Thou has been Thou for ever wilt be.

*Great is Thy faithfulness!*
*Great is Thy faithfulness!*
*Morning by morning new mercies I see;*
*All I have needed Thy hand hath provided,*
*Great is Thy faithfulness, Lord, unto me!*

Summer and winter, and springtime and
harvest,
Sun, moon and stars in their courses above,
Join with all nature in manifold witness
To Thy great faithfulness, mercy and love.

Pardon for sin and a peace that endureth,
Thine own dear presence to cheer and to
guide;
Strength for today and bright hope for
tomorrow,
Blessings all mine, with ten thousand beside!


**148**  William Williams.
Tr. Peter Williams.

**GUIDE ME, O THOU GREAT JEHOVAH,**
Pilgrim through this barren land;
I am weak, but Thou art mighty,
Hold me with Thy powerful hand:
Bread of heaven, Bread of heaven,
Feed me now and evermore,
Feed me now and evermore.

Open Thou the crystal fountain
Whence the healing stream doth flow;
Let the fiery, cloudy pillar
Lead me all my journey through:
Strong Deliverer, strong Deliverer,
Be Thou still my strength and shield,
Be Thou still my strength and shield.

When I tread the verge of Jordan
Bid my anxious fears subside;
Death of death, and hell's destruction,
Land me safe on Canaan's side:
Songs of praises, songs of praises,
I will ever give to Thee,
I will ever give to Thee.


**149**  John Bakewell.

**HAIL, THOU ONCE DESPISÉD JESUS,**
Hail, Thou Galilean King!
Thou didst suffer to release us,
Thou didst free salvation bring.
Hail, Thou agonising Saviour,
Bearer of our sin and shame,
By Thy merits we find favour,
Life is given through Thy name.

Paschal Lamb, by God appointed,
All our sins on Thee were laid.
With almighty love anointed,
Thou hast full atonement made.
All Thy people are forgiven
Through the virtue of Thy blood:
Opened is the gate of heaven,
Man is reconciled to God.

Jesus, hail! enthroned in glory,
There for ever to abide;
All the heavenly hosts adore Thee,
Seated at Thy Father's side:
There for sinners Thou art pleading,
There Thou dost our place prepare,
Ever for us interceding,
Till in glory we appear.

Worship, honour, power, and blessing
Thou art worthy to receive:
Loudest praises, without ceasing,
Right it is for us to give:
Come, O mighty Holy Spirit,
As our hearts and hands we raise,
Help us sing our Saviour's merits,
Help us sing Immanuel's praise.


**150**  James Montgomery.

**HAIL TO THE LORD'S ANOINTED,**
Great David's greater Son!
Hail, in the time appointed,
His reign on earth begun!
He comes to break oppression,
To set the captive free,
To take away transgression,
And rule in equity.

He comes, with succour speedy,
To those who suffer wrong;
To help the poor and needy,
And bid the weak be strong;
To give them songs for sighing,
Their darkness turn to light,
Whose souls, condemned and dying,
Were precious in His sight.

He shall come down like showers
Upon the fruitful earth;
Love, joy and hope, like flowers,
Spring in His path to birth;
Before Him, on the mountains,
Shall peace, the herald, go;
And righteousness, in fountains,
From hill to valley flow.

Kings shall fall down before Him,
And gold and incense bring;
All nations shall adore Him,
His praise all people sing;
To Him shall prayer unceasing
And daily vows ascend,
His kingdom still increasing,
A kingdom without end.

O'er every foe victorious,
He on His throne shall rest;
From age to age more glorious,
All-blessing and all-blessed.
The tide of time shall never
His covenant remove;
His name shall stand for ever,
His changeless name of Love.

**151** Dale Garratt.
Copyright © Scripture in Song/
CopyCare Ltd 1972.

**HALLELUJAH, FOR THE LORD OUR GOD**
The Almighty reigns.
Hallelujah, for the Lord our God
The Almighty reigns.
Let us rejoice and be glad
And give the glory unto Him.
Hallelujah, for the Lord our God
The Almighty reigns.

**152** Tim Cullen.
Copyright © Celebration/
Kingsway's Thankyou Music 1975.

**HALLELUJAH, MY FATHER,**
For giving us Your Son,
Sending Him into the world,
To be given up for men.
Knowing we would bruise Him
And smite Him from the earth.
Hallelujah, my Father,
In His death is my birth,
Hallelujah, my Father,
In His life is my life.

**153** William C. Dix.

**HALLELUJAH! SING TO JESUS;**
His the sceptre, His the throne;
Hallelujah! His the triumph,
His the victory alone.
Hark, the songs of holy Zion
Thunder like a mighty flood:
'Jesus out of every nation
Hath redeemed us by His blood.'

Hallelujah! not as orphans
Are we left in sorrow now;
Hallelujah! He is near us,
Faith believes, nor questions how.
Though the clouds from sight received Him
When the forty days were o'er,
Shall our hearts forget His promise,
'I am with you evermore'?

Hallelujah! Bread of heaven,
Thou on earth our food, our stay;
Hallelujah! here the sinful
Flee to Thee from day to day.
Intercessor, Friend of sinners,
Earth's Redeemer, plead for me
Where the songs of all the sinless
Sweep across the crystal sea.

Hallelujah! sing to Jesus;
His the sceptre, His the throne;
Hallelujah! His the triumph,
His the victory alone.
Hark, the songs of holy Zion
Thunder like a mighty flood:
'Jesus out of every nation
Hath redeemed us by His blood.'

**154** Philip Doddridge altd.

**HARK THE GLAD SOUND!** The Saviour comes,
The Saviour promised long;
Let every heart prepare a throne,
And every voice a song.

He comes the prisoners to release,
In Satan's bondage held;
The gates of brass before Him burst,
The iron fetters yield.

He comes the broken heart to bind,
The bleeding soul to cure,
And with the treasures of His grace
To enrich the humble poor.

Our glad hosannas, Prince of Peace,
Thy welcome shall proclaim;
And heaven's eternal arches ring
With Thy beloved name.

**155** Charles Wesley altd.

**HARK! THE HERALD-ANGELS SING**
'Glory to the new-born King!
Peace on earth, and mercy mild,
God and sinners reconciled!'
Joyful, all ye nations rise,
Join the triumph of the skies,
With the angelic host proclaim,
'Christ is born in Bethlehem.'
Hark! the herald angels sing
'Glory to the new-born King!'

Christ, by highest heaven adored,
Christ, the everlasting Lord,
Late in time behold Him come,
Offspring of a virgin's womb.
Veiled in flesh the Godhead see!
Hail the incarnate Deity!
Pleased as man with man to dwell,
Jesus, our Immanuel.
Hark! the herald angels sing,
'Glory to the newborn king.'

Hail the heaven-born Prince of Peace!
Hail, the Sun of righteousness!
Light and life to all He brings,
Risen with healing in His wings,
Mild, He lays His glory by;
Born that men no more may die;
Born to raise the sons of earth;
Born to give them second birth.
Hark! the herald angels sing:
'Glory to the newborn king.'

## 156 A. A. Pollard.

**HAVE THINE OWN WAY, LORD,**
Have Thine own way;
Thou art the Potter,
I am the clay.
Mould me and make me,
After Thy will,
While I am waiting
Yielded and still.

Have Thine own way, Lord,
Have Thine own way;
Search me and try me,
Master today.
Whiter than snow, Lord,
Wash me just now,
As in Thy presence
Humbly I bow.

Have Thine own way, Lord,
Have Thine own way;
Wounded and weary,
Help me, I pray.
Power, all power,
Surely is Thine;
Touch me and heal me,
Saviour divine.

Have Thine own way, Lord,
Have Thine own way;
Hold o'er my being
Absolute sway.
Fill with Thy Spirit
Till all shall see
Christ only, always,
Living in me.

## 157 Dave Bilbrough. Copyright © Kingsway's Thankyou Music 1990.

**HEALING GRACE,** *healing grace,*
*Show me more of Your healing grace.*
*Fill my life anew as I worship You,*
*For Your healing grace to me.*

My eyes have been opened
And now I can see,
The love of the Father
Given to me.

My Saviour, Deliverer,
The reason I sing,
To You I surrender,
For You are my King.

## 158 Graham Kendrick. Copyright © Make Way Music 1989.

**HEAR, O LORD, OUR CRY,**
Revive us, revive us again.
For the sake of Your glory,
Revive us, revive us again.
Lord, hear our cry.
Lord, hear our cry.

Hear, O Lord, our cry,
Revive us, revive us again.
For the sake of the children,
Revive us, revive us again.
Lord, hear our cry.
Lord, hear our cry.

## 159 David Fellingham. Copyright © Kingsway's Thankyou Music 1988.

**HEAR, O SHEPHERD** of Your people,
Let Your face shine and we will be saved.
Shine forth, O God, in this pagan darkness.
Awaken Your power, and come to restore.

*O Lord of hosts, turn again now,*
*Make Your church strong to speak out Your*
*word.*
*We'll not turn back from our great*
*commission*
*To reach the lost and save this land.*

Let Your power fall upon us,
Give strength unto the sons of Your right hand.
We now hear the call to seek You,
Awaken Your power, and come to restore.

## 160 Author unknown.

**HEAVENLY FATHER, I APPRECIATE YOU,**
Heavenly Father, I appreciate You,
I love You, adore You,
I bow down before You,
Heavenly Father, I appreciate You.

Son of God, what a wonder You are,
Son of God, what a wonder You are.
You cleansed my soul from sin,
You set the Holy Ghost within,
Son of God, what a wonder You are.

Holy Ghost, what a comfort You are,
Holy Ghost, what a comfort You are.
You lead us, You guide us,
You live right inside us,
Holy Ghost, what a comfort You are.

**161** John Pantry.
Copyright © Kingsway's
Thankyou Music 1990.

**HE CAME TO EARTH,** not to be served,
But gave His life to be a ransom for many;
The Son of God, the Son of man,
He shared our pain and bore our sins in His
   body.

*King of kings and Lord of lords,*
*I lift my voice in praise,*
*Such amazing love, but I do believe*
*This King has died for me.*

And so I stand, a broken soul,
To see the pain that I have brought to Jesus;
And yet each heart will be consoled,
To be made new, the joy of all believers.

And from now on, through all my days,
I vow to live each moment here for Jesus;
Not looking back, but giving praise
For all my Lord has done for this believer.

**162** Robert Whitney Manzano.
Copyright © Kingsway's
Thankyou Music 1984.

**HE GAVE ME BEAUTY** for ashes,
The oil of joy for mourning,
The garment of praise
For the spirit of heaviness.
That we might be trees of righteousness,
The planting of the Lord
That He might be glorified.

**163** Joan Parsons.
Copyright © Kingsway's
Thankyou Music 1978.

**HE HOLDS THE KEY** to salvation,
Jesus is over all.
He is the Lord of creation:

*Allelu, Alleluia.*
*Allelu, Alleluia Lord.*

He is the Rock ever standing,
No man could break Him down.
He is the Truth everlasting:

He is a Light in the darkness,
All men shall see His face.
He breaks all chains to redeem us:

All power to Him who is mighty,
All praise to Him who is God.
All glory now and for ever:

**164** Twila Paris.
Copyright © Straightway Music/
Word Music (UK)/CopyCare Ltd 1985.

**HE IS EXALTED,**
The King is exalted on high,
I will praise Him.
He is exalted,
Forever exalted
And I will praise His name!

He is the Lord,
Forever His truth shall reign.
Heaven and earth
Rejoice in His holy name.
He is exalted,
The King is exalted on high!

**165** Author unknown.

**HE IS LORD,** He is Lord,
He is risen from the dead
And He is Lord.
Every knee shall bow,
Every tongue confess
That Jesus Christ is Lord.

**166** Kandela Groves.
Copyright © Maranatha! Music/
CopyCare Ltd 1985.

**HE IS OUR PEACE,**
Who has broken down every wall;
He is our peace,
He is our peace.
He is our peace,
Who has broken down every wall;
He is our peace,
He is our peace.

Cast all your cares on Him,
For He cares for you;
He is our peace,
He is our peace.
Cast all your cares on Him,
For He cares for you;
He is our peace,
He is our peace.

**167** Chris Bowater.
Copyright © Sovereign Lifestyle Music Ltd 1981.

**HERE I AM,** *wholly available,*
*As for me, I will serve the Lord.*
*Here I am, wholly available;*
*As for me, I will serve the Lord.*

The fields are white unto harvest
But O, the labourers are so few,
So Lord I give myself to help the reaping,
To gather precious souls unto You.

The time is right in the nation
For works of power and authority;
God's looking for a people who are willing
To be counted in His glorious victory.

As salt are we ready to savour,
In darkness are we ready to be light?
God's seeking out a very special people
To manifest His truth and His might.

 **168**    William Rees.

**HERE IS LOVE** vast as the ocean,
Loving kindness as the flood,
When the Prince of life, our ransom
Shed for us His precious blood.
Who His love will not remember?
Who can cease to sing His praise?
He can never be forgotten
Throughout heaven's eternal days.

On the Mount of Crucifixion
Fountains opened deep and wide;
Through the floodgates of God's mercy
Flowed a vast and gracious tide.
Grace and love, like mighty rivers,
Poured incessant from above,
And heaven's peace and perfect justice
Kissed a guilty world in love.

**169**    Steve Hampton.
Copyright © Scripture in Song/
CopyCare Ltd 1978.

**HERE WE ARE,**
Gathered together as a family;
Bound as one,
Lifting up our voices
To the King of kings.
We cry:

> Abba, Father, worthy is Your name.
> Abba, Father, worthy is Your name.

Here, we are,
Singing together as a family;
Bound as one,
Lifting up our voices
To the King of kings.
We sing:

> Abba, Father, holy is Your name.
> Abba, Father, holy is Your name.

**170**    John Watson/Stuart Townend
Copyright © Ampelos Music (UK)/
Kingsway's Thankyou Music 1991.

**HE SHALL REIGN** as King of kings,
He shall reign as Lord of lords;
Messiah God, the living Word,
Hallelujah, hallelujah,
Let earth declare Him King!

**171**    Graham Kendrick.
Copyright © Kingsway's
Thankyou Music 1986.

**HE THAT IS IN US** *is greater than He*
*That is in the world.*
*He that is in us is greater than he*
*That is in the world.*

Therefore I will sing and I will rejoice
For His Spirit lives in me.
Christ the Living One has overcome
And we share in His victory.

All the powers of death and hell and sin
Lie crushed beneath His feet;
Jesus owns the Name above all names
Crowned with honour and majesty.

 **172**    Graham Kendrick.
Copyright © Make Way Music 1988.

**HE WALKED WHERE I WALK,**    *(echo)*
He stood where I stand,    *(echo)*
He felt what I feel,    *(echo)*
He understands.    *(echo)*
He knows my frailty,    *(echo)*
Shared my humanity,    *(echo)*
Tempted in every way,    *(echo)*
Yet without sin.    *(echo)*

> *God with us, so close to us.*    (all)
> *God with us, Immanuel!*

One of a hated race,    *(echo)*
Stung by the prejudice,    *(echo)*
Suffering injustice,    *(echo)*
Yet He forgives.    *(echo)*
Wept for my wasted years,    *(echo)*
Paid for my wickedness,    *(echo)*
He died in my place    *(echo)*
That I might live.    *(echo)*

**173**    Maggi Dawn.
Copyright © Kingsway's
Thankyou Music 1987.

**HE WAS PIERCED** for our transgressions,
And bruised for our iniquities;
And to bring us peace He was punished,
And by His stripes we are healed.

He was led like a lamb to the slaughter,
Although He was innocent of crime;
And cut off from the land of the living,
He paid for the guilt that was mine.

> *We like sheep have gone astray,*
> *Turned each one to his own way,*
> *And the Lord has laid on Him*
> *The iniquity of us all.*

(Descant)
*Like a lamb,*
*To the slaughter He came.*
*And the Lord laid on Him*
*The iniquity of us all.*

## 174

John Bunyan.

**HE WHO WOULD VALIANT BE**
'Gainst all disaster,
Let him in constancy
Follow the Master.
There's no discouragement
Shall make him once relent
His first avowed intent
To be a pilgrim.

Who so beset him round
With dismal stories,
Do but themselves confound—
His strength the more is.
No foes shall stay his might,
Though he with giants fight;
He will make good his right
To be a pilgrim.

Since, Lord, Thou dost defend
Us with Thy Spirit,
We know we at the end
Shall life inherit.
Then fancies flee away!
I'll fear not what men say,
I'll labour night and day
To be a pilgrim.

## 175

Author unknown.

**HIGHER, HIGHER,**
Higher, higher, higher,
Higher, higher, lift Jesus higher.
Higher, higher,
Higher, higher, higher,
Higher, higher, lift Jesus higher.

Cast your burdens onto Jesus,
He cares for you.
Cast your burdens onto Jesus,
He cares for you.

Lower, lower,
Lower, lower, lower,
Lower, lower, lower Satan lower.
Lower, lower,
Lower, lower, lower,
Lower, lower, lower Satan lower.

## 176

Author unknown.

**HIS NAME IS HIGHER** than any other,
His name is Jesus, His name is Lord.
His name is Wonderful,
His name is Counsellor,
His name is Prince of Peace,
The mighty God.
His name is higher than any other,
His name is Jesus, His name is Lord.

## 177

Audrey Mieir.

**HIS NAME IS WONDERFUL,**
His name is Wonderful
His name is Wonderful,
Jesus my Lord.
He is the mighty King,
Master of everything,
His name is Wonderful,
Jesus my Lord.

He's the great Shepherd,
The Rock of all ages,
Almighty God is He.
Bow down before Him,
Love and adore Him,
His name is wonderful,
Jesus my Lord.

## 178

Bill Anderson.

**HIS VOICE IS THE SEA**
And the sounding of the trumpets;
And the calling of the Shepherd is so sweet.
His face is the sun,
Brighter than the morning;
And all creation bows down at His feet.

*Jesus is Lord, and all the earth adores Him.*
*Jesus is Lord, He sits upon the throne.*
*When all men stand before Him,*
*Then every knee shall bow,*
*And every tongue cry 'Jesus is Lord.'*

His mouth is a sword
That rules o'er the nations,
And His sword will draw His children to His
side.
His eyes are a fire
That burns throughout the kingdom,
And the burning purifies the Master's bride.

## 179

Danny Daniels.

*(Men and women in canon)*
**HOLD ME LORD** in Your arms,
Fill me Lord with Your Spirit.
Touch my heart with Your love,
Let my life
Glorify Your name.

Singing Alleluia,
Singing Alleluia,
Singing Alleluia,
Singing Alleluia.

Alleluia, (Alleluia,)
Allelu, (Allelu,)
Alleluia, (Alleluia,)
Allelu, (Allelu.)

**180**

**HOLINESS UNTO THE LORD,**
Unto the King.
Holiness unto Your name
I will sing.

*Holiness unto Jesus,*
*Holiness unto You, Lord.*
*Holiness unto Jesus,*
*Holiness unto You Lord.*

I love You, I love Your ways,
I love Your name.
I love You, and all my days
I'll proclaim:

**181**

**HOLY, HOLY, HOLY** is the Lord God Almighty.
Holy, holy, holy is the Lord God Almighty.
All the angels cry out holy;
All the angels exalt Your name,
Crying holy, holy, holy,
Holy is the Lord.

Holy, holy, holy is the Lord God Almighty.
Holy, holy, holy is the Lord God Almighty.
All Your people cry out holy;
All Your people exalt Your name,
Crying holy, holy, holy,
Holy is the Lord.

Glory, glory, glory to the Lord God Almighty.
Glory, glory, glory to the Lord God Almighty.
The whole earth is filled with Your glory;
The whole earth will exalt Your name,
Crying holy, holy, holy,
Holy is the Lord.

**182**

**HOLY, HOLY, HOLY IS THE LORD,**
Holy is the Lord God Almighty.
Holy, holy, holy is the Lord,
Holy is the Lord God Almighty,
Who was and is and is to come,
Holy, holy, holy is the Lord.

Worthy, worthy, worthy is... *(etc.)*

Jesus, Jesus, Jesus is... *(etc.)*

Glory, glory, glory to... *(etc.)*

**183**

**HOLY, HOLY, HOLY, LORD GOD ALMIGHTY!**
Early in the morning
Our song shall rise to Thee:
Holy, holy, holy, merciful and mighty,
God in three Persons, blessèd Trinity!

Holy, holy, holy! all the saints adore Thee,
Casting down their golden crowns
Around the glassy sea;
Cherubim and seraphim falling down before
Thee,
Who were, and are, and evermore shall be.

Holy, holy, holy! though the darkness hide
Thee,
Though the eye of sinful man
Thy glory may not see;
Only Thou art holy, there is none beside Thee,
Perfect in power, in love and purity.

Holy, holy, holy, Lord God Almighty!
All Thy works shall praise Thy name
In earth, and sky, and sea;
Holy, holy, holy, merciful and mighty,
God in three Persons, blessèd Trinity!

**184**

**HOLY, HOLY, HOLY LORD,**
God of power and might,
Heaven and earth are filled with Your glory.
Holy, holy, holy Lord,
God of power and might,
Heaven and earth are filled with Your glory.
Hosanna, Hosanna in the highest!
Hosanna, Hosanna in the highest!

**185**

*(Men and women in canon)*
**HOLY IS THE LORD,**
Holy is the Lord.
Holy is the Lord,
Holy is the Lord.
Righteousness and mercy,
Judgement and grace.
Faithfulness and sovereignty;
Holy is the Lord,
Holy is the Lord.

**186**

**HOLY ONE,** holy One,
Blessed be the holy One,
Almighty ever-living God,
I worship only You.

*(Last time)*
Holy One.

**187**

**HOLY SPIRIT, LEAD ME TO MY FATHER,**
To bow before Him, and worship at His throne,
For He's my refuge, my strength and deliverer,
I will dwell in the shadow of Almighty God.

**188**

Chris Bowater.
Copyright © Sovereign Lifestyle Musc Ltd 1986.

## HOLY SPIRIT, WE WELCOME YOU.

Holy Spirit, we welcome You.
Move among us with holy fire,
As we lay aside all earthly desires,
Hands reach out and our hearts aspire.
Holy Spirit, Holy Spirit,
Holy Spirit, we welcome You.

Holy Spirit, we welcome You.
Holy Spirit, we welcome You.
Let the breeze of Your presence blow,
That Your children here might truly know
How to move in the Spirit's flow.
Holy Spirit, Holy Spirit,
Holy Spirit, we welcome You.

Holy Spirit, we welcome You.
Holy Spirit, we welcome You.
Please accomplish in me today
Some new work of loving grace, I pray;
Unreservedly have Your way.
Holy Spirit, Holy Spirit,
Holy Spirit, we welcome You.

**189**

Carl Tuttle.
Copyright © Mercy Publishing/
Kingsway's Thankyou Music 1985.

**HOSANNA**, hosanna, hosanna in the highest.
Hosanna, hosanna, hosanna in the highest.
Lord we lift up Your name, with hearts full of
    praise,
Be exalted, O Lord, my God,
Hosanna in the highest.

Glory, glory, glory to the King of kings.
Glory, glory, glory to the King of kings.
Lord, we lift up Your name, with hearts full of
    praise,
Be exalted, O Lord, my God,
Glory to the King of kings.

**190**

Keith & Melody Green.
Copyright © Birdwing Music/
Cherry Lane Music 1982.

### HOW I LOVE YOU,
*You are the One,*
*You are the One.*
*How I love You,*
*You are the One for me.*

I was so lost
But You showed the way,
'Cause You are the Way.
I was so lost
But You showed the way to me!

I was lied to
But You told the truth,
'Cause You are the Truth.
I was lied to
But You showed the truth to me!

I was dying
But You gave me life,
'Cause You are the Life.
I was dying
And You gave Your life for me!

*How I love You,*
*You are the One,*
*You are the One.*
*How I love You,*
*You are the One,*
*God's risen Son.*
*You are the One for me!*

Hallelujah!
You are the One,
You are the One.
Hallelujah!

**191**  Author unknown.

## HOW LOVELY IS THY DWELLING PLACE,
O Lord of hosts,
My soul longs and yearns for Your courts,
And my heart and flesh sing for joy
To the living God.
One day in Thy presence
Is far better to me than gold,
Or to live my whole life somewhere else;
And I would rather be
A doorkeeper in Your house
Than to take my fate upon myself.
You are my sun and my shield,
You are my lover from the start,
And the highway to Your city
Runs through my heart.

**192**

Leonard E. Smith Jnr.
Copyright © Kingsway's
Thankyou Music 1974, 1978.

*Popular version*

**HOW LOVELY ON THE MOUNTAINS** are the
    feet of Him
Who brings good news, good news,
Proclaiming peace, announcing news of
    happiness,
Our God reigns, our God reigns.

*Our God reigns, our God reigns,*
*Our God reigns, our God reigns.*

You watchmen lift your voices joyfully as one,
Shout for your King, your King.
See eye to eye the Lord restoring Zion:
Your God reigns, your God reigns!

Waste places of Jerusalem break forth with joy,
We are redeemed, redeemed.
The Lord has saved and comforted His people:
Your God reigns, your God reigns!

Ends of the earth, see the salvation of your
    God,
Jesus is Lord, is Lord.
Before the nations He has bared His holy arm:
Your God reigns, your God reigns!

*Original version*

**HOW LOVELY ON THE MOUNTAINS** are the
 feet of Him
Who brings good news, good news,
Announcing peace, proclaiming news of
 happiness,
Saying to Zion: Your God reigns.
Your God reigns, your God reigns,
Your God reigns, your God reigns.

He had no stately form, He had no majesty,
That we should be drawn to Him.
He was despised and we took no account of
 Him,
Yet now He reigns with the Most High.
Now He reigns, now He reigns,
Now He reigns with the Most High!

It was our sin and guilt that bruised and
 wounded Him,
It was our sin that brought Him down.
When we like sheep had gone astray, our
 Shepherd came
And on His shoulders bore our shame.
On His shoulders, on His shoulders,
On His shoulders He bore our shame.

Meek as a lamb that's led out to the
 slaughterhouse,
Dumb as a sheep before its shearer,
His life ran down upon the ground like pouring
 rain,
That we might be born again.
That we might be, that we might be,
That we might be born again.

Out from the tomb He came with grace and
 majesty,
He is alive, He is alive.
God loves us so, see here His hands, His feet,
 His side,
Yes, we know He is alive.
He is alive, He is alive,
He is alive, He is alive.

How lovely on the mountains are the feet of
 Him
Who brings good news, good news,
Announcing peace, proclaiming news of
 happiness:
Our God reigns, our God reigns.
Our God reigns, our God reigns,
Our God reigns, our God reigns.

**193** Phil Rogers.
 Copyright © Kingsway's
 Thankyou Music 1982.

**HOW PRECIOUS, O LORD,**
Is Your unfailing love,
We find refuge in the shadow of Your wings.
We feast, Lord Jesus, on the abundance of
 Your house
And drink from Your river of delights.
With You is the fountain of life,
In Your light we see light,
With You is the fountain of life,
In Your light we see light.

**194** John Newton.

**HOW SWEET THE NAME OF JESUS SOUNDS**
In a believer's ear!
It soothes his sorrows, heals his wounds,
And drives away his fear.

It makes the wounded spirit whole,
And calms the troubled breast;
'Tis manna to the hungry soul,
And to the weary, rest.

Dear name, the rock on which I build,
My shield and hiding place,
My never-failing treasury, filled
With boundless stores of grace!

Jesus! My Shepherd, Saviour, Friend,
My Prophet, Priest and King,
My Lord, my Life, my Way, my End,
Accept the praise I bring.

Weak is the effort of my heart,
And cold my warmest thought;
But when I see Thee as Thou art,
I'll praise Thee as I ought.

Till then I would Thy love proclaim
With every fleeting breath;
And may the music of Thy name
Refresh my soul in death.

**195**  Chris Welch.
 Copyright © Kingsway's
 Thankyou Music 1987.

**HOW YOU BLESS OUR LIVES,** Lord God!
How You fill our lives, Lord God!
I simply want to say I love You, Lord.
I simply want to say I bless You,
I simply want to say I adore You,
And I want to lift Your name even higher.

**196** Graham Kendrick.
 Copyright © Kingsway's
 Thankyou Music 1986.

**I AM A LIGHTHOUSE,** a shining and bright
 house,
Out in the waves of a stormy sea.
The oil of the Spirit keeps my lamp burning;
Jesus, my Lord, is the light on me.
And when people see the good things that I do,
They'll give praise to God who has sent us
 Jesus.
We'll send out a lifeboat of love and
 forgiveness
And give them a hand to get in.
(Repeat)

While the storm is raging, whoosh, whoosh,
And the wind is blowing, ooo, ooo,
And the waves are crashing,
Crash! crash! crash! crash!

**197**

**I AM A NEW CREATION,**
No more in condemnation,
Here in the grace of God I stand.
My heart is overflowing,
My love just keeps on growing,
Here in the grace of God I stand.

And I will praise You Lord,
Yes I will praise You Lord,
And I will sing of all that You have done.

A joy that knows no limit,
A lightness in my spirit,
Here in the grace of God I stand.

**198**

**I AM A WOUNDED SOLDIER** but I will not leave
   the fight,
Because the Great Physician is healing me.
So I'm standing in the battle, in the armour of
   His light,
Because His mighty power is real in me.

*I am loved, I am accepted,*
*By the Saviour of my soul.*
*I am loved, I am accepted*
*And my wounds will be made whole.*

**199**

**I AM NOT ASHAMED** *to belong to Jesus;*
*I am not afraid to stand my ground,*
*For there is no higher cause*
*Than working for the King.*
*To Him I lift my praise,*
*For I am not ashamed.*

Whom then shall I fear?
What shall daunt my spirit?
Sure and steadfast, anchored firm to the cross,
Standing with my brothers,
Serving God and others.
Though the world many ridicule, I'll still say:

At the King's returning,
Every soul will know Him,
All creation shall bow down to His name;
Brothers all, together
Serving Him forever,
He who gave His life for me, I will praise:

   *(Last chorus)*
   *We are not ashamed to belong to Jesus,*
   *We are not afraid to stand our ground,*
   *For there is no higher cause*
   *Than working for the King.*
   *To Him we lift our praise,*
   *For we are not ashamed.*

**200**

**I AM THE BREAD OF LIFE,**
He who comes to Me shall not hunger,
He who believes in Me shall not thirst.
No one can come to Me
Unless the Father draw him.

   *And I will raise him up,*
   *And I will raise him up,*
   *And I will raise him up on the last day.*

The bread that I will give
Is My flesh for the life of the world,
And he who eats of this bread,
He shall live for ever,
He shall live for ever.

Unless you eat
Of the flesh of the Son of man
And drink of His blood,
And drink of His blood,
You shall not have life within you.

I am the resurrection,
I am the life,
He who believes in Me
Even if he die,
He shall live for ever.

Yes, Lord, we believe
That You are the Christ,
The Son of God
Who has come
Into the world.

**201**

**I AM THE GOD THAT HEALETH THEE,**
I am the Lord, your healer.
I sent My word and healed your disease,
I am the Lord, your healer.

You are the God that healeth me,
You are the Lord, my healer.
You sent Your word and healed my disease,
You are the Lord, my healer.

**202**

**I AM TRUSTING THEE, LORD JESUS,**
Trusting only Thee!
Trusting Thee for full salvation,
Great and free.

I am trusting Thee for pardon,
At Thy feet I bow;
For Thy grace and tender mercy,
Trusting now.

I am trusting Thee for cleansing
In the crimson flood;
Trusting Thee to make me holy,
By Thy blood.

I am trusting Thee for power,
Thine can never fail;
Words which Thou Thyself shalt give me
Must prevail.

I am trusting Thee to guide me,
Thou alone shalt lead;
Every day and hour supplying
All my need.

I am trusting Thee, Lord Jesus;
Never let me fall;
I am trusting Thee for ever,
And for all.

## 203
Marc Nelson.
Copyright © Mercy Publishing/
Kingsway's Thankyou Music 1987.

**I BELIEVE IN JESUS:**
*I believe He is the Son of God,*
*I believe He died and rose again,*
*I believe He paid for us all.*

(Men)    And I believe He's here now,
(Women)  I believe that He is here.
(All)    Standing in our midst.
(Men)    Here with the power to heal now,
(Women)  With the power to heal,
(All)    And the grace to forgive.

*I believe in You, Lord;*
*I believe You are the Son of God,*
*I believe You died and rose again,*
*I believe You paid for us all.*

(Men)    And I believe You're here now.
(Women)  I believe that You're here.
(All)    Standing in our midst.
(Men)    Here with the power to heal now,
(Women)  With the power to heal,
(All)    And the grace to forgive.

## 204
Peter & Hanneke Jacobs.
Copyright © Maranatha! Music/
CopyCare Ltd 1985.

**I CAN ALMOST SEE** Your holiness,
As I look around this place,
With my hands stretched out,
To receive Your love,
I can see You on each face.

*Spirit of God, lift me up,*
*Spirit of God, lift me up,*
*Fill me again with Your love,*
*Sweet Spirit of God.*
    (Repeat)

## 205
William Y. Fullerton.

**I CANNOT TELL** why He, whom angels
    worship,
Should set His love upon the sons of men,
Or why, as Shepherd, He should seek the
    wanderers,
To bring them back, they know not how or
    when.
But this I know, that He was born of Mary,
When Bethlehem's manger was His only home,
And that He lived at Nazareth and laboured,
And so the Saviour, Saviour of the world, is
    come.

I cannot tell how silently He suffered,
As with His peace He graced this place of tears,
Or how His heart upon the cross was broken,
The crown of pain to three-and-thirty years.
But this I know, He heals the broken-hearted,
And stays our sin, and calms our lurking fear,
And lifts the burden from the heavy-laden,
For yet the Saviour, Saviour of the world, is
    here.

I cannot tell how He will win the nations,
How He will claim His earthly heritage,
How satisfy the needs and aspirations
Of east and west, of sinner and of sage.
But this I know, all flesh shall see His glory,
And He shall reap the harvest He has sown,
And some glad day His sun shall shine in
    splendour,
When He the Saviour, Saviour of the world is
    known.

I cannot tell how all the lands shall worship,
When, at his bidding, every storm is stilled,
Or who can say how great the jubilation
When all the hearts of men with love are filled.
But this I know, the skies will thrill with rapture,
And myriad, myriad human voices sing,
And earth to heaven, and heaven to earth, will
    answer:
'At last the Saviour, Saviour of the world, is
    King!'

## 206
Chris Bowater.
Copyright © Sovereign Lifestyle Music Ltd. 1981.

**I DELIGHT GREATLY IN THE LORD,**
My soul rejoices in my God.
I delight greatly in the Lord,
My soul rejoices in my God.
For He has clothed me with garments of
    salvation,
And arrayed me in a robe of righteousness.
He has clothed me with garments of salvation,
And arrayed me in a robe of righteousness.

**207**

**I EXALT YOU,**
Just and true are all Your ways.
I exalt You,
And glorify Your name.
(Repeat)

For You are resplendent in Your majesty,
There is no other God beside You;
Magnificent in power and in glory,
You are Jehovah God Almighty.
Holy is the Lord of hosts,
Holy is the Lord.
Holy is the Lord of hosts,
Holy is the Lord!

**208**

**IF I WERE A BUTTERFLY,**
I'd thank You, Lord, for giving me wings.
And if I were a robin in a tree,
I'd thank You, Lord, that I could sing.
And if I were a fish in the sea,
I'd wiggle my tail and I'd giggle with glee;
But I just thank You Father,
For making me 'me'.

*For You gave me a heart*
*And You gave me a smile,*
*You gave me Jesus*
*And You made me Your child,*
*And I just thank You, Father,*
*For making me 'me'.*

If I were an elephant,
I'd thank You, Lord, by raising my trunk.
And if I were a kangaroo,
You know I'd hop right up to You.
And if I were an octopus,
I'd thank You, Lord, for my fine looks;
But I just thank You, Father,
For making me 'me'.

If I were a wiggily worm,
I'd thank You, Lord, that I could squirm.
And if I were a billy goat,
I'd thank You, Lord, for my strong throat.
And if I were a fuzzy-wuzzy bear,
I'd thank You, Lord, for my fuzzy-wuzzy hair;
But I just thank You, Father,
For making me 'me'.

**209**

**I GET SO EXCITED, LORD,**
Every time I realise
I'm forgiven, I'm forgiven.
Jesus, Lord, You've done it all,
You've paid the price,
I'm forgiven, I'm forgiven.

Hallelujah, Lord,
My heart just fills with praise,
My feet start dancing, my hands rise up,
And my lips they bless Your name.
I'm forgiven, I'm forgiven, I'm forgiven.
I'm forgiven, I'm forgiven, I'm forgiven.

Living in Your presence, Lord,
Is life itself,
I'm forgiven, I'm forgiven.
With the past behind, grace for today
And a hope to come,
I'm forgiven, I'm forgiven.

**210**

**I GIVE YOU ALL THE HONOUR**
And praise that's due Your name,
For You are the King of Glory,
The Creator of all things.

*And I worship You,*
*I give my life to You,*
*I fall down on my knees.*
*Yes, I worship You,*
*I give my life to You,*
*I fall down on my knees.*

As Your Spirit moves upon me now
You meet my deepest need,
And I lift my hands up to Your throne,
Your mercy I've received.

You have broken chains that bound me,
You've set this captive free,
I will lift my voice to praise Your name,
For all eternity.

**211**

**I GIVE YOU NOW** all I have;
I give to you my everything.
You have the power inside of you
To overcome all the hosts of darkness.

*Go, go into the world,*
*Tell them I'm alive,*
*Go into the streets,*
*Tell them that I live,*
*Ooh, that I live in you.*
*Go, go into the world,*
*Claim it for your King,*
*Go into the streets,*
*Dry those people's tears,*
*Ooh, make the old things new.*

**212**

**I HAVE A DESTINY** *I know I shall fulfil,*
*I have a destiny in that city on a hill.*
*I have a destiny and it's not an empty wish,*
*For I know I was born for such a time as*
*    this.*

Long before the ages You predestined me
To walk in all the works You have prepared for
    me.
You've given me a part to play in history
To help prepare a bride for eternity.

I did not choose You but You have chosen me
And appointed me for bearing fruit abundantly.
I know You will complete the work begun in
    me,
By the power of Your Spirit working mightily.

**213**

**I HAVE FOUND** such joy in my salvation
Since I gave my heart to You,
I have found the reason I'm living
So in love, so near to You.

*    I worship You, my Lord,*
*    With all my life, praise Your name,*
*    I worship You, worship You, my Lord.*

Oh my Lord, my life I'm giving,
A living sacrifice to You,
Oh my Lord, the reason I'm living
Is to serve and worship You.

**214**

**I HAVE MADE A COVENANT** with My chosen,
Given My servant My word.
I have made Your name to last for ever,
Built to outlast all time.

*    I will celebrate Your love for ever, Yahweh,*
*    Age on age my words proclaim Your love.*
*    For I claim that love is built to last for ever,*
*    Founded firm Your faithfulness.*

Yahweh, that assembly of those who love You
Applaud Your marvellous word.
Who in the skies can compare with Yahweh?
Who can rival Him?

Happy the people who learn to acclaim You,
They rejoice in Your light.
You are our glory and You are our courage,
Our hope belongs to You.

I have revealed My chosen servant
And He can rely on Me,
Given Him My love to last for ever,
He shall rise in My name.

He will call to Me, 'My Father, my God!'
For I make Him My firstborn Son.
I cannot take back My given promise,
I've called Him to shine like the sun.

**215**

**I HEARD THE VOICE OF JESUS SAY:**
'Come unto Me and rest;
Lay down, thou weary one, lay down
Thy head upon My breast.'
I came to Jesus as I was,
Weary and worn and sad,
I found in Him a resting place,
And He has made me glad.

I heard the voice of Jesus say:
'Behold I freely give
The living water, thirsty one,
Stoop down and drink and live.'
I came to Jesus, and I drank
Of that life-giving stream;
My thirst was quenched, my soul revived,
And now I live in Him.

I heard the voice of Jesus say:
'I am this dark world's light;
Look unto Me, thy morn shall rise,
And all thy day be bright.'
I looked to Jesus, and I found
In Him my Star, my Sun;
And in that light of life I'll walk,
Till travelling days are done.

**216**

**I HEAR THE SOUND OF RUSTLING** in the
    leaves of the trees,
The Spirit of the Lord has come down on the
    earth.
The Church that seemed in slumber has now
    risen from its knees
And dry bones are responding with the fruits of
    new birth.
Oh this is now a time for declaration,
The word will go to all men everywhere;
The Church is here for healing of the nations,
Behold the day of Jesus drawing near.

*    My tongue will be the pen of a ready writer,*
*    And what the Father gives to me I'll sing;*
*    I only want to be His breath,*
*    I only want to glorify the King.*

And all around the world the body waits
    expectantly,
The promise of the Father is now ready to fall.
The watchmen on the tower all exhort us to
    prepare
And the church responds—a people who will
    answer the call.
And this is not a phase which is passing,
It's the start of an age that is to come.
And where is the wise man and the scoffer?
Before the face of Jesus they are dumb.

A body now prepared by God and ready for
    war,
The prompting of the Spirit is our word of
    command.
We rise, a mighty army, at the bidding of the
    Lord,
The devils see and fear, for their time is at
    hand.
And children of the Lord hear our commission
That we should love and serve our God as one.
The Spirit won't be hindered by division
In the perfect work that Jesus has begun.

**217**    Dave Moody.

**I HEAR THE SOUND OF THE ARMY OF THE
    LORD,**
I hear the sound of the army of the Lord.
It's the sound of praise,
It's the sound of war,
The army of the Lord,
The army of the Lord,
The army of the Lord is marching on.

**218**    Arthur Tannous.

**I JUST WANT TO PRAISE YOU,**
Lift my hands and say: 'I love You.'
You are everything to me
And I exalt Your holy name on high.
I just want to praise You,
Lift my hands and say: 'I love You.'
You are everything to me
And I exalt Your holy name,
I exalt Your holy name,
I exalt Your holy name on high.

**219**    Dave Bilbrough.

**I JUST WANT TO PRAISE YOU,** I just want to
    sing.
I just want to give You, Lord, my everything,
In every situation, in everything I do,
To give You my devotion, for my delight is
    You.

    *Lord, I lift You high.*
    *Your love will never die.*

**220**    D.W. Whittle.

**I KNOW NOT WHY GOD'S WONDROUS
    GRACE**
To me hath been made known;
Nor why unworthy as I am
He claimed me for His own.

*But I know whom I have believèd;*
*And am persuaded that He is able*
*To keep that which I've committed*
*Unto Him against that day.*

I know not how this saving faith
To me He did impart;
Or how believing in His word
Wrought peace within my heart.

I know not how the Spirit moves,
Convincing men of sin;
Revealing Jesus through the Word,
Creating faith in Him.

I know not what of good or ill
May be reserved for me,
Of weary ways or golden days
Before His face I see.

I know not when my Lord may come;
I know not how, nor where;
If I shall pass the vale of death,
Or 'meet Him in the air'.

**221**    Brian Doerksen.

**I LIFT MY EYES UP** to the mountains,
Where does my help come from?
My help comes from You, Maker of heaven,
Creator of the earth.

    *O how I need You, Lord,*
    *You are my only hope;*
    *You're my only prayer.*
    *So I will wait for You*
    *To come and rescue me,*
    *Come and give me life.*

**222**    Eddie Espinosa.

**I LIFT MY HANDS,**
I raise my voice,
I give my heart to You my Lord,
And I rejoice.
There are many, many reasons why I do the
    things I do,
O but most of all, I praise You,
Most of all I praise You,
Jesus, most of all I praise You because You're
    You.

I lift my hands,
I raise my voice,
I give my life to You my Lord
And I rejoice.
There are many, many reasons why I do the
    things I do,
O but most of all, I love You,
Most of all I love You,
Jesus, most of all I love You because You're
    You.

I lift my hands,
I raise my voice,
I give my love to You my Lord,
And I rejoice.
There are many, many reasons why I do the
   things I do,
O but most of all, I love You,
Most of all I love You,
Jesus, most of all I love You because You're
   You.


**223**

**I LIFT MY HANDS** *(echo)*
To the coming King, *(echo)*
To the great I AM, *(echo)*
To You I sing, *(echo)*
For You're the One *(echo)*
Who reigns within my heart. *(all)*

*And I will serve no foreign god,*
*Or any other treasure.*
*You are my heart's desire,*
*Spirit without measure.*
*Unto Your name*
*I will bring my sacrifice.*


**224**

**I LIFT MY VOICE** to praise Your name,
That through my life I might proclaim
The praises of the One who reigns:
Jesus, my Lord.

Like a mighty flame that burns so bright,
I am a bearer of His light.
No longer I, for He is my life:
Jesus, my Lord.

*Jesus, Jesus, alive in me.*
*Jesus, Jesus, setting me free.*


**225**

**I LIVE,** I live because He is risen,
I live, I live with power over sin,
I live, I live because He is risen,
I live, I live to worship Him.

Thank You Jesus, thank You Jesus,
Because You're alive,
Because You're alive,
Because You're alive I live.

**226**

**I LOVE YOU, LORD,** and I lift my voice
To worship You, O my soul rejoice.
Take joy, my King, in what You hear,
May it be a sweet, sweet sound in Your ear.
Let me


**227**

**I LOVE YOU MY LORD**
For giving to me Your great salvation,
Setting me free from sin and death
And the kingdom of Satan's destruction.
There's power in the blood
To cleanse all my sin, I know I'm forgiven;
I'm reigning in life, I'm living by faith,
I'm now united with Christ.

*(1st part)*
I confess with my mouth that Jesus is Lord,
Jesus is Lord, and believe in my heart
He's been raised from the dead.
I confess with my mouth that Jesus is Lord,
Jesus is Lord, and now I have life,
Now I have life by the Spirit of God.

*(2nd part)*
I confess with my mouth that Jesus is Lord
And believe in my heart
He's been raised from the dead.
I confess with my mouth that Jesus is my Lord
And now I have life by the Spirit of God.


**228**

**I LOVE YOU WITH THE LOVE OF THE LORD,**
Yes, I love you with the love of the Lord.
I can see in you the glory of my King,
And I love you with the love of the Lord.


**229**

**I'M ACCEPTED,** I'm forgiven,
I am fathered by the true and living God.
I'm accepted, no condemnation,
I am loved by the true and living God.
There's no guilt or fear as I draw near
To the Saviour and Creator of the world.
There is joy and peace
As I release my worship to You, O Lord.

**I'M GONNA THANK THE LORD,** He set me free,
I'm gonna thank the Lord, He set me free,
For my Saviour He redeemed me,
For my Saviour rescued me.
Yes, I'm gonna thank the Lord, He set me free.

I'm gonna clap my hands and stamp my
    feet... *(etc.)*

I'm gonna sing and shout aloud for joy... *(etc.)*

I'm gonna raise my hands in victory... *(etc.)*

**I'M IN LOVE WITH YOU,**
For You have called me child.
I'm in love with You,
For You have called me child.
You reached out and touched me,
You heard my lonely cry;
I will praise Your name forever,
And give You all my life.

**IMMANUEL,**
*God is with us,*
*Immanuel,*
*He is here.*
*Immanuel,*
*He is among us,*
*Immanuel,*
*His kingdom is here.*

Wonderful Counsellor, they laughed at His
    wisdom,
The Mighty God on a dusty road.
Everlasting Father, a friend of sinners,
The Prince of peace in a cattle stall.

He was despised and rejected,
A man of sorrows acquainted with grief.
From Him we turned and hid our faces;
He was despised, Him we did not esteem.

But He was wounded for our transgressions,
He was bruised for our iniquities.
On Him was the punishment that made us
    whole,
And by His stripes we are healed.

He was oppressed, He was afflicted,
And yet He opened not His mouth.
Like a lamb that is led to the slaughter,
Like a sheep before his shearers He did not
    speak.

**IMMANUEL, O IMMANUEL,**
Bowed in awe I worship at Your feet,
And sing Immanuel, God is with us;
Sharing my humanness, my shame,
Feeling my weaknesses, my pain,
Taking the punishment, the blame,
Immanuel.
And now my words cannot explain,
All that my heart cannot contain,
How great are the glories of Your name,
Immanuel.

**IMMORTAL, INVISIBLE,** God only wise,
In light inaccessible hid from our eyes,
Most blessèd, most glorious, the Ancient of
    Days,
Almighty, victorious, Thy great name we
    praise.

Unresting, unhasting, and silent as light,
Nor wanting, nor wasting, Thou rulest in
    might;
Thy justice like mountains high soaring above
Thy clouds which are fountains of goodness
    and love.

To all life Thou givest, to both great and small;
In all life Thou livest, the true life of all;
We blossom and flourish as leaves on the tree,
And wither and perish; but naught changeth
    Thee.

Great Father of glory, pure Father of light,
Thine angels adore Thee, all veiling their sight;
All laud we would render: O help us to see
'Tis only the splendour of light hideth Thee.

Immortal, invisible, God only wise,
In light inaccessible hid from our eyes,
Most blessèd, most glorious, the Ancient of
    Days,
Almighty, victorious, Thy great name we
    praise.

**I'M NOT ALONE** *for my Father is with me,*
*With me wherever I go.*
*Speaking words of faith, of courage and of*
    *love,*
*He's with me, he loves me wherever I go.*

Waking in the morning,
Getting ready for school,
Walking down the road;
In class, at work, or at play,
He's with me, He loves me, wherever I go.

And when I find myself in a mess,
I can trust in Him;
Call on His name and watch Him move,
He's with me, He loves me, wherever I go.

All of my life, everywhere that I go,
I will walk with Him;
Praising Him and blessing His name,
He's with me, He loves me, wherever I go.

**236** Graham Kendrick.
Copyright © Kingsway's
Thankyou Music 1986.

**I'M SPECIAL** because God has lov'd me,
For He gave the best thing that He had to save
me;
His own Son Jesus, crucified to take the blame,
For all the bad things I have done.
Thank You Jesus, thank You Lord,
For loving me so much.
I know I don't deserve anything,
Help me feel Your love right now
To know deep in my heart
That I'm Your special friend.

**237** Jamie Owens-Collins.
Copyright © Fairhill Music/
Word Music (UK)/CopyCare Ltd 1984.

**IN HEAVENLY ARMOUR** we'll enter the land,
The battle belongs to the Lord.
No weapon that's fashioned against us will
stand,
The battle belongs to the Lord.

*And we sing glory, honour,*
*Power and strength to the Lord.*
*We sing glory, honour,*
*Power and strength to the Lord.*

When the power of darkness comes in like a
flood,
The battle belongs to the Lord.
He's raised up a standard, the power of His
blood,
The battle belongs to the Lord.

When your enemy presses in hard, do not fear,
The battle belongs to the Lord.
Take courage, my friend, your redemption is
near.
The battle belongs to the Lord.

**238** Anna L. Waring.

**IN HEAVENLY LOVE ABIDING,**
No change my heart shall fear;
And safe is such confiding,
For nothing changes here:
The storm may roar without me,
My heart may low be laid;
But God is round about me,
And can I be dismayed?

Wherever He may guide me,
No want shall turn me back;
My Shepherd is beside me,
And nothing can I lack:
His wisdom ever waketh,
His sight is never dim;
He knows the way He taketh,
And I will walk with Him.

Green pastures are before me,
Which yet I have not seen;
Bright skies will soon be o'er me,
Where darkest clouds have been;
My hope I cannot measure,
My path to life is free;
My Saviour has my treasure,
And He will walk with me.

**239** Randy Speir.
Copyright © Randy Speir/
Kingsway's Thankyou Music 1981.

**IN HIM WE LIVE AND MOVE**
*And have our being,*
*In Him we live and move*
*And have our being.*

Make a joyful noise,
Sing unto the Lord,
Tell Him of your love,
Dance before Him.
Make a joyful noise,
Sing unto the Lord,
Tell Him of your love:
Hallelujah!

**240** David Fellingham.
Copyright © Kingsway's
Thankyou Music 1990.

**IN MAJESTY HE COMES,**
The Lamb who once was slain;
Riding in majesty, faithful and true,
Eyes ablaze, crowns on His head,
Robe dipped in blood from His suffering,
He is the Word of God,
Coming again, King of kings.

*We shall rise,*
*We shall meet Him in the air*
*When He comes again,*
*And we will worship Him, worship Him,*
*Give Him praise forever more,*
*King of kings and Lord of lords.*

**241** David Graham.
Copyright © C. A. Music USA/
Word Music (UK)/CopyCare Ltd 1980.

**IN MOMENTS LIKE THESE** I sing out a song,
I sing out a love song to Jesus.
In moments like these I lift up my hands,
I lift up my hands to the Lord.

Singing, I love You, Lord,
Singing, I love You, Lord,
Singing, I love You, Lord,
I love You.

**242** Bob Kilpatrick.
Copyright © Bob Kilpatrick Ministries/
CopyCare Ltd 1978.

**IN MY LIFE, LORD,** be glorified, be glorified,
In my life, Lord, be glorified today.

In Your church, Lord, be glorified, be glorified,
In Your church, Lord, be glorified today.

**243** Christina G. Rossetti.

**IN THE BLEAK MIDWINTER,**
Frosty wind made moan;
Earth stood hard as iron,
Water like a stone.
Snow had fallen, snow on snow,
Snow on snow;
In the bleak midwinter,
Long ago.

Our God, heaven cannot hold Him,
Nor earth sustain,
Heaven and earth shall flee away
When He comes to reign.
In the bleak midwinter
A stable-place sufficed
The Lord God Almighty,
Jesus Christ.

Angels and archangels
May have gathered there,
Cherubim and seraphim
Thronged the air.
But His mother only,
In her maiden bliss,
Worshipped the Belovèd
With a kiss.

What can I give Him,
Poor as I am?
If I were a shepherd,
I would bring a lamb.
If I were a wise man,
I would do my part;
Yet what I can I give him—
Give my heart.

**244**  Brent Chambers.
Copyright © Scripture in Song/
CopyCare Ltd 1977.

**IN THE PRESENCE OF YOUR PEOPLE**
I will praise Your name,
For alone You are holy,
Enthroned in the praises of Israel.
Let us celebrate Your goodness
And Your steadfast love
May Your name be exalted
Here on earth and in heaven above.

Lai, lai, lai-lai-lai-lai-lai-lai...(etc.)

**245** Graham Kendrick.
Copyright © Kingsway's
Thankyou Music 1986.

**IN THE TOMB SO COLD** they laid Him,
Death its victim claimed.
Powers of hell they could not hold Him;
Back to life He came!

*Christ is risen! (Christ is risen!)*
*Death has been conquered. (Death has been*
*    conquered.)*
*Christ is risen! (Christ is risen!)*
*He shall reign for ever.*

Hell had spent its fury on Him,
Left Him crucified.
Yet, by blood, He boldly conquered,
Sin and death defied.

Now the fear of death is broken,
Love has won the crown.
Prisoners of the darkness listen,
Walls are tumbling down.

Raised from death to heaven ascending
Love's exalted King.
Let His song of joy, unending,
Through the nations ring!

**246**  Bruce Clewett.
Copyright © Kingsway's
Thankyou Music 1983.

**IN THROUGH THE VEIL** now we enter,
Boldly approaching Your throne,
Bearing a sacrifice of fragrance sweet;
The fruit of some seeds You have sown.
From our lips we offer these praises,
May You be blessed as we sing.
Lord we adore You, like incense before You
Our worship ascends to the King.
Welling up within our hearts
Is a song of praise to You,
We lift up our hands with our voice.
Blessings and honour,
Glory and power be unto You,
Let us rejoice, rejoice.
Blessings and honour,
Glory and power be unto You,
Let us rejoice.

**247**
Mike Kerry.
Copyright © Kingsway's
Thankyou Music 1982.

**IN THY PRESENCE** there's fullness of joy,
Fullness of joy, fullness of joy.
At Thy right hand are pleasures for ever,
Pleasures for evermore.

I keep the Lord before me,
I shall not be moved,
My heart is glad and my soul rejoices,
I shall dwell in safety.

And in Thy presence there's fullness of joy,
Fullness of joy, fullness of joy.
At Thy right hand are pleasures for ever,
Pleasures for evermore.

**248**
Paul Armstrong.
Copyright © Springtide/Word Music (UK)/
CopyCare Ltd 1980.

**I RECEIVE YOUR LOVE,**
I receive Your love,
In my heart I receive Your love, O Lord.
I receive Your love
By Your Spirit within me,
I receive, I receive Your love.

I confess Your love,
I confess Your love,
From my heart I confess Your love, O Lord.
I confess Your love
By Your Spirit within me,
I confess, I confess Your love.

**249**
Author unknown.

**I SEE THE LORD,** I see the Lord,
He is high and lifted up
And His train fills the temple,
He is high and lifted up
And His train fills the temple.
The angels cry, Holy,
The angels cry, Holy,
The angels cry, Holy is the Lord.

**250**
John Wimber.
Copyright © Mercy Publishing/
Kingsway's Thankyou Music 1980.

**ISN'T HE BEAUTIFUL,** beautiful isn't He?
Prince of Peace, Son of God, isn't He?
Isn't He wonderful, wonderful isn't He?
Counsellor, Almighty God, isn't He, isn't He,
   isn't He?

**251**
E. H. Sears.

**IT CAME UPON THE MIDNIGHT CLEAR,**
That glorious song of old,
From angels bending near the earth
To touch their harps of gold:
'Peace on the earth, goodwill to men
From heaven's all gracious King!'
The world in solemn stillness lay
To hear the angels sing.

Still through the cloven skies they come,
With peaceful wings unfurled,
And still their heavenly music floats
O'er all the weary world:
Above its sad and lowly plains
They bend on hovering wing,
And ever o'er its Babel sounds
The blessèd angels sing.

Yet with woes of sin and strife
The world has suffered long,
Beneath the angel-strain have rolled
Two thousand years of wrong;
And man, at war with man, hears not
The love-song which they bring:
O hush the noise, ye men of strife,
And hear the angels sing.

For lo! the days are hastening on,
By prophet bards foretold,
When with the ever-circling years
Comes round the age of gold;
When peace shall over all the earth
Its ancient splendours fling,
And all the world send back the song
Which now the angels sing.

**252**
W. W. How.

**IT IS A THING MOST WONDERFUL,**
Almost too wonderful to be,
That God's own Son should come from heaven
And die to save a child like me.

And yet I know that it is true;
He came to this poor world below,
And wept, and toiled, and mourned, and died,
Only because He loved us so.

I cannot tell how He could love
A child so weak and full of sin;
His love must be most wonderful,
If He could die my love to win.

It is most wonderful to know
His love for me so free and sure;
But 'tis more wonderful to see
My love for Him so faint and poor.

And yet I want to love Thee, Lord;
O light the flame within my heart,
And I will love Thee more and more,
Until I see Thee as Thou art.

**253**
Tim Blomdahl.
Copyright © Bible Temple Music/
Integrity's Hosanna! Music.
Adm. Kingsway's Thankyou Music.

**IT IS GOOD FOR ME** to draw near unto God,
Lord, I put my trust in Thee,
That I may declare all Thy works, O my God,
Lord, I put my trust in Thee.
My flesh and my heart they fail me,
But God is the strength of my life,
You are my portion both now and evermore,
There is none that I desire but Thee.

**254** Sally Ellis.
Copyright © Kingsway's
Thankyou Music 1980.

**IT IS NO LONGER I THAT LIVETH**
But Christ that liveth in me,
It is no longer I that liveth
But Christ that liveth in me.
He lives, He lives,
Jesus is alive in me.
It is no longer I that liveth
But Christ that liveth in me.

The life that I live in the body
I live by faith in the Son.
The life that I live in the body
I live by faith in the Son.
He loves, He loves,
Jesus gave Himself for me.
The life that I live in the body
I live by faith in the Son.

**255** Gary Pfeiffer.
Copyright © Fred Bock Music/
Kingsway's Thankyou Music 1973.

**IT'S A HAPPY DAY,** and I thank God for the
weather.
It's a happy day, living it for my Lord.
It's a happy day, things are gonna get better,
Living each day by the promises in God's word.

It's a grumpy day, and I can't stand the
weather.
It's a grumpy day, living it for myself.
It's a grumpy day, and things aren't gonna get
better,
Living each day with my Bible up on my shelf.

**256** Len Magee.
Copyright © Len Magee Music 1977.

**IT'S THE PRESENCE OF YOUR SPIRIT, LORD,
WE NEED,**
It's the presence of Your Spirit, Lord, we need,
So help us, Lord, to worship You,
It's the presence of Your Spirit, Lord, we need.

It's the presence of Your Spirit, Lord, we love,
It's the presence of Your Spirit, Lord, we love,
So help us, Lord, to worship You,
It's the presence of Your Spirit, Lord, we love.

For the moving of Your Spirit, Lord, we
pray…(etc.)

**257** Michael Christ.
Copyright © Mercy Publishing/
Kingsway's Thankyou Music 1985.

**IT'S YOUR BLOOD** that cleanses me,
It's Your blood that gives me life.
It's Your blood that took my place,
In redeeming sacrifice;
Washes me whiter than the snow, than the
snow,
My Jesus, God's precious sacrifice.

**258** Dave Renehan.
Copyright © Kingsway's
Thankyou Music 1982.

**I WANNA SING,** wanna sing.
I wanna sing, wanna sing
For Jesus, for Jesus, for Jesus,
Oh I wanna sing for Him.

I wanna clap, wanna clap.
I wanna clap, wanna clap
For Jesus, for Jesus, for Jesus,
Oh I wanna clap for Him.

I wanna dance, praise, work, love, live…(etc.)

**259** Graham Kendrick.
Copyright © Make Way Music 1988.

**I WANT TO BE A HISTORY MAKER,** (echo)
I want to be a world shaker, (echo)
To be a pen on history's pages, (echo)
Faithful to the end of the ages. (echo)

*I want to see Your kingdom come,*
*I want to see Your will be done*
*On the earth.*
*I want to see Your kingdom come,*
*I want to see Your will be done*
*On the earth as it is in heaven.*

I believe I was called and chosen (echo)
Long before the world's creation, (echo)
Called to be a holy person, (echo)
Called to bear good fruit for heaven. (echo)

We want to be the generation (echo)
Taking the news to every nation, (echo)
Filled with the Spirit without measure, (echo)
Working for a heavenly treasure. (echo)

**260** Mark Altrogge.
Copyright © People of Destiny/
CopyCare Ltd 1982.

**I WANT TO SERVE THE PURPOSE OF GOD**
In my generation.
I want to serve the purpose of God
While I am alive.
I want to give my life
For something that will last forever.
O I delight, I delight to do Your will.

I want to build with silver and gold
In my generation.
I want to build with silver and gold
While I am alive.
I want to give my life
For something that will last forever.
O I delight, I delight to do Your will.

*What is on Your heart?*
*Tell me what to do;*
*Let me know Your will*
*And I will follow You.*
*(Repeat)*

I want to see the kingdom of God
In my generation.
I want to see the kingdom of God
While I am alive.
I want to live my life
For something that will last forever.
O I delight, I delight to do Your will.

I want to see the Lord come again
In my generation.
I want to see the Lord come again
While I am alive.
I want to give my life
For something that will last forever.
O I delight, I delight to do Your will.
O I delight, I delight to do Your will.

 **261**   C. Simmonds.
Copyright © C. Simmonds 1964.

## I WANT TO WALK WITH JESUS CHRIST,
All the days I live of this life on earth;
To give to Him complete control
Of body and of soul.

> *Follow him, follow him, yield your life to*
> *Him,*
> *He has conquered death, He is King of*
> *kings;*
> *Accept the joy which He gives to those*
> *Who yield their lives to Him.*

I want to learn to speak to Him,
To pray to Him, confess my sin;
To open my life and let Him in,
For joy will then be mine:

I want to learn to speak of Him,
My life must show that He lives in me;
My deeds, my thoughts, my words must speak
All of His love for me:

I want to learn to read His word,
For this is how I know the way
To live my life as pleases Him,
In holiness and joy:

O Holy Spirit of the Lord,
Enter now into this heart of mine;
Take full control of my selfish will
And make me wholly Thine:

**262**   Chris Christensen.
Copyright © Integrity's Hosanna! Music.
Adm. Kingsway's Thankyou Music 1986.

## I WAS MADE TO PRAISE YOU,
I was made to glorify Your name,
In every circumstance
To find a chance to thank You.
I was made to love You
I was made to worship at Your feet
And to obey You Lord.
I was made for You.

I will always praise You,
I will always glorify Your name.
In every circumstance
I'll find a chance to thank You.
I will always love You,
I will always worship at Your feet,
And I'll obey You, Lord.
I was made for You.

**263**   Joan Parsons.
Copyright © Kingsway's
Thankyou Music 1978.

## I WAS ONCE IN DARKNESS, now my eyes can see,
I was lost but Jesus sought and found me.
O what love He offers, O what peace He gives,
I will sing for evermore, He lives.

Hallelujah Jesus! Hallelujah Lord!
Hallelujah Father, I am shielded by His word.
I will live for ever, I will never die,
I will rise up to meet Him in the sky.

 **264**   Graham Kendrick.
Copyright © Make Way Music 1988.

## I WILL BUILD MY CHURCH,   *(Men)*
I will build My church,   *(Women)*
And the gates of hell   *(Men)*
And the gates of hell   *(Women)*
Shall not prevail   *(Men)*
Shall not prevail   *(Women)*
Against it.   *(All)*
*(Repeat)*

So you powers in the heavens above, bow
down!
And you powers on the earth below, bow
down!
And acknowledge that Jesus,
Jesus, Jesus, is Lord, is Lord.

**265**   Victor Rubbo.
Copyright © Mercy Publishing/
Kingsway's Thankyou Music 1982.

*(Men and women in canon)*
## I WILL CALL upon the Lord,
Who is worthy to be praised.
I will call upon the Lord,
Who is worthy to be praised.

*(Together)*
So shall I be saved,
So shall I be saved from my enemies.

 **266**   Michael O'Shields.
Copyright © Word Music (UK)/
CopyCare Ltd 1981.

## I WILL CALL UPON THE LORD,
Who is worthy to be praised,
So shall I be saved from mine enemies.

The Lord liveth, and blessed be my Rock
And may the God of my salvation be exalted.
The Lord liveth, and blessed be my Rock
And may the God of my salvation be exalted.

**267** D. J. Butler.
Copyright © Mercy Publishing/
Kingsway's Thankyou Music 1987.

**I WILL CHANGE YOUR NAME,**
You shall no longer be called
Wounded, outcast, lonely or afraid.
I will change your name,
Your new name shall be,
Confidence, joyfulness, overcoming one;
Faithfulness, friend of God,
One who seeks My face.

**268** Leona Von Brethorst.
Copyright © Maranatha! Music/
CopyCare Ltd 1976, 1983.

**I WILL ENTER HIS GATES** with thanksgiving in
   my heart,
I will enter His courts with praise,
I will say this is the day that the Lord has made,
I will rejoice for He has made me glad.
He has made me glad,
He has made me glad,
I will rejoice for He has made me glad.
He has made me glad,
He has made me glad,
I will rejoice for He has made me glad.

**269** Brent Chambers.
Copyright © Scripture in Song/
CopyCare Ltd 1977.

**I WILL GIVE THANKS TO THEE,**
O Lord, among the people,
I will sing praises to Thee
Among the nations.
For Thy steadfast love is great,
Is great to the heavens,
And Thy faithfulness,
Thy faithfulness to the clouds.

Be exalted, O God,
Above the heavens,
Let Thy glory be over all the earth.
Be exalted, O God,
Above the heavens,
Let Thy glory be over all the earth.

   (Last time only:)
Be exalted, O God,
Above the heavens,
Let Thy glory be over all the earth.
Be exalted, O God,
Above the heavens,
Let Thy glory, let Thy glory,
Let Thy glory be over all the earth.

**270** Tommy Walker.
Copyright © Kingsway's
Thankyou Music 1985.

**I WILL GIVE YOU PRAISE,**
I will sing Your song,
I will bless Your holy name;
For there is no other god,
Who is like unto You,
You're the only way.

Only You are the Author of life,
Only You can bring the blind their sight,
Only You are called Prince of Peace,
Only You promised You'd never leave.
Only You are God.

**271** Scott Palazzo.
Copyright © Mercy Publishing/
Kingsway's Thankyou Music 1985.

**I WILL MAGNIFY** Thy name
Above all the earth.
I will magnify Thy name
Above all the earth.

I will sing unto Thee
The praises of my heart.
I will sing unto Thee
The praises of my heart.

**272** Mark Altrogge.
Copyright © People of Destiny/
CopyCare Ltd 1987.

**I WILL PRAISE YOU ALL MY LIFE;**
I will sing to You with my whole heart.
I will trust in You, my hope and my help,
My Maker and my faithful God.

   *O faithful God, O faithful God,*
   *You lift me up and You uphold my cause;*
   *You give me life, You dry my eyes,*
   *You're always near, You're a faithful God.*

**273** Author unknown.

**I WILL REJOICE IN YOU AND BE GLAD,**
I will extol Your love more than wine,
Draw me after You and let us run together,
I will rejoice in You and be glad.

**274** David Fellingham.
Copyright © Kingsway's
Thankyou Music 1982.

**I WILL REJOICE, I WILL REJOICE,**
I will rejoice in the Lord with my whole heart,
I will rejoice, I will rejoice,
I will rejoice in the Lord.
You anoint my head with oil
And my cup surely overflows,
Goodness and love shall follow me
All the days that I dwell in Your house.

**275**

**I WILL RISE AND BLESS YOU, LORD,**
Lift my hands and shout Your praise,
I will tell of the marvellous things You have
  done
And declare Your faithfulness.
I will rise and bless You, Lord,
Lift You high and dance for joy.
Oh nothing can separate me
From Your wonderful, wonderful love.

**276**

**I WILL SEEK YOUR FACE,** *O Lord;*
*I will seek Your face, O Lord;*
*I will seek Your face, O Lord;*
*I will seek Your face, O Lord.*

Lord, how awesome is Your presence;
Who can stand in Your light?
Those who by Your grace and mercy,
Are made holy in Your sight.

I will dwell in Your presence
All the days of my life;
There to gaze upon Your glory
And to worship only You.

**277**

**I WILL SING OF THE MERCIES** of the Lord for
  ever,
I will sing, I will sing.
I will sing of the mercies of the Lord for ever,
I will sing of the mercies of the Lord.

With my mouth will I make known
Thy faithfulness, Thy faithfulness.
With my mouth will I make known
Thy faithfulness to all generation.

**278**

**I WILL SING THE WONDROUS STORY**
Of the Christ who died for me;
How He left His home in glory
For the cross on Calvary.
I was lost but Jesus found me,
Found the sheep that went astray;
Threw His loving arms around me,
Drew me back into His way.

I was bruised but Jesus healed me,
Faint was I from many a fall;
Sight was gone, and fears possessed me,
But He freed me from them all.
Days of darkness still come o'er me;
Sorrow's paths I often tread,
But the Saviour still is with me,
By His hand I'm safely led.

He will keep me till the river
Rolls its waters at my feet,
Then He'll bear me safely over,
All my joys in Him complete.
Yes, I'll sing the wondrous story
Of the Christ who died for me;
Sing it with the saints in glory,
Gathered by the crystal sea.

**279**

**I WILL SING UNTO THE LORD** as long as I live,
I will sing praise to my God while I have my
  being.
My meditation of Him shall be sweet,
I will be glad, I will be glad in the Lord.
Bless thou the Lord, O my soul,
Praise ye the Lord.
Bless thou the Lord, O my soul,
Praise ye the Lord.
Bless thou the Lord, O my soul,
Praise ye the Lord.
Bless thou the Lord, O my soul,
Praise ye the Lord.

**280**

**I WILL SPEAK OUT** for those who have no
  voices,
I will stand up for the rights of all the
  oppressed;
I will speak truth and justice,
I'll defend the poor and the needy,
I will lift up the weak in Jesus' name.

I will speak out for those who have no choices,
I will cry out for those who live without love;
I will show God's compassion
To the crushed and broken in spirit,
I will lift up the weak in Jesus' name.

**281**

**I WILL WORSHIP YOU, LORD,** with all of my
  might,
I will praise You with a psalm;
I will worship You, Lord, with all of my might,
I will praise You all day long.

For Thou, O Lord, art glorious,
And Thy name is greatly to be praised;
May my heart be pure and holy in Thy sight,
As I worship You with all of my might.

**I WORSHIP YOU, ALMIGHTY GOD,**
There is none like You.
I worship You, O Prince of Peace,
That is what I love to do.
I give You praise,
For You are my righteousness.
I worship You, Almighty God,
There is none like You.

**JEHOVAH JIREH,** God will provide,
Jehovah Rophe, God heals;
Jehovah M'keddesh, God who sanctifies,
Jehovah Nissi, God is my banner.

Jehovah Rohi, God my shepherd,
Jehovah Shalom, God is peace;
Jehovah Tsidkenu, God our righteousness,
Jehovah Shammah, God who is there.

**JEHOVAH JIREH, MY PROVIDER,**
His grace is sufficient for me, for me, for me.
Jehovah Jireh, my Provider,
His grace is sufficient for me.

My God shall supply all my needs
According to His riches in glory;
He will give His angels charge over me,
Jehovah Jireh cares for me, for me, for me,
Jehovah Jireh cares for me.

**JESUS CHRIST IS RISEN TODAY;** Hallelujah!
Our triumphant holy day; Hallelujah!
Who did once upon the cross; Hallelujah!
Suffer to redeem our loss; Hallelujah!

Hymns of praise then let us sing; Hallelujah!
Unto Christ our heavenly King; Hallelujah!
Who endured the cross and grave; Hallelujah!
Sinners to redeem and save: Hallelujah!

But the pains, which He endured; Hallelujah!
Our salvation have procured; Hallelujah!
Now in heaven above He's King; Hallelujah!
Where the angels ever sing: Hallelujah!

**JESUS HAS SAT DOWN** at God's right hand,
He is reigning now on David's throne.
God has placed all things beneath His feet,
His enemies will be His footstool.

For the government is now upon His
    shoulder,
For the government is now upon His
    shoulder,
And of the increase of His government and
    peace
There will be no end, there will be no end,
There will be no end.

God has now exalted Him on high,
Given Him a name above all names.
Every knee will bow and tongue confess
That Jesus Christ is Lord.

Jesus is now living in His church,
Men who have been purchased by His blood,
They will serve their God, a royal priesthood,
And they will reign on earth.

Sound the trumpets, good news to the poor,
Captives will go free, the blind will see,
The kingdom of this world will soon become
The kingdom of our God.

**JESUS, HOW LOVELY YOU ARE,**
*You are so gentle, so pure and kind.*
*You shine as the morning star,*
*Jesus, how lovely You are.*

Hallelujah, Jesus is my Lord and King;
Hallelujah, Jesus is my everything.

Hallelujah, Jesus died and rose again;
Hallelujah, Jesus forgave all my sin.

Hallelujah, Jesus is meek and lowly;
Hallelujah, Jesus is pure and holy.

Hallelujah, Jesus is the Bridegroom;
Hallelujah, Jesus will take His Bride soon.

**JESUS, I LOVE YOU;**
I bow down before You.
Praises and worship
To our King.

Alleluia, alleluia;
Alleluia, allelu.

**JESUS IS KING** and I will extol Him,
Give Him the glory, and honour His name.
He reigns on high, enthroned in the heavens,
Word of the Father, exalted for us.

We have a hope that is steadfast and certain,
Gone through the curtain and touching the
    throne.
We have a Priest who is there interceding,
Pouring His grace on our lives day by day.

We come to Him our Priest and Apostle,
Clothed in His glory and bearing His name,
Laying our lives with gladness before Him,
Filled with His Spirit we worship the King.

O Holy One, our hearts do adore You,
Thrilled with Your goodness we give You our
    praise.
Angels in light with worship surround Him,
Jesus, our Saviour, for ever the same.

**290**  David J. Mansell.
Copyright © Word Music (UK)/
CopyCare Ltd 1982.

**JESUS IS LORD!** creation's voice proclaims it,
For by His power each tree and flower
Was planned and made.
Jesus is Lord! the universe declares it,
Sun, moon and stars in heaven
Cry, 'Jesus is Lord!'

*Jesus is Lord! Jesus is Lord!*
*Praise Him with Hallelujahs*
*For Jesus is Lord!*

Jesus is Lord! yet from His throne eternal
In flesh He came to die in pain
On Calvary's tree.
Jesus is Lord! from Him all life proceeding,
Yet gave His life a ransom
Thus setting us free.

Jesus is Lord! o'er sin the mighty conqueror,
From death He rose, and all His foes
Shall own His Name.
Jesus is Lord! God sent His Holy Spirit
To show by works of power
That Jesus is Lord.

**291**  Marilyn Baker.
Copyright © Word Music (UK)/
CopyCare Ltd 1986.

**JESUS IS LORD OF ALL,**
Satan is under His feet,
Jesus is reigning on high
And all power is given to Him
In heaven and earth.

We are joined to Him,
Satan is under our feet,
We are seated on high
And all authority is given
To us through Him.

One day we'll be like Him,
Perfect in every way,
Chosen to be His bride,
Ruling and reigning with Him
For evermore.

**292**  Chris Bowater.
Copyright © Sovereign Lifestyle Music Ltd 1982.

**JESUS, I WORSHIP YOU,**
Worship, honour and adore Your lovely name.
Jesus, I worship You,
Lord of lords and King of kings, I worship You,
From a thankful heart I sing;
I worship You.

**293**  John Barnett.
Copyright © Mercy Publishing/
Kingsway's Thankyou Music 1988.

**JESUS, JESUS,**
Holy and anointed One,
Jesus.
Jesus, Jesus,
Risen and exalted One,
Jesus.

Your name is like honey on my lips,
Your Spirit like water to my soul,
Your word is a lamp unto my feet,
Jesus I love You, I love You.

**294**  Chris Bowater.
Copyright © Sovereign Lifestyle
Music Ltd. 1979, 1991.

**JESUS, JESUS, JESUS,**
Your love has melted my heart.
Jesus, Jesus, Jesus,
Your love has melted my heart.

**295**  Chris Rolinson.
Copyright © Kingsway's
Thankyou Music 1988.

**JESUS, KING OF KINGS,**
We worship and adore You.
Jesus, Lord of heaven and earth,
We bow down at Your feet.
Father, we bring to You our worship;
Your sovereign will be done.
On earth Your kingdom come
Through Jesus Christ, Your only Son.

Jesus, Sovereign Lord,
We worship and adore You.
Jesus, Name above all names,
We bow down at Your feet.
Father, we offer You our worship;
Your sovereign will be done.
On earth Your kingdom come
Through Jesus Christ, Your only Son.

Jesus, Light of the world,
We worship and adore You.
Jesus, Lord Immanuel,
We bow down at Your feet.
Father, for Your delight we worship;
Your sovereign will be done,
On earth Your kingdom come
Through Jesus Christ, Your only Son.

## 296
Christian F. Gellert.
Tr. Frances E. Cox

**JESUS LIVES!** thy terrors now
Can, O death, no more appal us;
Jesus lives! by this we know,
Thou, O grave, canst not enthral us.
Hallelujah!

Jesus lives! henceforth is death
But the gate of life immortal;
This shall calm our trembling breath,
When we pass its gloomy portal.
Hallelujah!

Jesus lives! for us He died;
Then, alone to Jesus living,
Pure in heart may we abide,
Glory to our Saviour giving.
Hallelujah!

Jesus lives! our hearts know well,
Naught from us His love shall sever;
Life, nor death, nor powers of hell,
Tear us from His keeping ever.
Hallelujah!

Jesus lives! to Him the throne
Over all the world is given:
May we go where He is gone,
Rest and reign with Him in heaven.
Hallelujah!

## 297
Charles Wesley.

**JESUS, LOVER OF MY SOUL,**
Let me to Thy bosom fly,
While the nearer waters roll,
While the tempest still is high;
Hide me, O my Saviour, hide,
Till the storm of life is past;
Safe into the haven guide,
O receive my soul at last.

Other refuge have I none,
Hangs my helpless soul on Thee;
Leave, ah, leave me not alone,
Still support and comfort me.
All my trust on Thee is stayed,
All my help from Thee I bring;
Cover my defenceless head
With the shadow of Thy wing.

Thou, O Christ, art all I want;
More than all in Thee I find;
Raise the fallen, cheer the faint,
Heal the sick, and lead the blind.
Just and holy is Thy name,
I am all unrighteousness,
False and full of sin I am,
Thou art full of truth and grace.

Plenteous grace with Thee is found,
Grace to cover all my sin;
Let the healing streams abound,
Make and keep me pure within.
Thou of life the fountain art;
Freely let me take of Thee;
Spring Thou up within my heart,
Rise to all eternity.

## 298
Naida Hearn.
Copyright © Scripture in Song/
CopyCare Ltd 1974, 1979.

**JESUS, NAME ABOVE ALL NAMES,**
Beautiful Saviour, Glorious Lord;
Emmanuel, God is with us,
Blessèd Redeemer, Living Word.

## 299
Graham Kendrick.
Copyright © Kingsway's
Thankyou Music 1986.

**JESUS PUT THIS SONG INTO OUR HEARTS,**
Jesus put this song into our hearts,
It's a song of joy no one can take away,
Jesus put this song into our hearts.

Jesus taught us how to live in harmony,
Jesus taught us how to live in harmony,
Different faces, different races, He made us
    one,
Jesus taught us how to live in harmony.

Jesus taught us how to be a family,
Jesus taught us how to be a family,
Loving one another with the love that He gives,
Jesus taught us how to be a family.

Jesus turned our sorrow into dancing,
Jesus turned our sorrow into dancing,
Changed our tears of sadness into rivers of joy,
Jesus turned our sorrow into a dance.

## 300
Chris Rolinson.
Copyright © Kingsway's
Thankyou Music 1988.

**JESUS, SEND MORE LABOURERS,**
For, Lord, we see the need;
The land is ready for harvest,
The fields are ripe indeed.

*Oh Lord, but start with me,*
*Jesus, begin with me,*
*Who will go for You, Lord?*
*Who will go for You, Lord?*
*Here I am, Lord,*
*Send me,*
*Send me, Lord,*
*Send me.*

Lord, we love our country,
Countless lives to be won;
Jesus, bring revival,
That through us Your will be done.

Lord, we sense Your moving,
Touching our lives with power;
We are ready to serve You,
To go this day, this hour.

## 301    Isaac Watts.

JESUS SHALL REIGN where'er the sun
Doth his successive journeys run;
His kingdom stretch from shore to shore,
Till moons shall wax and wane no more.

For Him shall endless prayer be made,
And praises throng to crown His head;
His name like sweet perfume shall rise
With every morning sacrifice.

People and realms of every tongue
Dwell on His love with sweetest song,
And infant voices shall proclaim
Their early blessings on His name.

Blessings abound where'er He reigns;
The prisoner leaps to lose his chains;
The weary find eternal rest,
And all the sons of want are blessed.

Let every creature rise and bring
Peculiar honours to our King;
Angels descend with songs again,
And earth repeat the loud Amen!

## 302    Chris Bowater.
Copyright © Sovereign Lifestyle Music Ltd. 1988.

JESUS SHALL TAKE THE HIGHEST HONOUR,
Jesus shall take the highest praise.
Let all earth join heaven in exalting
The Name which is above all other names.
Let's bow the knee in humble adoration,
For at His name every knee must bow;
Let every tongue confess He is Christ, God's
    only Son.
Sovereign Lord we give you glory now,

*For all honour and blessing and power,*
*Belongs to You, belongs to You;*
*All honour and blessing and power,*
*Belongs to You, belongs to You,*
*Lord Jesus Christ, Son of the living God.*

## 303    Graham Kendrick.
Copyright © Kingsway's
Thankyou Music 1977.

JESUS, STAND AMONG US
At the meeting of our lives,
Be our sweet agreement
At the meeting of our eyes,
O Jesus, we love You, so we gather here,
Join our hearts in unity and take away our fear.

So to You we're gathering
Out of each and every land,
Christ the love between us
At the joining of our hands.
O Jesus, we love You, so we gather here,
Join our hearts in unity and take away our fear.

*(Optional verse for Communion:)*
Jesus, stand among us
At the breaking of the bread,
Join us as one body
As we worship You, our Head.
O Jesus, we love You, so we gather here,
Join our hearts in unity and take away our fear.

## 304    William Pennefather.

JESUS, STAND AMONG US,
IN THY RISEN POWER,
Let this time of worship
Be a hallowed hour.

Breathe Thy Holy Spirit
Into every heart,
Bid the fears and sorrows
From each soul depart.

Thus with quickened footsteps
We'll pursue our way,
Watching for the dawning
Of eternal day.

## 305    Dave Bryant.
Copyright © Kingsway's
Thankyou Music 1978.

JESUS TAKE ME AS I AM,
I can come no other way.
Take me deeper into You,
Make my flesh life melt away.
Make me like a precious stone,
Crystal clear and finely honed,
Life of Jesus shining through,
Giving glory back to You.

## 306    Hilary Davies.
Copyright © Samsongs/Coronation Music/
Kingsway's Thankyou Music 1988.

JESUS, THE NAME ABOVE ALL NAMES,
For evermore the same,
And lifting up our hands we exalt You;
Come among us once again,
And glorify Your name,
So everyone will know
You are Emmanuel.

*Emmanuel, Emmanuel,*
*Emmanuel, God is with us.*

## 307    Charles Wesley.

JESUS! THE NAME HIGH OVER ALL,
In hell, or earth, or sky;
Angels and men before it fall,
And devils fear and fly,
And devils fear and fly.

Jesus! the name to sinners dear,
The name to sinners given;
It scatters all their guilty fear,
It turns their hell to heaven,
It turns their hell to heaven.

Jesus! the prisoners' fetters breaks,
And bruises Satan's head;
Power into strengthless souls it speaks,
And life into the dead,
And life into the dead.

O that the world might taste and see
The riches of His grace!
The arms of love that compass me
Would all mankind embrace,
Would all mankind embrace.

His only righteousness I show,
His saving grace proclaim;
'Tis all my business here below
To cry: 'Behold the Lamb!'
To cry: 'Behold the Lamb!'

Happy if with my latest breath
I might but gasp His name;
Preach Him to all, and cry in death:
'Behold, behold the Lamb!'
'Behold, behold the Lamb!'

 **308** St Bernard of Clairvaux.
Tr. Edward Caswall.

**JESUS, THE VERY THOUGHT OF THEE**
With sweetness fills the breast;
But sweeter far Thy face to see,
And in Thy presence rest.

Nor voice can sing, nor heart can frame,
Nor can the memory find
A sweeter sound than Thy blessed name,
O Saviour of mankind!

O hope of every contrite heart,
O joy of all the meek,
To those who fall how kind Thou art,
How good to those who seek!

But what to those who find? Ah, this
Nor tongue nor pen can show:
The love of Jesus, what it is
None but His loved ones know.

Jesus, Thy mercies are untold
Through each returning day;
Thy love exceeds a thousandfold
Whatever we can say.

Jesus, our only joy be Thou,
As Thou our prize wilt be;
Jesus, be Thou our glory now,
And through eternity.

 **309** John Gibson.
Copyright © Kingsway's
Thankyou Music 1987.

**JESUS, WE CELEBRATE YOUR VICTORY:**
*Jesus, we revel in Your love.*
*Jesus, we rejoice, You've set us free;*
*Jesus, Your death has brought us life.*

It was for freedom that Christ has set us free,
No longer to be subject to a yoke of slavery;
So we're rejoicing in God's victory,
Our hearts responding to His love.

His Spirit in us releases us from fear,
The way to Him is open, with boldness we
    draw near;
And in His presence our problems disappear,
Our hearts responding to His love.

**310** Paul Kyle.
Copyright © Kingsway's
Thankyou Music 1980.

**JESUS, WE ENTHRONE YOU,**
We proclaim You our King,
Standing here in the midst of us
We raise You up with our praise.
And as we worship, build a throne,
And as we worship, build a throne,
And as we worship, build a throne,
Come Lord Jesus and take Your place.

**311** Marilyn Baker.
Copyright © Springtide/
Word Music (UK)/CopyCare Ltd 1981.

**JESUS, YOU ARE CHANGING ME,**
By Your Spirit You're making me like You.
Jesus, You're transforming me,
That Your loveliness may be seen in all I do.
You are the potter and I am the clay,
Help me to be willing to let You have Your way.
Jesus, You are changing me,
As I let You reign supreme within my heart.

**312** David Fellingham.
Copyright © Kingsway's
Thankyou Music 1985.

**JESUS, YOU ARE THE RADIANCE** of the
    Father's glory,
You are the Son, the appointed heir,
Through whom all things are made.
You are the One who sustains all things by
    Your powerful word.
You have purified us from sin,
You are exalted, O Lord,
Exalted, O Lord,
To the right hand of God.

    *(Last time)*
Crowned with glory,
Crowned with honour,
We worship You.

**313** Isaac Watts.

### JOIN ALL THE GLORIOUS NAMES
Of wisdom, love, and power,
That ever mortals knew,
That angels ever bore:
All are too mean to speak His worth,
Too mean to set my Saviour forth.

Great Prophet of my God,
My tongue would bless Thy name:
By Thee the joyful news
Of our salvation came:
The joyful news of sins forgiven,
Of hell subdued and peace with heaven.

Jesus, my great High Priest,
Offered His blood, and died;
My guilty conscience seeks
No sacrifice beside:
His powerful blood did once atone,
And now it pleads before the throne.

My Saviour and my Lord,
My Conqueror and my King,
Thy sceptre and Thy sword,
Thy reigning grace I sing:
Thine is the power; behold, I sit
In willing bonds beneath Thy feet.

Now let my soul arise,
And tread the tempter down:
My Captain leads me forth
To conquest and a crown.
March on, nor fear to win the day,
Though death and hell obstruct the way.

Should all the hosts of death,
And powers of hell unknown,
Put their most dreadful forms
Of rage and malice on,
I shall be safe; for Christ displays
Superior power and guardian grace.

**314** Isaac Watts.

### JOY TO THE WORLD! The Lord is come;
Let earth receive her King.
Let every heart prepare Him room,
And heaven and nature sing,
And heaven and nature sing,
And heaven, and heaven and nature sing!

Joy to the earth the Saviour reigns;
Your sweetest songs employ.
While fields and streams and hills and plains
Repeat the sounding joy,
Repeat the sounding joy,
Repeat, repeat the sounding joy!

He rules the world with truth and grace,
And makes the nations prove
The glories of His righteousness,
The wonders of His love,
The wonders of His love,
The wonders, wonders of His love.

**315** Fred Dunn.
Copyright © Kingsway's
Thankyou Music 1977, 1980.

### JUBILATE, EVERYBODY,
Serve the Lord in all your ways,
And come before His presence singing,
Enter now His courts with praise.
For the Lord our God is gracious,
And His mercy's everlasting,
Jubilate, Jubilate, Jubilate Deo.

**316** Charlotte Elliot.

### JUST AS I AM, without one plea
But that Thy blood was shed for me,
And that Thou bid'st me come to Thee,
O Lamb of God, I come.

Just as I am, and waiting not
To rid my soul of one dark blot,
To Thee, whose blood can cleanse each spot,
O Lamb of God, I come.

Just as I am, though tossed about
With many a conflict, many a doubt,
Fightings and fears within, without,
O Lamb of God, I come.

Just as I am, poor, wretched, blind;
Sight, riches, healing of the mind,
Yea, all I need, in Thee to find,
O Lamb of God, I come.

Just as I am, Thou wilt receive,
Wilt welcome, pardon, cleanse, relieve,
Because Thy promise I believe,
O Lamb of God, I come.

Just as I am, Thy love unknown
Has broken every barrier down;
Now to be Thine, yea, Thine alone,
O Lamb of God, I come.

Just as I am, of that free love
The breadth, length, depth and height to prove,
Here for a season, then above,
O Lamb of God, I come.

**317** Patty Kennedy.
Copyright © Mercy Publishing/
Kingsway's Thankyou Music 1982.

### JUST LIKE YOU PROMISED, You've come,
Just like You told us, You're here,
And our desire is that You know
We love You, we worship You,
We welcome You here.

**318**
Jane Norton.
Copyright © Kingsway's
Thankyou Music 1986.

KING FOREVER, Lord Messiah,
He who was, and is, and is to come;
Prince of glory, name of Jesus,
Be Your praise and worship ever sung.

*And we will sing hosanna to Jesus,*
*We exalt and raise Your name above;*
*And we proclaim the glory of Jesus,*
*Prince of peace, and worthy King of love.*

Lord anointed, our salvation,
He whom angels call the Word of God;
True and faithful, Lamb of mercy,
Now receive our worship and our love.

**319**
Graham Kendrick.
Copyright © Make Way Music 1988.

KING OF KINGS, Lord of lords,
Lion of Judah, Word of God.
King of kings, Lord of lords,
Lion of Judah, Word of God.

And here He comes, the King of glory comes!
In righteousness he comes to judge the earth.
And here He comes, the King of glory comes!
With justice He'll rule the earth.

**320**
Chris Bowater.
Copyright © Sovereign Lifestyle Music Ltd 1988.

LAMB OF GOD, Holy One,
Jesus Christ, Son of God,
Lifted up willingly to die,
That I the guilty one may know
The blood once shed, still freely flowing,
Still cleansing, still healing.

*I exalt You, Jesus my sacrifice;*
*I exalt You, my Redeemer and my Lord.*
*I exalt You, worthy Lamb of God,*
*And in honour I bow down before Your*
*    throne.*

**321**
James Edmeston altd.

LEAD US, HEAVENLY FATHER, LEAD US
O'er the world's tempestuous sea;
Guard us, guide us, keep us, feed us,
For we have no help but Thee;
Yet possessing every blessing
If our God our Father be.

Saviour, breathe forgiveness o'er us;
All our weakness Thou dost know,
Thou didst tread this earth before us,
Thou didst feel its keenest woe;
Tempted, taunted, yet undaunted,
Through the desert Thou didst go.

Spirit of God, descending,
Fill our hearts with heavenly joy,
Love with every passion blending,
Pleasure that can never cloy;
Thus provided, pardoned, guided,
Nothing can our peace destroy.

**322**
Graham Kendrick.
Copyright © Kingsway's
Thankyou Music 1983.

LED LIKE A LAMB to the slaughter
In silence and shame,
There on Your back You carried a world
Of violence and pain.
Bleeding, dying, bleeding, dying.

*You're alive, You're alive*
*You have risen, Alleluia!*
*And the power and the glory is given,*
*Alleluia, Jesus, to You.*

At break of dawn, poor Mary,
Still weeping she came,
When through her grief she heard Your voice
Now speaking her name.
Mary, Master, Mary, Master.

At the right hand of the Father
Now seated on high
You have begun Your eternal reign
Of justice and joy.
Glory, glory, glory, glory.

**323**
Graham Kendrick.
Copyright © Kingsway's
Thankyou Music 1984.

LET GOD ARISE
*And let His enemies*
*Be scattered;*
*And let those who hate Him*
*Flee before Him.*
*Let God arise,*
*And let His enemies*
*Be scattered;*
*And let those who hate Him*
*Flee away.*

*(Men)*
But let the righteous be glad,
Let them exult before God,
Let them rejoice with gladness,
Building up a highway for the King,
We go in the name of the Lord,
Let the shout go up
In the name of the Lord.

*(Women)*
The righteous be glad,
Let them exult before God,
O let them rejoice
For the King,
In the name of the Lord.

**324**

**LET GOD SPEAK** *and I will listen,*
*Let God speak, there's things I'm needing to*
*put right.*
*Let God speak and I will obey what He says,*
*Please God, I want to hear Your voice*
*tonight.*

Lord I want to hear Your voice,
Lord I want to hear Your voice,
Lord I want to hear Your voice
Tonight, tonight.

**325**

**LET ME HAVE MY WAY AMONG YOU,**
Do not strive, do not strive.
Let me have My way among you,
Do not strive, do not strive.
For Mine is the power and the glory
For ever and ever the same.
Let Me have My way among you,
Do not strive, do not strive.

We'll let You have Your way among us,
We'll not strive, we'll not strive.
We'll let You have Your way among us,
We'll not strive, we'll not strive.
For Yours is the power and the glory
For ever and ever the same.
We'll let You have Your way among us,
We'll not strive, we'll not strive.

Let My peace rule within your hearts,
Do not strive, do not strive.
Let My peace rule within your hearts,
Do not strive, do not strive.
For Mine is the power and the glory,
For ever and ever the same.
Let My peace rule within your hearts,
Do not strive, do not strive.

We'll let Your peace rule within our hearts,
We'll not strive, we'll not strive.
We'll let Your peace rule within our hearts,
We'll not strive, we'll not strive.
For Yours is the power and the glory,
For ever and ever the same.
We'll let Your peace rule within our hearts,
We'll not strive, we'll not strive.

**326**

**LET OUR PRAISE TO YOU BE AS INCENSE,**
Let our praise to You be as pillars of Your
throne.
Let our praise to You be as incense,
As we come before You and worship You
alone.
As we see You in Your splendour,
As we gaze upon Your majesty,
As we join the hosts of angels
And proclaim together Your holiness.

Holy, holy, holy,
Holy is the Lord.
Holy, holy, holy,
Holy is the Lord.

**327**

**LET PRAISES RING,** let praises ring,
Lift voices up to love Him,
Lift hearts and hands to touch Him,
O let praises ring.
And fill the skies with anthems high
That tell His excellencies,
As priests and kings who rule with Him
Through all eternity;

*Let praises ring, let praises ring,*
*To our glorious King.*

Let praises ring, let praises ring,
Bow down in adoration,
Cry out His exaltation,
O let praises ring.
And lift the name above all names
Till every nation knows
The love of God has come to men,
His mercies overflow.

**328**

*(1st part)*
**LET THERE BE GLORY AND HONOUR** *and*
*praises,*
*Glory and honour to Jesus,*
*Glory, honour, glory and honour to Him.*
*Let there be glory and honour and praises,*
*Glory and honour to Jesus,*
*Glory, honour, glory and honour to Him.*

*(2nd part)*
*Glory, glory and honour to Jesus,*
*Glory, honour, glory and honour to Him.*
*Glory, glory and honour to Jesus,*
*Glory, honour, glory and honour to Him.*

*(1st and 2nd parts)*
Keep your light shining brightly
As the darkness covers the earth,
For a people that walk in darkness
They shall see, they shall see a great light.

## 329

Dave Bilbrough.
Copyright © Kingsway's
Thankyou Music 1979.

**LET THERE BE LOVE** shared among us,
Let there be love in our eyes,
May now Your love sweep this nation,
Cause us O Lord to arise.
Give us a fresh understanding
Of brotherly love that is real,
Let there be love shared among us,
Let there be love.

## 330

Author Unknown.

**LET US BREAK BREAD TOGETHER, WE ARE ONE.**
Let us break bread together, we are one.
We are one as we stand
With our face to the risen Son.
O Lord, have mercy on us.

Let us drink wine together, we are one… *(etc.)*

Let us praise God together, we are one… *(etc.)*

## 331

Ian White.
Copyright © Little Misty Music 1985.

**LET US GO TO THE HOUSE OF THE LORD.**
*Let us go to the house of the Lord.*
*Let us go to the house of the Lord.*

I rejoiced with those who said to me
'Let us go to the house of the Lord'.
Our feet are standing in your gates, Jerusalem;
Like a city built together,
Where the people of God go up
To praise the name of the Lord.

For peace for our Jerusalem
And loved ones this we pray;
May all men be secure where they must live.
And to all my friends and brothers,
May the peace be within you
For the sake of the house of the Lord.

## 332

Pale Sauni.
Copyright © Scripture in Song/
CopyCare Ltd 1983.

**LET US PRAISE HIS NAME WITH DANCING**
And with the tambourine.
Let us praise His name with dancing,
Make a joyful noise and sing.

*Dance, dance, dance before the King.*
*Dance, dance, celebrate and sing.*

Let us celebrate with dancing;
The King has set us free.
Let us celebrate with dancing,
Rejoice in victory.

## 333

John Milton.

**LET US WITH A GLADSOME MIND**
Praise the Lord, for He is kind:

*For His mercies shall endure,*
*Ever faithful, ever sure.*

Let us blaze His name abroad,
For of gods He is the God:

He, with all-commanding might,
Filled the new-made world with light:

He the golden-tressèd sun
Caused all day his course to run:

And the silver moon by night,
'Mid her spangled sisters bright:

He His chosen race did bless
In the wasteful wilderness:

All things living He doth feed,
His full hand supplies their need:

Let us with gladsome mind
Praise the Lord, for He is kind:

## 334

John Watson.
Copyright © Ampelos Music/
Kingsway's Thankyou Music 1986.

**LET YOUR LIVING WATER FLOW** over my soul.
Let Your Holy Spirit come and take control
Of every situation that has troubled my mind.
All my cares and burdens onto You I roll.

*Jesus, Jesus, Jesus.*
*Father, Father, Father.*
*Spirit, Spirit, Spirit.*

Come now, Holy Spirit, and take control.
Hold me in Your loving arms and make me
whole.
Wipe away all doubt and fear and take my
pride,
Draw me to Your love and keep me by Your
side.

Give your life to Jesus, let Him fill Your soul.
Let Him take You in His arms and make you
whole.
As you give your life to Him He'll set You free.
You will live and reign with Him eternally.

## 335

Graham Kendrick.
Copyright © Make Way Music 1989.

**LIFT HIGH THE CROSS.**
*Lift high the cross.*
*In majesty,*
*In victory.*

Here raged the fight, *(Women echo)*
Darkness and light. *(Women echo)*
All heaven and hell *(Women echo)*
Battled here. *(All)*

Here once for all *(Women echo)*
Was sacrificed *(Women echo)*
The Lamb of God, *(Women echo)*
Jesus Christ. *(All)*

Raise now your voices give glory and praise
    Him, *(Leader–All echo)*
For He has poured out His blood as a
    ransom. *(Leader–All echo)*
Hell's power is broken and heaven stands
    open, *(Leader–All echo)*
Lift high the cross. *(All)*

 **336**
Steven L. Fry.
Copyright © Birdwing Music/Cherry Lane 1974.

**LIFT UP YOUR HEADS** to the coming King,
Bow before Him and adore Him, sing
To His majesty, let your praises be
Pure and holy, giving glory
To the King of kings.

**337**
Graham Kendrick.
Copyright © Make Way Music 1991.

**LIFT UP YOUR HEADS** O you gates,
Swing wide you everlasting doors.
Lift up your heads O ye gates,
Swing wide you everlasting doors.

    *That the King of Glory may come in.*
    *That the King of glory may come in.*
    *That the King of glory may come in.*
    *That the King of glory may come in.*

Up from the dead He ascends,
Through every rank of heavenly power.
Let heaven prepare the highest place,
Throw wide the everlasting doors:

With trumpet blast and shouts of joy,
All heaven greets the risen King.
With angel choirs come line the way,
Throw wide the gates and welcome Him.

**338**
Terry Manship.
Copyright © Kingsway's
Thankyou Music 1986.

**LIFT UP YOUR HEADS, O YE GATES,**
*And be ye lifted up, ye everlasting doors.*
*Lift up your heads, O ye gates,*
*And be ye lifted up, ye everlasting doors;*
*And the King of glory shall come in,*
*The King of glory shall come in,*
*The King of glory shall come in.*

*(Women)*
Who is the King of glory?
What is His name?
    *(Men)*
The Lord strong and mighty,
The Lord mighty in battle, strong to save.

*(Women)*
Who shall ascend the hill,
The hill of the Lord?
    *(Men)*
Even he that hath clean hands
And a pure heart with which to praise his God.

**339**
Mick Gisbey.
Copyright © Kingsway's
Thankyou Music 1987.

**LIGHT A FLAME** *within my heart*
*That burning bright;*
*Fan the fire of joy in me*
*To set the world alight.*
*Let my flame begin to spread,*
*My life to glow;*
*God of light may I reflect*
*Your love to all I know.*

From heaven's splendour
He comes to earth,
While all the angels celebrate
The goodness of His birth.

We too exalt You,
Our glorious King;
Jesus our Saviour
Paid the price to take away our sin.

 **340**
Chris Rolinson.
Copyright © The Central Board of Finance
of the C of E.

**LIGHTEN OUR DARKNESS,** Lord we
    pray; *(echo)*
And in Your mercy defend us *(echo)*
From all perils and dangers of this
    night, *(echo)*
For the love of Your only Son, *(all)*
Our Saviour Jesus Christ.
Amen, Amen.
Amen, Amen.

**341**
Graham Kendrick.
Copyright © Make Way Music 1988.

**LIGHT HAS DAWNED** that ever shall blaze,
Darkness flees away.
Christ the light has shone in our hearts,
Turning night to day.

    *We proclaim Him King of kings,*
    *We lift high His name.*
    *Heaven and earth shall bow at His feet*
    *When He comes to reign.*

Saviour of the world is He,
Heaven's King come down.
Judgement, love and mercy meet
At His thorny crown.

Life has sprung from hearts of stone,
By the Spirit's breath.
Hell shall let her captives go,
Life has conquered death.

Blood has flowed that cleanses from sin,
God His love has proved.
Men may mock and demons may rage,
We shall not be moved!

**342** Craig Musseau.
Copyright © Mercy Publishing/
Kingsway's Thankyou Music 1990.

**LIGHT OF THE WORLD,** shine Your light
Into my heart.
God of love, pierce my soul
With Your mercy.

*So we might see Your glory,*
*So we might see Your face.*
*So we can feel Your heartbeat,*
*And hear You call our name.*

Fire of God, burn away
What is not holy.
Jesus, take our hearts
And make them new.

**343** Maggi Dawn.
Copyright © Kingsway's
Thankyou Music 1991.

**LIKE A GENTLE BREEZE,** like a mighty wind,
Like a roaring fire,
You will visit us, you will cleanse our souls,
And our hearts inspire,
Bringing peace to us, like a healing balm,
Or a gentle dove;
O come to us, O bring to us
God's gifts of love.

Come with holy fire,
Melt these hearts of clay.
Let them beat with love
That will never fade.
Holy Spirit come,
Holy Spirit come,
Holy Spirit come again.

**344** Frances Ridley Havergal.

**LIKE A RIVER GLORIOUS** is God's perfect
    peace,
Over all victorious, in its bright increase:
Perfect, yet it floweth fuller every day;
Perfect, yet it groweth deeper all the way.

Stayed upon Jehovah, hearts are fully blest;
Finding, as He promised, perfect peace and
    rest.

Hidden in the hollow of His blessèd hand,
Never foe can follow, never traitor stand;
Not a surge of worry, not a shade of care,
Not a blast of hurry touch the Spirit there.

Every joy or trial falleth from above,
Traced upon our dial by the sun of love.
We may trust Him fully, all for us to do;
They who trust Him wholly find Him wholly
    true.

**345** Ted Sandquist.
Copyright © Lion of Judah Music/
U.N. Music Publishing Ltd./
CopyCare Ltd 1976.

**LION OF JUDAH** on the throne,
I shout Your name, let it be known
That You are the King of kings,
You are the Prince of peace,
May Your kingdom's reign never cease.
Hail to the King!
Hail to the King!

Lion of Judah come to earth,
I want to thank You for Your birth,
For the living Word,
For Your death on the tree,
For Your resurrection victory.
Hallelujah! Hallelujah!

Lion of Judah come again,
Take up Your throne Jerusalem,
Bring release to this earth
And the consummation
Of Your kingdom's reign, let it come.
Maranatha! Maranatha!

Lion of Judah on the throne,
I shout Your name, let it be known
That You are the King of kings,
You are the Prince of peace,
May Your kingdom's reign never cease.
Hail to the King!
Hail to the King!
You are my King!

**346** David J. Hadden & Bob Sylvester.
Copyright © Restoration Music Ltd./
Sovereign Lifestyle Music Ltd. 1982.

**LIVING UNDER THE SHADOW OF HIS WING**
We find security,
Standing in His presence we will bring
Our worship, worship, worship to the King.

Bowed in adoration at His feet
We dwell in harmony,
Voices joined together that repeat,
Worthy, worthy, worthy is the Lamb.

Heart to heart embracing in His love
Reveals His purity,
Soaring in my spirit like a dove,
Holy, holy, holy is the Lord.


**347**  Charles Wesley.

**LO, HE COMES WITH CLOUDS DESCENDING,**
Once for favoured sinners slain;
Thousand thousand saints attending
Swell the triumph of His train:
Alleluia!
Alleluia!
Alleluia!
God appears on earth to reign.

Every eye shall now behold Him
Robed in glorious majesty;
Those who set at naught and sold Him,
Pierced and nailed Him to the tree,
Deeply wailing,
Deeply wailing,
Deeply wailing,
Shall their true Messiah see.

Those dear tokens of His passion
Still His dazzling body bears;
Cause of endless exultation
To His ransomed worshippers:
With what rapture,
With what rapture,
With what rapture,
Gaze we on those glorious scars.

Yea, Amen, let all adore Thee,
High on Thine eternal throne;
Saviour, take the power and glory,
Claim the kingdom for Thine own:
Come, Lord Jesus!
Come, Lord Jesus!
Come, Lord Jesus!
Everlasting God, come down!


**348**  Martin F. Ball.
Copyright © Restoration Music Ltd./
Sovereign Lifestyle Music Ltd. 1982.

**LOOK AND SEE THE GLORY OF THE KING,**
*Sense the presence of the Lord amongst His
      people,
Feel Him fill the temple of our lives
As He sits upon the throne of our praise.*

We are His church,
We are all God's own people,
We all proclaim that He is King, He is King.

At God's right hand
Jesus Christ is exalted,
His rule is now, and shall be for evermore.


**349**  Thomas Kelly.

**LOOK, YE SAINTS, THE SIGHT IS GLORIOUS;**
See the Man of Sorrows now,
From the fight returned victorious;
Every knee to Him shall bow:
Crown Him! Crown Him!
Crown Him! Crown Him!
Crowns become the Victor's brow.

Crown the Saviour, angels, crown Him;
Rich the trophies Jesus brings;
In the seat of power enthrone Him,
While the vault of heaven rings:
Crown Him! Crown Him!
Crown Him! Crown Him!
Crown the Saviour, King of kings!

Sinners in derision crowned Him,
Mocking thus the Saviour's claim;
Saints and angels throng around Him,
Own His title, praise His name:
Crown Him! Crown Him!
Crown Him! Crown Him!
Spread abroad the Victor's fame.

Hark, those bursts of acclamation!
Hark, those loud triumphant chords!
Jesus takes the highest station:
O what joy the sight affords!
Crown Him! Crown Him!
Crown Him! Crown Him!
King of kings, and Lord of lords!


**350**  Noel Richards.
Copyright © Kingsway's
Thankyou Music 1982.

**LORD AND FATHER, KING FOR EVER,**
Throned with majesty and power,
We adore You, we exalt You,
Worship we bring, our offering,
Worship we bring to You our King.


**351**  Chris Rolinson.
Copyright © Kingsway's
Thankyou Music 1988.

**LORD, COME AND HEAL YOUR CHURCH,**
Take our lives and cleanse with Your fire.
Let Your deliverance flow,
As we lift Your name up higher.

*We will draw near,
And surrender our fear;
Lift our hands to proclaim
Holy Father, You are here.*

Spirit of God, come in
And release our hearts to praise You.
Make us whole, for
Holy we'll become, and serve You.

Show us Your power, we pray,
That we might share in Your glory.
We shall arise and go
To proclaim Your works most holy.

**352** G. H. Bourne.

## LORD, ENTHRONED IN HEAVENLY SPLENDOUR,

First-begotten from the dead,
Thou alone, our strong defender,
Liftest up Thy people's head.
Alleluia! Alleluia!
Jesus, true and living Bread.

Here our humblest homage pay we,
Here in loving reverence bow;
Here for faith's discernment pray we
Lest we fail to know Thee now.
Alleluia! Alleluia!
Thou art here, we ask not how.

Though the lowliest form doth veil Thee
As of old in Bethlehem,
Here as there Thine angels hail Thee
Branch and Flower of Jesse's stem.
Alleluia! Alleluia!
We in worship join with them.

Paschal Lamb, Thine offering, finished
Once for all when Thou wast slain,
In its fullness undiminished
Shall for evermore remain,
Alleluia! Alleluia!
Cleansing souls from every stain.

Life-imparting, heavenly Manna,
Stricken Rock with streaming side,
Heaven and earth with loud hosanna
Worship Thee, the Lamb who died,
Alleluia! Alleluia!
Risen, ascended, glorified!

**353** Sue Hutchinson.
Copyright © Springtide/
Word Music (UK)/CopyCare Ltd 1979.

## LORD GOD, HEAVENLY KING,

You are our God, to You we sing;
Receive the worship of our hearts,
The adoration of our lips;
How we love You,
Lord God, heavenly King.

**354** Graham Kendrick.
Copyright © Kingsway's
Thankyou Music 1986.

## LORD HAVE MERCY on us,

Come and heal our land.
Cleanse with Your fire, heal with Your touch,
Humbly we bow and call upon You now.
O Lord, have mercy on us,
O Lord, have mercy on us.
    (Last time only)
O Lord, have mercy on us.

**355** Stuart Townend.
Copyright © Kingsway's
Thankyou Music 1990.

## LORD HOW MAJESTIC YOU ARE,

My eyes meet Your gaze
And my burden is lifted.
Your word is a lamp to my feet,
Your hand swift to bless
And Your banner a shield.

*You are my everything,*
*You who made earth and sky and sea,*
*All that You've placed inside of me*
*Calls out Your name.*
*To You I bow,*
*The King who commands my every breath,*
*The Man who has conquered sin and death,*
*My Lord and my King,*
*My everything.*

Lord, how resplendent You are,
When I think of Your heavens,
The work of Your fingers—
What is man, that You are mindful of him,
Yet You've crowned him with glory
And caused him to reign!

**356** Dave Bilbrough.
Copyright © Kingsway's
Thankyou Music 1987.

## LORD, I WILL CELEBRATE YOUR LOVE,

From deep within my heart,
I celebrate Your love;
I celebrate Your love given to me.

You are the one that I adore;
Lord, in Your presence is life for evermore;
The one that I adore.
You are my Lord.

Healing me, releasing me,
More and more reveal Yourself in me,
My Lord, my Lord!

**357** Patrick Appleford.
Copyright © Josef Weinberger Ltd 1960.

## LORD JESUS CHRIST,

You have come to us,
You are one with us,
Mary's son.
Cleansing our souls from all their sin,
Pouring Your love and goodness in;
Jesus, our love for You we sing,
Living Lord.

*(Optional communion verse:)*
Lord Jesus Christ,
Now and every day,
Teach us how to pray,
Son of God.
You have commanded us to do
This in remembrance, Lord, of You:
Into our lives Your power breaks through,
Living Lord.

Lord Jesus Christ,
You have come to us,
Born as one of us,
Mary's son.
Led out to die on Calvary,
Risen from death to set us free,
Living Lord Jesus, help us see
You are Lord.

Lord Jesus Christ,
We would come to You,
Live our lives for You,
Son of God.
All Your commands we know are true,
Your many gifts will make us new,
Into our lives Your power breaks through,
Living Lord.

**358**

**LORD JESUS, HERE I STAND** before You,
To worship You, glorify Your name,
I humbly bow the knee before Your majesty,
Give You the glory, give You the praise.
I love You, lay my life before You,
I trust You for my every need;
I lift my hands to You, surrender everything,
You are my Saviour, My Lord and King.

**359**

**LORD, KEEP MY HEART TENDER,**
Reaching with outstretched hands
To Jesus Christ,
Feeling my hardness melt,
Knowing how Jesus felt
Possessed by love,
Warm Calvary love.

Lord, keep my heart tender,
Reaching with outstretched hands
For healing grace;
Believe the word revealed—
'By His stripes we are healed'—
Possessed by love,
Whole Calvary love.

Lord, keep my heart tender,
Reaching with outstretched hands
To those in need;
Finding, as tears I weep,
Compassion's well is deep,
Possessed by love,
Fresh Calvary love.

Lord, keep my heart tender,
Reaching with outstretched hands
To God most high;
Worshipping with desire,
My heart consumed by fire,
Possessed by love,
Strong Calvary love.

**360**

**LORD MAKE ME AN INSTRUMENT,**
An instrument of worship.
I lift up my hands in Your name.
Lord make me an instrument,
An instrument of worship.
I lift up my hands in Your name.

I'll sing You a love song,
A love song of worship,
I'll lift up my hands in Your name.
I'll sing You a love song,
A love song to Jesus,
I'll lift up my hands in Your name.

For we are a symphony,
A symphony of worship.
We lift up our hands in Your name.
For we are a symphony,
A symphony of worship.
We lift up our hands in Your name.

We'll sing You a love song,
A love song of worship,
We'll lift up our hands in Your name.
We'll sing you a love song,
A love song to Jesus,
We'll lift up our hands in Your name.

**361**

**LORD OF LORDS,** King of kings,
Maker of heaven and earth and all good things,
We give You glory.
Lord Jehovah, Son of Man,
Precious Prince of Peace and the great I AM,
We give You glory.

*Glory to God!*
*Glory to God!*
*Glory to God Almighty*
*In the highest!*

Lord, You're righteous in all Your ways.
We bless Your holy name and we will give You
praise,
We give You glory.
You reign for ever in majesty,
We praise You and lift You up for eternity,
We give You glory.

**362**

**LORD, THE LIGHT OF YOUR LOVE** is shining,
In the midst of the darkness, shining;
Jesus, Light of the world, shine upon us,
Set us free by the truth You now bring us,
Shine on me, shine on me.

*Shine, Jesus, shine,*
*Fill this land with the Father's glory;*
*Blaze, Spirit, blaze,*
*Set our hearts on fire.*
*Flow, river, flow,*
*Flood the nations with grace and mercy;*
*Send forth Your word,*
*Lord, and let there be light.*

Lord, I come to Your awesome presence,
From the shadows into Your radiance;
By the blood I may enter Your brightness,
Search me, try me, consume all my darkness.
Shine on me, shine on me.

As we gaze on Your kingly brightness
So our faces display Your likeness.
Ever changing from glory to glory,
Mirrored here may our lives tell Your story.
Shine on me, shine on me.

**363** Graham Kendrick.
Copyright © Make Way Music 1991.

**LORD WE COME** in Your name,
Gathered here to worship You.
Join us all in harmony,
Spirit, come.

*And join our hearts together in love,* (men)
*Join our hearts together in love,* (women)
*Join our hearts together in love,* (men)
*Join our hearts,* (women)
*And come like the dew on the mountains*
*descending.* (all)
*Join our hearts together in love,* (men)
*Join our hearts together in love,* (women)
*Join our hearts together in love,* (men)
*Join our hearts,* (women)
*For there the Lord has commanded the*
*blessing.* (all)

O how good, how beautiful    *(women)*
When we live in unity
Flowing like anointing oil    *(men)*
On Jesus' head.

*So join our hearts…*(etc.)

So let us all agree
To make strong our bonds of peace.
Here is life forever more,
Spirit, come.

*And join our hearts…*(etc.)

 **364** Mick Ray.
Copyright © Kingsway's
Thankyou Music 1987.

**LORD, WE GIVE YOU PRAISE;**
Our prayer of thanks to You we bring.
We sing our songs to You,
For praise belongs to You;
Lord, we give You praise.

Your love goes on and on;
You never change, You never turn.
Our hands we raise to You,
And bring our praise to You;
Lord, we give You praise.

**365** Trish Morgan, Ray Goudie,
Ian Townend, Dave Bankhead.
Copyright © Kingsway's
Thankyou Music 1986.

**LORD, WE LONG FOR YOU** to move in power;
There's a hunger deep within our hearts,
To see healing in our nation.
Send Your Spirit to revive us:

*Heal our nation,*
*Heal our nation,*
*Heal our nation,*
*Pour out Your Spirit on this land.*

Lord we hear Your Spirit, coming closer,
A mighty wave to break upon our land,
Bringing justice, and forgiveness.
God we cry to You, 'Revive us':

**366** Dave Bilbrough.
Copyright © Kingsway's
Thankyou Music 1984.

**LORD, WE WORSHIP YOU,**
Lord, we worship You,
Lord, we worship You,
Lord, we worship You.

In humble adoration
We lift our voices to You,
And sing in acclamation
Our song of praise to You.

**367** Simon and Lorraine Fenner.
Copyright © Kingsway's
Thankyou Music 1989.

**LORD, YOU ARE CALLING** the people of Your
   kingdom
To battle in Your name against the enemy;
To stand before You, a people who will serve
   You,
Till Your kingdom is released throughout the
   earth.

*Let Your kingdom come,*
*Let Your will be done*
*On earth as it is in heaven.*
*(Repeat)*

At the name of Jesus every knee must bow;
The darkness of this age must flee away.
Release Your power to flow throughout the
   land;
Let Your glory be revealed as we praise.

**368**  Lynn DeShazo.
Copyright © Integrity's Hosanna! Music
Adm. Kingsway's Thankyou Music 1985.

**LORD, YOU ARE MORE PRECIOUS** than silver,
Lord, You are more costly than gold.
Lord, You are more beautiful than diamonds,
And nothing I desire compares with You.

**369**  Graham Kendrick.
Copyright © Kingsway's
Thankyou Music 1986.

**LORD, YOU ARE SO PRECIOUS TO ME,**
Lord, You are so precious to me,
And I love You,
Yes, I love You,
Because You first loved me.

Lord, You are so gracious to me,
Lord, You are so gracious to me,
And I love You,
Yes, I love You,
Because You first loved me.

**370**  Ian Smale.
Copyright © Kingsway's
Thankyou Music 1983.

**LORD, YOU PUT A TONGUE IN MY MOUTH**
And I want to sing to You,
Lord, You put a tongue in my mouth
And I want to sing to You,
Lord, You put a tongue in my mouth
And I want to sing only to You.
Lord Jesus, free us in our praise;
Lord Jesus, free us in our praise.

Lord, You put some hands on my arms
Which I want to raise to You... *(etc.)*

Lord, You put some feet on my legs
And I want to dance to You... *(etc.)*

**371**  Don Moen.
Copyright © Integrity's Hosanna! Music.
Adm. Kingsway's Thankyou Music 1986.

**LORD, YOU'RE FAITHFUL AND JUST,**
In You I put my trust, mighty God,
Everlasting Father.
Your word is faithful and true,
What You promised You will do, oh Lord.
Your word endures forever.

*You're faithful, faithful, and Your mercy*
*  never ends;*
*The world will pass away, but Your words*
*  are here to stay.*
*You're wonderful, Counsellor, Mighty God.*
*Lord Jehovah, You are the great I AM.*

**372**  Craig Musseau.
Copyright © Mercy Publishing/
Kingsway's Thankyou Music 1990.

**LORD, YOUR GLORY FILLS MY HEART,**
Your presence deep within me stirs my soul.
O Lord, how awesome are Your ways,
Your majesty surrounding all the earth.

*All wisdom and honour and glory for ever,*
*All power and greatness and splendour,*
*They are Yours above all others, my Lord.*

Lord, Your Spirit moves me now,
I see a picture of Your holiness.
O Lord, I look into Your eyes,
And feel a fire burn into my heart.

**373**  Tom Shirey.
Copyright © Mercy Publishing/
Kingsway's Thankyou Music 1987.

**LORD, YOUR NAME IS HOLY,**
Lord, Your name is holy,
Holy Lord,
You are holy,
Lord, You are holy,
Holy Lord.

*I love You, Lord,*
*I glorify and praise Your holy name.*
*Lord, I love You, Lord,*
*I glorify and praise Your holy name.*

Lord, Your name is mighty,
Lord, Your name is mighty,
Mighty Lord,
You are mighty,
Lord, You are mighty,
Mighty Lord.

**374**  Barry Taylor.
Copyright © Kingsway's
Thankyou Music 1990.

**LORD, YOUR NAME IS WONDERFUL,**
*At Your name the captives shall go free.*
*We declare the mighty name of Jesus,*
*And proclaim Your holy victory.*

At Your name the kingdoms fall;
We declare You Lord of all.
At Your name the enemy shall flee,
You are mighty,
You are mighty Lord of all.
Mighty Lord of all.

*(Last time)*
Mighty Lord of all!

**375** Dave Bilbrough.
Copyright © Kingsway's
Thankyou Music 1984.

**LOVE BEYOND MEASURE,** mercy so free,
Your endless resources given to me.
Strength to the weary, healing our lives,
Your love beyond measure has opened my
    eyes,
Opened my eyes.

**376** Christina Rossetti (1830-94).

**LOVE CAME DOWN AT CHRISTMAS,**
Love all lovely, Love divine;
Love was born at Christmas,
Star and angels gave the sign.

Worship we the Godhead,
Love Incarnate, Love divine;
Worship we our Jesus:
But wherewith for sacred sign?

Love shall be our token,
Love be yours and love be mine,
Love to God and all men,
Love for plea and gift and sign.

**377** Charles Wesley.

**LOVE DIVINE,** all loves excelling,
Joy of heaven to earth come down!
Fix in us Thy humble dwelling,
All Thy faithful mercies crown.
Jesus, Thou art all compassion,
Pure unbounded love Thou art;
Visit us with Thy salvation,
Enter every trembling heart.

Breathe, O breathe Thy loving Spirit
Into every troubled breast!
Let us all in Thee inherit,
Let us find Thy promised rest.
Take away the love of sinning;
Alpha and Omega be;
End of faith, as its beginning,
Set our hearts at liberty.

Come, Almighty to deliver,
Let us all Thy grace receive!
Suddenly return, and never,
Never more Thy temples leave.
Thee we would be always blessing,
Serve Thee as Thy hosts above,
Pray, and praise Thee without ceasing,
Glory in Thy perfect love.

Finish then Thy new creation,
Pure and spotless let us be;
Let us see Thy great salvation
Perfectly restored in Thee!
Changed from glory into glory,
Till in heaven we take our place;
Till we cast our crowns before Thee,
Lost in wonder, love and praise.

**378** Robert Lowry.

**LOW IN THE GRAVE HE LAY,**
Jesus, my Saviour,
Waiting the coming day,
Jesus, my Lord:

> *Up from the grave He arose,*
> *With a mighty triumph o'er His foes;*
> *He arose a Victor from the dark domain,*
> *And He lives for ever with His saints to*
>     *reign:*
> *He arose! He arose!*
> *Alleluia! Christ arose!*

Vainly they watch His bed,
Jesus, my Saviour;
Vainly they seal the dead,
Jesus, my Lord:

Death cannot keep his prey,
Jesus, my Saviour;
He tore the bars away,
Jesus, my Lord:

**379** Jack W. Hayford.
Copyright © Rocksmith Music/
Leosong Copyright Service 1976.

**MAJESTY,** worship His majesty,
Unto Jesus be glory, honour and praise.
Majesty, kingdom authority,
Flow from His throne unto His own,
His anthem raise.
So exalt, lift up on high the name of Jesus,
Magnify, come glorify Christ Jesus the King.
Majesty, worship His majesty,
Jesus who died, now glorified,
King of all kings.

**380** Dave Bilbrough.
Copyright © Kingsway's
Thankyou Music 1988.

**MAKE A JOYFUL MELODY,**
Join together in harmony,
We are a part of a family,
The family of God.

His Spirit is our guarantee
That He lives in you and me,
We are a part of a family,
The family of God.

> *Lord, we praise You, praise You,*
> *Your love is great!*
> *Lord, we praise You, praise You,*
> *We celebrate!*

**381**

**MAKE ME A CHANNEL OF YOUR PEACE**
Where there is hatred let me bring Your love;
Where there is injury, Your pardon, Lord;
And where there's doubt, true faith in You.

*Oh, Master, grant that I may never seek*
*So much to be consoled as to console;*
*To be understood as to understand;*
*To be loved as to love with all my soul.*

Make me a channel of Your peace.
Where there's despair in life let me bring hope;
Where there is darkness, only light;
And where there's sadness, ever joy.

Make me a channel of Your peace.
It is in pardoning that we are pardoned,
In giving to all men that we receive,
And in dying that we're born to eternal life.

**382**

**MAKE ME, LORD, A DREAMER** for Your
    kingdom;
Plant in my heart heavenly desires.
Grant faith that can say, impossibilities shall
    be,
And vision lest a world should perish not
    knowing Thee.

Make me, Lord, a dreamer for Your kingdom;
I would aspire to greater goals in God.
So cause faith to rise, to motivate each word
    and deed,
A faith that's well convinced that Jesus meets
    every need.

Make me, Lord, a dreamer for Your kingdom;
Dreams that will change a world that's lost its
    way.
May dreams that first found their birth in Your
    omnipotence,
Come alive in me, becoming reality.

*(As verse 1)*

**383**

*MAKE US ONE, LORD, make us one, Lord,*
*By Your Spirit, make us one, Lord.*
*We are members of one body,*
*Make us one, Lord, we pray.*

Every tribe and nation
Is represented here,
Watching with each other
As the day of Christ draws near;
Worshipping the Saviour
Who died to set us free,
We belong together;
We are family.

**384**

**MAKE WAY,** make way, for Christ the King
In splendour arrives.
Fling wide the gates and welcome Him
Into your lives.

*Make way! (Make way!)*
*Make way! (Make way!)*
*For the King of kings*
*(For the King of kings)*
*Make way! (Make way!)*
*Make way! (Make way!)*
*And let His kingdom in.*

He comes the broken hearts to heal,
The prisoners to free.
The deaf shall hear, the lame shall dance,
The blind shall see.

And those who mourn with heavy hearts,
Who weep and sigh;
With laughter, joy and royal crown
He'll beautify.

We call you now to worship Him
As Lord of all.
To have no gods before Him,
Their thrones must fall!

**385** Philipp Bliss.

**MAN OF SORROWS!** what a name
For the Son of God, who came
Ruined sinners to reclaim!
Hallelujah! what a Saviour!

Bearing shame and scoffing rude,
In my place condemned He stood;
Sealed my pardon with His blood:
Hallelujah! what a Saviour!

Guilty, vile, and helpless, we;
Spotless Lamb of God was He:
Full atonement—can it be?
Hallelujah! what a Saviour!

Lifted up was He to die,
'It is finished!' was His cry:
Now in heaven exalted high:
Hallelujah! what a Saviour!

When He comes, our glorious King,
All His ransomed home to bring,
Then anew this song we'll sing:
'Hallelujah! what a Saviour!'

**386** Frances Ridley Havergal.

**MASTER, SPEAK! THY SERVANT HEARETH,**
Longing for Thy gracious word,
Longing for Thy voice that cheereth;
Master, let it now be heard.
I am listening, Lord, for Thee;
What hast Thou to say to me?

Speak to me by name, O Master,
Let me know it is to me;
Speak, that I may follow faster,
With a step more firm and free,
Where the Shepherd leads the flock
In the shadow of the rock.

Master, speak! though least and lowest,
Let me not unheard depart;
Master, speak! for O Thou knowest
All the yearning of my heart,
Knowest all its truest need;
Speak and make me blessed indeed.

Master, speak! and make me ready,
When Thy voice is truly heard,
With obedience glad and steady
Still to follow every word.
I am listening, Lord, for Thee;
Master, speak! O speak to me!

 **387**    Dave Bilbrough.
Copyright © Kingsway's
Thankyou Music 1990.

**MAY MY LIFE** declare the honour of Your
    name,
Reveal the heart of Christ who came
To light the darkest place
With sacrificial love

*(Last time)*
Sacrificial love

Cause me, Lord, to reach out in the Father's
    name,
To glorify the Lamb once slain,
To light the darkest place
With sacrificial love.

> *Teach me, Lord, to make my life as an*
>     *offering,*
>     *To tell the world that Jesus Christ is King,*
> *For the glory of God.*

**388**    Graham Kendrick.
Copyright © Kingsway's
Thankyou Music 1986.

**MAY THE FRAGRANCE** of Jesus fill this
    place. *(Men)*
May the fragrance of Jesus fill this
    place. *(Women)*
May the fragrance of Jesus fill this
    place. *(Men)*
Lovely fragrance of Jesus, *(Women)*
Rising from the sacrifice *(All)*
Of lives laid down in adoration.

May the glory of Jesus fill His church. *(Men)*
May the glory of Jesus fill His
    church. *(Women)*
May the glory of Jesus fill His church. *(Men)*
Radiant glory of Jesus, *(Women)*
Shining from our faces *(All)*
As we gaze in adoration.

May the beauty of Jesus fill my life. *(Men)*
May the beauty of Jesus fill my life. *(Women)*
May the beauty of Jesus fill my life. *(Men)*
Perfect beauty of Jesus, *(Women)*
Fill my thoughts my words my deeds *(All)*
My all I give in adoration.

 **389**    Chris Christensen.
Copyright © Integrity's Hosanna! Music.
Adm. Kingsway's Thankyou Music 1986.

**MAY WE BE A SHINING LIGHT** to the nations,
A shining light to the peoples of the earth;
Till the whole world sees the glory of Your
    name,
May Your pure light shine through us.

May we bring a word of hope to the nations,
A word of life to the peoples of the earth;
Till the whole world knows there's salvation
    through Your name,
May Your mercy flow through us.

May we be a healing balm to the nations,
A healing balm to the peoples of the earth;
Till the whole world knows the power of Your
    name,
May Your healing flow through us.

May we sing a song of joy to the nations,
A song of praise to the peoples of the earth;
Till the whole world rings with the praises of
    Your name,
May Your song be sung through us.

May Your kingdom come to the nations,
Your will be done to the peoples of the earth;
Till the whole world knows that Jesus Christ is
    Lord,
May Your kingdom come in us,
May Your kingdom come in us,
May Your kingdom come on earth.

**390**    Graham Kendrick.
Copyright © Kingsway's
Thankyou Music 1986.

**MEEKNESS AND MAJESTY,**
Manhood and Deity,
In perfect harmony,
The Man who is God.
Lord of eternity
Dwells in humanity,
Kneels in humility
And washes our feet.

> *O what a mystery,*
> *Meekness and majesty.*
> *Bow down and worship*
> *For this is your God,*
> *This is your God.*

Father's pure radiance,
Perfect in innocence,
Yet learns obedience
To death on a cross.
Suffering to give us life,
Conquering through sacrifice,
And as they crucify
Prays: 'Father forgive.'

Wisdom unsearchable,
God the invisible,
Love indestructible
In frailty appears.
Lord of infinity,
Stooping so tenderly,
Lifts our humanity
To the heights of His throne.

Sweet the rain's new fall
Sunlit from heaven,
Like the first dewfall
On the first grass.
Praise for the sweetness
Of the wet garden,
Sprung in completeness
Where His feet pass.

Mine is the sunlight!
Mine is the morning
Born of the one light
Eden saw play!
Praise with elation,
Praise every morning,
God's re-creation
Of the new day!

**391**  Maggi Dawn.
Copyright © Kingsway's
Thankyou Music 1987.

**MIGHTY GOD**, gracious King, strong Deliverer;
You have heard all our prayers, and You've
    answered;
So we give to You our deep appreciation,
You're the living God, You are Lord;
You're the living God, You are Lord.

**392**  Jude Del Hierro.
Copyright © Mercy Publishing/
Kingsway's Thankyou Music 1987.

**MORE LOVE** (more love),
**MORE POWER** (more power),
More of You in my life.
More love (more love),
More power (more power),
More of You in my life.

*And I will worship You with all my heart,*
*And I will worship You with all my mind,*
*And I will worship You with all of my*
    *strength,*
*For You are my Lord.*

(Last time)
And I will seek Your face with all of my heart,
And I will seek Your face with all of my mind,
And I will seek Your face with all of my
    strength,
For You are my Lord,
You are my Lord.

**393**  Eleanor Farjeon.
Copyright © David Higham Associates Ltd.

**MORNING HAS BROKEN**
Like the first morning;
Blackbird has spoken
Like the first bird.
Praise for the singing!
Praise for the morning!
Praise for them, springing
Fresh from the Word!

**394**  Patricia Morgan.
Copyright © Kingsway's
Thankyou Music 1984.

**MOVE HOLY SPIRIT,**
We ask You to
Fill us afresh.
We receive You.

**395**  Frederick W. Faber.

**MY GOD, HOW WONDERFUL THOU ART,**
Thy majesty how bright!
How beautiful Thy mercy-seat,
In depths of burning light!

How dread are Thine eternal years,
O everlasting Lord,
By prostrate spirits day and night
Incessantly adored!

How beautiful, how beautiful
The sight of Thee must be,
Thine endless wisdom, boundless power,
And awesome purity!

O how I fear Thee, Living God,
With deepest, tenderest fears,
And worship Thee with trembling hope
And penitential tears!

Yet I may love Thee too, O Lord,
Almighty as Thou art,
For Thou hast stooped to ask of me
The love of my poor heart.

No earthly father loves like Thee;
No mother e'er so mild,
Bears and forbears as Thou hast done
With me, Thy sinful child.

Father of Jesus, love's reward,
What rapture will it be
Prostrate before Thy throne to lie,
And gaze, and gaze on Thee.

**396**

**MY HEART IS FULL** of admiration   *(Men)*
For You, my Lord, my God and King.
Your excellence my inspiration,   *(Women)*
Your words of grace have made my spirit sing.

You love what's right and hate all evil,   *(Men)*
Therefore your God sets You on high,
And on Your head pours oil of
   gladness,   *(Women)*
While fragrance fills Your royal palaces.

   *All the glory, honour and power*
   *Belong to You, belong to You.*
   *Jesus, Saviour, Anointed One,*
   *I worship You, I worship You.*

Your throne, O God, will last forever,   *(All)*
Justice will be Your royal decree.
In majesty, ride out victorious,
For righteousness, truth and humility.

**397**

**MY LORD HE IS THE FAIREST OF THE FAIR,**
He is the lily of the valley,
The bright and morning star.
His love is written deep within my heart,
He is the never-ending fountain
Of everlasting life.
And He lives, He lives, He lives,
He lives in me.

**398**

**MY LORD, WHAT LOVE IS THIS**
That pays so dearly,
That I, the guilty one
May go free!

   *Amazing love, O what sacrifice,*
   *The Son of God given for me.*
   *My debt He pays, and my death He dies,*
   *That I might live, that I might live.*
      *(Last time only)*
   *That I might live!*

And so they watched Him die,
Despised, rejected;
But oh, the blood He shed
Flowed for me!

And now, this love of Christ
Shall flow like rivers;
Come wash your guilt away,
Live again!

**399**

**MY PEACE** I give unto you,
It's a peace that the world cannot give,
It's a peace that the world cannot understand,
Peace to know, peace to live,
My peace I give unto you.

My joy…, My love… *(etc.)*

**400**

**MY SONG IS LOVE UNKNOWN,**
My Saviour's love to me:
Love to the loveless shown,
That they might lovely be.
O who am I, that for my sake
My Lord should take frail flesh and die?

He came from His blessed throne
Salvation to bestow;
But men made strange, and none
The longed-for Christ would know:
But O! my Friend, my Friend indeed,
Who at my need His life did spend.

Sometimes they strew His way,
And His sweet praises sing;
Resounding all the day
Hosannas to their King:
Then 'Crucify!' is all their breath,
And for His death they thirst and cry.

They rise and needs will have
My dear Lord made away;
A murderer they save,
The Prince of life they slay,
Yet cheerful He to suffering goes,
That He His foes from thence might free.

In life no house, no home
My Lord on earth might have;
In death, no friendly tomb,
But what a stranger gave.
What may I say? Heaven was His home;
And mine the tomb wherein He lay.

Here might I stay and sing,
No story so divine;
Never was love, dear King!
Never was grief like Thine.
This is my Friend, in whose sweet praise
I all my days could gladly spend.

**401**

**MY SOUL LONGS FOR YOU,** O my God,
I seek You with all of my heart.
In this dry and thirsty land
My voice cries out to You;
Only Your presence can satisfy my need.

And so I enter into Your sanctuary,
To behold Your glory.
I'll give You my praise as long as I live,
Raise my hands, my life I'll give
To You, oh I love You Lord.

**402** Andy Park.
Copyright © Mercy Publishing/
Kingsway's Thankyou Music 1988.

**NO-ONE BUT YOU, LORD**
Can satisfy the longing in my heart.
Nothing I do, Lord
Can take the place of drawing near to You.

*Only You can fill my deepest longing,*
*Only You can breathe in me new life,*
*Only You can fill my heart with laughter,*
*Only You can answer my heart's cry.*

Father, I love You,
Come satisfy the longing in my heart.
Fill me, overwhelm me,
Until I know Your love deep in my heart.

**403** Philip Lawson Johnston.
Copyright © Kingsway's
Thankyou Music 1989.

**NOT UNTO US** *but unto Your name*
*Be glory honour and praise.*
*Not unto us but unto Your name*
*Be glory honour and praise.*

Yours is the greatness and power.
You alone deserve all the fame.
Yours is the splendour and majesty.
From everlasting You're the same.

Yours is the glorious kingdom.
You alone are the King over all.
The earth is under Your dominion now.
You say when nations rise or fall.

**404** Bill Anderson.
Copyright © Kingsway's
Thankyou Music 1985.

**NOT WITHOUT A CAUSE** do we go marching
forth to war,
Not without a cause that we'll see
righteousness restored.
Clean your weapons, stir your hearts, shed all
fears before we start,
When we stand to do our part we shall say:

*'Not without a right do we unsheath our*
*silent swords,*
*Not without a fight but we will crown Him*
*Lord of lords.*
*Lift your banner, lift it high, Jesus is our*
*battle cry.*
*As we've lived, so we shall die, by His side.'*

Not without a foe do we prepare ourselves to
fight,
Not without a shout will we scale hell's
unconquered height.
Let the hosts of Satan pray, when we rise as
one that day,
Let them run in disarray, when we say:

Not without a cheer will we hear bells and
trumpets ring,
Not without a tear we'll set Him on the throne
of kings.
Eyes on fire and faces grim, we will free
Jerusalem,
Through the gates we'll follow Him, as we say:

**405** Martin Rinkart.
Tr. Catherine Winkworth.

**NOW THANK WE ALL OUR GOD,**
With hearts and hands and voices;
Who wondrous things has done,
In whom His world rejoices;
Who from our mother's arms
Has blessed us on our way
With countless gifts of love,
And still is ours today.

O may this bounteous God
Through all our life be near us,
With ever joyful hearts
And blessèd peace to cheer us;
And keep us in His grace,
And guide us when perplexed,
And free us from all ills
In this world and the next.

All praise and thanks to God
The Father now be given,
The Son, and Him who reigns
With them in highest heaven,
The one eternal God,
Whom earth and heaven adore;
For thus it was, is now,
And shall be evermore.

**406** Joey Holder.
Copyright © Far Lane Music Publishing/
Kingsway's Thankyou Music 1984.

**NOW UNTO THE KING** eternal,
Unto the King immortal,
Unto the King invisible,
The only wise God,
The only wise God.
*(Repeat)*

Unto the King be glory and honour,
Unto the King forever,
Unto the King be glory and honour forever
And ever, amen, amen.

**407**  Elizabeth Porter Head.

**O BREATH OF LIFE, COME SWEEPING THROUGH US,**
Revive Thy church with life and power.
O Breath of Life, come, cleanse, renew us,
And fit Thy church to meet this hour.

O Wind of God, come, bend us, break us,
Till humbly we confess our need;
Then in Thy tenderness remake us,
Revive, restore; for this we plead.

O Breath of Love, come, breathe within us,
Renewing thought and will and heart:
Come, love of Christ, afresh to win us,
Revive Thy church in every part.

Revive us, Lord! is zeal abating
While harvest fields are vast and white?
Revive us, Lord, the world is waiting,
Equip Thy church to spread the light.

**408**  Tr. Frederick Oakeley altd.

**O COME, ALL YE FAITHFUL,**
Joyful and triumphant,
O come ye, O come ye to Bethlehem;
Come and behold Him,
Born the King of angels;

*O come, let us adore Him,*
*O come, let us adore Him,*
*O come, let us adore Him,*
*Christ the Lord!*

God of God,
Light of light,
Lo, He abhors not the virgin's womb;
Very God,
Begotten, not created:

Sing, choirs of angels,
Sing in exultation,
Sing, all ye citizens of heaven above;
Glory to God
In the highest:

Yea, Lord, we greet Thee,
Born this happy morning,
Jesus, to Thee be glory given;
Word of the Father
Now in flesh appearing:

**409**  Author Unknown.

**O COME LET US ADORE HIM,**
O come let us adore Him,
O come let us adore Him,
Christ the Lord.

For He alone is worthy...*(etc.)*

We'll give Him all the glory...*(etc.)*

**410**  Tr. John Mason Neale altd.

**O COME, O COME, IMMANUEL,**
And ransom captive Israel,
That mourns in lonely exile here
Until the Son of God appear.

*Rejoice, rejoice! Immanuel*
*Shall come to thee, O Israel.*

O come, O come, Thou Lord of might
Who to Thy tribes on Sinai's height
In ancient times didst give the law
In cloud, and majesty, and awe.

O come, Thou Rod of Jesse, free
Thine own from Satan's tyranny;
From depths of hell Thy people save
And give them victory o'er the grave.

O come, Thou Dayspring, come and cheer
Our spirits by Thine advent here;
Disperse the gloomy clouds of night,
And death's dark shadows put to flight.

O come, Thou Key of David, come
And open wide our heavenly home;
Make safe the way that leads on high,
And close the path to misery.

**411**  Charles Wesley.

**O FOR A HEART TO PRAISE MY GOD,**
A heart from sin set free;
A heart that always feels Thy blood
So freely shed for me;

A heart resigned, submissive, meek,
My great Redeemer's throne,
Where only Christ is heard to speak,
Where Jesus reigns alone;

A humble, lowly, contrite heart,
Believing, true, and clean;
Which neither life nor death can part
From Him who dwells within;

A heart in every thought renewed,
And full of love divine;
Perfect and right, and pure, and good:
A copy, Lord, of Thine.

Thy nature, gracious Lord, impart;
Come quickly from above;
Write Thy new name upon my heart,
Thy new best name of love.

**412** Charles Wesley.

**O FOR A THOUSAND TONGUES** to sing
My great Redeemer's praise,
My great Redeemer's praise!
The glories of my God and King,
The triumphs of His grace!

Jesus! the name that charms our fears,
That bids our sorrows cease,
That bids our sorrows cease;
'Tis music in the sinner's ears,
'Tis life, and health, and peace.

See all your sins on Jesus laid;
The Lamb of God was slain,
The Lamb of God was slain;
His soul was once an offering made
For every soul of man.

He breaks the power of cancelled sin,
He sets the prisoner free,
He sets the prisoner free;
His blood can make the foulest clean,
His blood availed for me.

He speaks and, listening to His voice,
New life the dead receive,
New life the dead receive.
The mournful, broken hearts rejoice,
The humble poor believe.

Hear Him, ye deaf; His praise, ye dumb,
Your loosened tongues employ,
Your loosened tongues employ;
Ye blind, behold your Saviour come;
And leap, ye lame, for joy!

My gracious Master and my God,
Assist me to proclaim,
Assist me to proclaim,
To spread through all the earth abroad
The honours of Thy name.

**413** Joanne Pond.
Copyright © Kingsway's
Thankyou Music 1980.

**O GIVE THANKS** to the Lord,
All you His people,
O give thanks to the Lord for He is good.
Let us praise, let us thank,
Let us celebrate and dance,
O give thanks to the Lord for He is good.

**414** Graham Kendrick.
Copyright © Kingsway's
Thankyou Music 1979.

**O GOD MY CREATOR,** create in me
That river of water that flows full and free.
Let it bring life to the dead and stagnant sea;
Spring up, O well, and flow on out of me.

We come to the throne
Where flows the living stream,
And drink from the water,
And drink from the water,
And drink from the water that flows from
    Thee.

O God my Creator, create in me
That new way of living that flows full and free.
Let it bring life to the wilderness of man;
Spring up, O well, and flood this thirsty land.

**415** Isaac Watts.

**O GOD, OUR HELP IN AGES PAST,**
Our hope for years to come,
Our shelter from the stormy blast,
And our eternal home.

Under the shadow of Thy throne
Thy saints have dwelt secure;
Sufficient is Thine arm alone,
And our defence is sure.

Before the hills in order stood,
Or earth received her frame,
From everlasting Thou art God,
To endless years the same.

A thousand ages in Thy sight
Are like an evening gone,
Short as the watch that ends the night
Before the rising sun.

Time, like an ever-rolling stream,
Bears all its sons away;
They fly forgotten, as a dream
Dies at the opening day.

O God, our help in ages past,
Our hope for years to come,
Be Thou our guard while troubles last,
And our eternal home.

**416** Graham Kendrick.
Copyright © Make Way Music 1991.

**O HEAVEN, IS IN MY HEART.**
*O, heaven is in my heart.*

The kingdom of our God is here,    *(Leader)*
Heaven is in my heart.    *(All)*
The presence of His majesty,    *(Leader)*
Heaven is in my heart.    *(All)*
And in His presence joy abounds,    *(Leader)*
Heaven is in my heart.    *(All)*
The light of holiness surrounds,    *(Leader)*
Heaven is in my heart.    *(All)*

His precious life on me He spent, *(All)*
Heaven is in my heart.
To give me life without an end,
Heaven is in my heart.
In Christ is all my confidence,
Heaven is in my heart.
The hope of my inheritance,
Heaven is in my heart.

We are a temple for His throne, *(Women)*
Heaven is in my heart. *(All)*
And Christ is the foundation stone, *(Women)*
Heaven is in my heart. *(All)*
He will return to take us home, *(Women)*
Heaven is in my heart. *(All)*
The Spirit and the Bride say 'Come!' *(Women)*
Heaven is in my heart.

**417** Shona Sauni.
Copyright © Scripture in Song/
CopyCare Ltd 1982.

**O I WILL SING UNTO YOU WITH JOY,** O Lord,
For You're the rock of my salvation,
Come before You with thanksgiving
And extol You with a song.
For You're the greatest King above all else,
You hold the depths of the earth in Your hand.
O I will sing unto You with joy, O Lord,
For You're the rock of my salvation.
    *(Last time)*
O I will sing unto You with joy, O Lord,
For You're the rock of my salvation.

**418** John Ernest Bode.

**O JESUS, I HAVE PROMISED**
To serve Thee to the end;
Be Thou for ever near me,
My Master and my Friend;
I shall not fear the battle
If Thou art by my side,
Nor wander from the pathway
If Thou wilt be my Guide.

O let me feel Thee near me;
The world is ever near;
I see the sights that dazzle,
The tempting sounds I hear;
My foes are ever near me,
Around me and within;
But Jesus, draw Thou nearer,
And shield my soul from sin.

O let me hear Thee speaking
In accents clear and still,
Above the storms of passion,
The murmurs of self-will;
O speak to reassure me,
To hasten, or control;
O speak, and make me listen,
Thou Guardian of my soul.

O Jesus, Thou hast promised
To all who follow Thee
That where Thou art in glory
There shall Thy servants be;
And, Jesus, I have promised
To serve Thee to the end;
O give me grace to follow
My Master and my Friend.

O let me see Thy footmarks,
And in them plant mine own;
My hope to follow duly
Is in Thy strength alone.
O guide me, call me, draw me,
Uphold me to the end;
And then in heaven receive me,
My Saviour and my Friend.

**419** John Wimber.
Copyright © Mercy Publishing/
Kingsway's Thankyou Music 1979.

**O LET THE SON OF GOD ENFOLD YOU**
With His Spirit and His love,
Let Him fill your heart and satisfy your soul.
O let Him have the things that hold you,
And His Spirit like a dove
Will descend upon your life and make you
    whole.

    *Jesus, O Jesus,*
    *Come and fill Your lambs.*
    *Jesus, O Jesus,*
    *Come and fill Your lambs.*

O come and sing this song with gladness
As your hearts are filled with joy,
Lift your hands in sweet surrender to His name.
O give Him all your tears and sadness,
Give Him all your years of pain,
And you'll enter into life in Jesus' name.

**420** Philips Brooks.

**O LITTLE TOWN OF BETHLEHEM,**
How still we see thee lie!
Above thy deep and dreamless sleep
The silent stars go by.
Yet in the dark streets shineth
The everlasting light;
The hopes and fears of all the years
Are met in thee tonight.

O morning stars, together
Proclaim the holy birth,
And praises sing to God the King,
And peace to men on earth;
For Christ is born of Mary,
And gathered all above,
While mortals sleep, the angels keep
Their watch of wondering love.

How silently, how silently,
The wondrous gift is given!
So God imparts to human hearts
The blessings of His heaven.
No ear may hear His coming;
But in this world of sin,
Where meek souls will receive Him, still
The dear Christ enters in.

O holy Child of Bethlehem,
Descend to us, we pray;
Cast out our sin, and enter in;
Be born in us today.
We hear the Christmas angels
The great glad tidings tell;
O come to us, abide with us,
Our Lord Immanuel!

**421**
Chris Roe/Dave Markee.
Copyright © Kingsway's
Thankyou Music 1990.

**O LORD, GIVE ME AN UNDIVIDED HEART**
To follow You.
O Lord, give me an undiminished love,
To see what You see, to do what You do,
O Lord, give me an undivided heart.

O Lord, give me an unrelenting mind
To seek Your face.
O Lord, give me an undefeated faith,
To see victory in all that I do,
To worship in spirit and truth.
To see less of me, and much more of You,
O Lord, give me an undivided heart.
O Lord, give me an undivided heart.

**422**
Carl Tuttle.
Copyright © Mercy Publishing/
Kingsway's Thankyou Music 1985.

**O LORD, HAVE MERCY ON ME,** and heal me;
O Lord, have mercy on me, and free me.
Place my feet upon a rock,
Put a new song in my heart, in my heart.
O Lord, have mercy on me.

O Lord, may Your love and Your grace, protect
me;
O Lord, may Your ways and Your truth, direct
me.
Place my feet upon a rock,
Put a new song in my heart, in my heart,
O Lord, have mercy on me.

**423**
Taizé.
Copyright © Les Presses de Taizé (France)/
Harper Collins 1982, 1983 and 1984.

**O LORD, HEAR MY PRAYER,**
O Lord, hear my prayer:
When I call answer me.
O Lord, hear my prayer,
O Lord, hear my prayer:
Come and listen to me.

**424**
Wendy Churchill.
Copyright © Word Music (UK)/
CopyCare Ltd 1980.

**O LORD, MOST HOLY GOD,**
Great are Your purposes,
Great is Your will for us,
Great is Your love.
And we rejoice in You,
And we will sing to You,
O Father, have Your way,
Your will be done.

For You are building
A temple without hands,
A city without walls
Enclosed by fire.
A place for You to dwell,
Built out of living stones,
Shaped by a Father's hand
And joined in love.

**425**
Stuart K. Hine.
Copyright © Stuart K. Hine/
Kingsway's Thankyou Music 1953.

**O LORD MY GOD!** when I in awesome wonder
Consider all the works Thy hand hath made,
I see the stars, I hear the mighty thunder,
Thy power throughout the universe displayed:

*Then sings my soul, my Saviour God to
    Thee,
How great Thou art! How great Thou art!
Then sings my soul, my Saviour God, to
    Thee,
How great Thou art! How great Thou art!*

When through the woods and forest glades I
    wander
And hear the birds sing sweetly in the trees;
When I look down from lofty mountain
    grandeur,
And hear the brook, and feel the gentle breeze;

And when I think that God His Son not sparing,
Sent Him to die—I scarce can take it in.
That on the cross my burden gladly bearing,
He bled and died to take away my sin:

When Christ shall come with shout of
    acclamation
And take me home—what joy shall fill my
    heart!
Then shall I bow in humble adoration
And there proclaim, my God, how great Thou
    art!

**426**
Phil Lawson Johnston.
Copyright © Kingsway's
Thankyou Music 1982.

**O LORD OUR GOD,** how majestic is Your name,
The earth is filled with Your glory.
O Lord our God, You are robed in majesty,
You've set Your glory above the heavens.

*We will magnify, we will magnify*
*The Lord enthroned in Zion.*
*We will magnify, we will magnify*
*The Lord enthroned in Zion.*

O Lord our God, You have established a
    throne,
You reign in righteousness and splendour.
O Lord our God, the skies are ringing with Your
    praise,
Soon those on earth will come to worship.

O Lord our God, the world was made at Your
    command,
In You all things now hold together.
Now to Him who sits on the throne and to the
    Lamb,
Be praise and glory and power for ever.

**427**

**O LORD OUR GOD, YOU ARE A GREAT GOD,**
Your majesty beyond compare.
Who is a God like unto You,
And who like me could know Your care?

It's good, dear Lord, to know Your greatness,
It's good, dear Lord, to know Your care.
It's good just to be in Your presence,
It's good just to know that You are there.

**428**

**O LORD, OUR LORD,** *how excellent is Your*
    *name in all the earth.*
*O Lord, our Lord, how excellent is Your*
    *name in all the earth.*

You have set Your glory above the heavens,
From children's lips You have ordained praise.
You have set the moon and the stars in place,
And You still remember me.

What is man that You are mindful of him,
The son of man that you take care of him?
You have put everything beneath his feet,
And made him ruler of Your works.

**429**

**O LORD, THE CLOUDS ARE GATHERING,**
The fire of judgement burns,
How we have fallen!
O Lord, You stand appalled
To see Your laws of love so scorned,
And lives so broken.

*Have mercy, Lord*   (Men)
*Have mercy, Lord*   (Women)
*Forgive us, Lord*   (Men)
*Forgive us, Lord*   (Women)
*Restore us, Lord*
*Revive Your church again* { (All)
*Let justice flow*   (Men)
*Let justice flow*   (Women)
*Like rivers*   (Men)
*Like rivers*   (Women)
*And righteousness like a* { (All)
*Never failing stream.*

O Lord, over the nations now
Where is the dove of peace?
Her wings are broken.
O Lord, while precious children starve
The tools of war increase;
Their bread is stolen.

O Lord, dark powers are poised to flood
Our streets with hate and fear;
We must awaken!
O Lord, let love reclaim the lives
That sin would sweep away
And let Your kingdom come.

Yet, O Lord, Your glorious cross shall tower
Triumphant in this land,
Evil confounding.
Through the fire Your suffering church display
The glories of her Christ:
Praises resounding!

**430**

**O LORD, YOU ARE MY GOD,**
I will exalt You and praise Your name,
I will exalt You and praise Your name.
For in Your perfect faithfulness
You have done marvellous things.
O Lord, You are my God,
I will exalt You and praise Your name.

**431**

**O LORD, YOU ARE MY LIGHT,**
*O Lord, You are my salvation,*
*You have delivered me from all my fear,*
*For You are the defence of my life.*

For my life is hidden with Christ in God,
You have concealed me in Your love,
You've lifted me up, placed my feet on a rock;
I will shout for joy in the house of God.

**432** Keith Green.
Copyright © Birdwing Music/
Cherry Lane Music Ltd.

**O LORD, YOU'RE BEAUTIFUL,**
Your face is all I seek,
For when Your eyes are on this child,
Your grace abounds to me.

O Lord, please light the fire
That once burned bright and clear,
Replace the lamp of my first love
That burns with holy fear!

I wanna take Your word
And shine it all around,
But first help me just to live it Lord!
And when I'm doing well,
Help me to never seek a crown,
For my reward is giving glory to You.

O Lord, You're beautiful,
Your face is all I seek,
For when Your eyes are on this child,
Your grace abounds to me.


**433** Graham Kendrick.
Copyright © Kingsway's
Thankyou Music 1986.

**O LORD YOUR TENDERNESS**
Melting all my bitterness,
O Lord, I receive Your love.
O Lord, Your loveliness
Changing all my ugliness,
O Lord, I receive Your love.
O Lord, I receive Your love,
O Lord, I receive Your love.


**434** George Matheson.

**O LOVE THAT WILT NOT LET ME GO,**
I rest my weary soul in thee:
I give thee back the life I owe,
That in thine ocean depths its flow
May richer, fuller be.

O light that followest all my way,
I yield my flickering torch to thee:
My heart restores its borrowed ray,
That in thy sunshine's blaze its day
May brighter, fairer be.

O joy that seekest me through pain,
I cannot close my heart to thee:
I trace the rainbow through the rain,
And feel the promise is not vain,
That morn shall tearless be.

O cross that liftest up my head,
I dare not ask to fly from thee:
I lay in dust life's glory dead,
And from the ground there blossoms red
Life that shall endless be.


**435** Maggi Dawn.
Copyright © Kingsway's
Thankyou Music 1986.

*O MAGNIFY THE LORD* with me,
*And let us exalt His name together.*
*O magnify the Lord with me,*
*And let us exalt His name together.*

I called to the Lord and He answered,
Saved me from all of my trouble;
He delivered me from all my fear,
So I'll rejoice, I'll rejoice!

We will boast about the Lord,
Tell of the things He has done;
Let the whole world hear about it,
And they'll rejoice, they'll rejoice!

We will magnify Jesus together;
We will magnify You, O Lord.
We will magnify Jesus together;
We will magnify You, O Lord.


**436** Geoff Roberts.
Copyright © Kingsway's
Thankyou Music 1990.

**O MY LORD, YOU ARE MOST GLORIOUS,**
King of kings and Prince of Peace.
By Your word this world was created;
By Your love I have been set free.
And I lift my hands in worship up to Your
    throne,
I will declare how much You mean to me.
You are my Lord, it's You I worship;
Son of God, You reign in majesty.


**437** William W. How.

**O MY SAVIOUR, LIFTED**
From the earth for me,
Draw me, in Thy mercy,
Nearer unto Thee.

Lift my earthbound longings,
Fix them, Lord, above;
Draw me with the magnet
Of Thy mighty love.

And I come, Lord Jesus;
Dare I turn away?
No! Thy love hath conquered,
And I come today.

Bringing all my burdens,
Sorrow, sin, and care;
At Thy feet I lay them,
And I leave them there.

## 438

Cecil F. Alexander.

**ONCE IN ROYAL DAVID'S CITY,**
Stood a lowly cattle shed,
Where a mother laid her baby,
In a manger for His bed.
Mary was that mother mild,
Jesus Christ, her little child.

He came down to earth from heaven,
Who is God and Lord of all,
And His shelter was a stable,
And His cradle was a stall:
With the poor and meek and lowly
Lived on earth our Saviour holy.

And through all His wondrous childhood
He would honour and obey,
Love and watch the lowly mother
In whose gentle arms He lay.
Christian children all should be
Mild, obedient, good as He.

For He is our childhood's pattern:
Day by day like us He grew;
He was little, weak and helpless;
Tears and smiles like us He knew:
And He feeleth for our sadness,
And He shareth in our gladness.

And our eyes at last shall see Him
Through His own redeeming love;
For that child, so dear and gentle,
Is our Lord in heaven above;
And He leads His children on
To the place where He is gone.

Not in that poor lowly stable,
With the oxen standing by,
We shall see Him, but in heaven,
Set at God's right hand on high;
When like stars His children crowned,
All in white shall wait around.

## 439

Graham Kendrick.
Copyright © Kingsway's
Thankyou Music 1981.

**ONE SHALL TELL ANOTHER,**
And he shall tell his friend,
Husbands, wives and children
Shall come following on.
From house to house in families
Shall more be gathered in,
And lights will shine in every street,
So warm and welcoming.

*Come on in and taste the new wine,*
*The wine of the kingdom,*
*The wine of the kingdom of God.*
*Here is healing and forgiveness,*
*The wine of the kingdom,*
*The wine of the kingdom of God.*

Compassion of the Father
Is ready now to flow,
Through acts of love and mercy
We must let it show.
He turns now from His anger
To show a smiling face
And longs that men should stand beneath
The fountain of His grace.

He longs to do much more than
Our faith has yet allowed,
To thrill us and surprise us
With His sovereign power.
Where darkness has been darkest
The brightest light will shine,
His invitation comes to us,
It's yours and it is mine.

## 440

Andy Park.
Copyright © Mercy Publishing/
Kingsway's Thankyou Music 1989.

**ONE THING I ASK,** one thing I seek,
That I may dwell in Your house, O Lord.
All of my days, all of my life,
That I may see You, Lord.
Hear me, O Lord, hear me when I cry;
Lord, do not hide Your face from me.
You have been my strength,
You have been my shield,
And You will lift me up.

*One thing I ask,*
*One thing I desire*
*Is to see You,*
*Is to see You.*

## 441

Gerrit Gustafson.
Copyright © Integrity's Hosanna! Music.
Adm. Kingsway's Thankyou Music 1989.

**ONLY BY GRACE** can we enter,
Only by grace can we stand;
Not by our human endeavour,
But by the blood of the Lamb.
Into Your presence You call us,
You call us to come.
Into Your presence You draw us,
And now by Your grace we come,
Now by Your grace we come.

Lord, if You mark our transgressions,
Who would stand?
Thanks to Your grace we are cleansed
By the blood of the Lamb.

## 442

Sabine Baring-Gould.

**ONWARD, CHRISTIAN SOLDIERS,**
Marching as to war,
With the cross of Jesus
Going on before!
Christ, the royal Master,
Leads against the foe;
Forward into battle,
See, His banners go!

*Onward, Christian soldiers,*
*Marching as to war,*
*With the cross of Jesus*
*Going on before.*

At the name of Jesus
Satan's host doth flee;
On then, Christian soldiers,
On to victory!
Hell's foundations quiver
At the shout of praise;
Brothers, lift your voices;
Loud your anthems raise:

Like a mighty army
Moves the church of God:
Brothers we are treading
Where the saints have trod.
We are not divided
All one body we,
One in hope and doctrine,
One in charity.

Crowns and thrones may perish,
Kingdoms rise and wane,
But the church of Jesus
Constant will remain;
Gates of hell can never
'Gainst that church prevail;
We have Christ's own promise,
And that cannot fail:

Onward, then, ye people!
Join our happy throng;
Blend with ours your voices
In the triumph-song:
Glory, laud, and honour
Unto Christ the King!
This through countless ages
Men and angels sing:

**443**  Robert Cull.
Copyright © Maranatha! Music/
CopyCare Ltd 1976.

**OPEN OUR EYES, LORD,**
We want to see Jesus,
To reach out and touch Him
And say that we love Him.
Open our ears, Lord,
And help us to listen,
Open our eyes, Lord,
We want to see Jesus.

**444**  Carl Tuttle.
Copyright © Mercy Publishing/
Kingsway's Thankyou Music 1985.

**OPEN YOUR EYES,** see the glory of the King.
Lift up your voice and His praises sing.
I love You, Lord, I will proclaim:
Allelujah, I bless Your name.

**445**  Henry W. Baker.

**O PRAISE YE THE LORD!**
Praise Him in the height;
Rejoice in His word,
Ye angels of light;
Ye heavens adore Him
By whom ye were made,
And worship before Him,
In brightness arrayed.

O praise ye the Lord!
Praise Him upon earth,
In tuneful accord,
Ye sons of new birrth;
Praise Him who hath brought you
His grace from above,
Praise Him who hath taught you
To sing of His love.

O praise ye the Lord,
All things that give sound;
Each jubilant chord,
Re-echo around:
Loud organs, His glory
Forthtell in deep tone,
And sweet harp, the story
Of what He hath done.

O praise ye the Lord!
Thanksgiving and song
To Him be outpoured
All ages along;
For love in creation,
For heaven restored,
For grace of salvation,
O praise ye the Lord!

**446**  Paulus Gerhardt.
Tr. James W. Alexander.

**O SACRED HEAD, ONCE WOUNDED,**
With grief and pain weighed down,
How scornfully surrounded
With thorns, Thine only crown!
How pale art Thou with anguish,
With sore abuse and scorn!
How does that visage languish,
Which once was bright as morn!

O Lord of life and glory,
What bliss till now was Thine!
I read the wondrous story,
I joy to call Thee mine.
Thy grief and Thy compassion
Were all for sinners' gain;
Mine, mine was the transgression,
But Thine the deadly pain.

What language shall I borrow
To praise Thee, heavenly friend,
For this, Thy dying sorrow,
Thy pity without end?
Lord, make me Thine for ever,
Nor let me faithless prove;
O let me never, never
Abuse such dying love!

Be near me, Lord, when dying;
O show Thyself to me;
And for my succour flying,
Come, Lord, to set me free:
These eyes, new faith receiving,
From Jesus shall not move;
For he who dies believing,
Dies safely through Thy love.

 **447** Phil Rogers.
Copyright © Kingsway's
Thankyou Music 1984.

**O TASTE AND SEE** that the Lord is good,
How blessèd is the man who hides himself in
 Him.
I sought the Lord and He answered me
And set me free from all my fears.

I will give thanks to Him, for He is good,
His steadfast love to me will never end.
I will give thanks to Him, for He is good,
His steadfast love to me will never end.

**448** Phil Rogers.
Copyright © Kingsway's
Thankyou Music 1988.

**O, THAT YOU WOULD BLESS ME,**
And enlarge my borders,
That Your hand would be with me,
O Lord, O Lord.
O, that You would keep me,
Keep me from all evil,
So that I may not be ashamed,
O Lord, O Lord.

*May Your kingdom come,*
*May Your will be done*
*On earth as it is in heaven;*
*May Your kingdom come,*
*May Your will be done*
*Through me, O Lord, O Lord.*

O, that You would fill me,
Fill me with Your Spirit,
So that I may know Your power,
O Lord, O Lord.
O, that You would use me
To fulfil Your purposes,
That through me Your glory would shine,
O Lord, O Lord.

 **449** Dave Bilbrough.
Copyright © Kingsway's
Thankyou Music 1988.

**O, THE JOY OF YOUR FORGIVENESS,**
Slowly sweeping over me;
Now in heartfelt adoration
This praise I'll bring
To You, my King,
I'll worship You, my Lord.

 **450** Dave Bilbrough.
Copyright © Kingsway's
Thankyou Music 1980.

**O THE VALLEYS SHALL RING**
With the sound of praise,
And the lion shall lie with the lamb.
Of His government there shall be no end
And His glory shall fill the earth.

May Your will be done,
May Your kingdom come,
Let it rule, let it reign in our lives.
There's a shout in the camp as we answer the
 call,
Hail the King, Hail the Lord of lords.

**451** Charles Wesley.

**O THOU WHO CAMEST FROM ABOVE**
The pure celestial fire to impart,
Kindle a flame of sacred love
On the mean altar of my heart.

There let it for Thy glory burn
With inextinguishable blaze,
And trembling to its source return,
In humble prayer and fervent praise.

Jesus, confirm my heart's desire
To work, and speak, and think for Thee;
Still let me guard the holy fire,
And still stir up Thy gift in me.

Ready for all Thy perfect will,
My acts of faith and love repeat,
Till death Thy endless mercies seal,
And make the sacrifice complete.

**452** Noel & Tricia Richards.
Copyright © Kingsway's
Thankyou Music 1989.

**OUR CONFIDENCE IS IN THE LORD,**
The source of our salvation.
Rest is found in Him alone,
The Author of creation.
We will not fear the evil day,
Because we have a refuge;
In ev'ry circumstance we say,
Our hope is built on Jesus.

He is our fortress,
We will never be shaken.
He is our fortress,
We will never be shaken.
We will put our trust in God.
We will put our trust in God.

**453**
Rich Mullins.
Copyright © Ed Grant Inc/
Leosong Copyright Service 1989.

OUR GOD IS AN AWESOME GOD,
He reigns from heaven above,
With wisdom, power and love,
Our God is an awesome God!
Our God is an awesome God,
He reigns from heaven above,
With wisdom power and love,
Our God is an awesome God!

**454**
Patricia Morgan.
Copyright © Kingsway's
Thankyou Music 1986.

OUT OF YOUR GREAT LOVE, You have
    relented.
Out of Your great love, You have shown us
    grace.
Though we've caused You pain, and we have
    hurt You,
Out of Your great love, You've turned again.

**455**
Steven Fry.
Copyright © Birdwing Music/
BMG Music Publishing Ltd 1986.

O, WE ARE MORE THAN CONQUERORS.
*O, we are more than conquerors,*
*And who can separate us from*
*The love, The love of God.*
*O yes, we are,*
*We are more than conquerors.*
*O, we are more than conquerors.*

For He has promised to fulfill His will in us,
He said that He would guide us with His eye;
For He has blessed us with all gifts in Christ,
And we are His delight.

For He's within to finish what's begun in me,
He opens doors that no one can deny;
He makes a way where there's no other way,
And gives me wings to fly.

**456**
Robert Grant.

O WORSHIP THE KING,
All glorious above;
O gratefully sing
His power and His love:
Our Shield and Defender,
The Ancient of days,
Pavilioned in splendour
And girded with praise.

O tell of His might,
O sing of His grace,
Whose robe is the light,
Whose canopy space;
His chariots of wrath
The deep thunder-clouds form,
And dark is His path
On the wings of the storm.

The earth, with its store
Of wonders untold,
Almighty, Thy power
Hath founded of old;
Hath 'stablished it fast,
By a changeless decree,
And round it hath cast,
Like a mantle, the sea.

Thy bountiful care
What tongue can recite?
It breathes in the air,
It shines in the light;
It streams from the hills,
It descends to the plain,
And sweetly distils
In the dew and the rain.

Frail children of dust,
And feeble as frail,
In Thee do we trust,
Nor find Thee to fail;
Thy mercies how tender,
How firm to the end,
Our Maker, Defender,
Redeemer, and Friend!

**457**
John S. B. Monsell.

O WORSHIP THE LORD in the beauty of
    holiness,
Bow down before Him, His glory proclaim;
With gold of obedience and incense of
    lowliness,
Kneel and adore Him; the Lord is His name.

Low at His feet lay thy burden of carefulness,
High on His heart He will bear it for thee,
Comfort thy sorrows, and answer thy
    prayerfulness,
Guiding thy steps as may best for thee be.

Fear not to enter His courts in the slenderness
Of the poor wealth thou wouldst reckon as
    thine;
Truth in its beauty, and love in its tenderness,
These are the offerings to lay on His shrine.

These, though we bring them in trembling and
    fearfulness,
He will accept for the name that is dear;
Mornings of joy give for evenings of
    tearfulness,
Trust for our trembling, and hope for our fear.

O worship the Lord in the beauty of holiness,
Bow down before Him, His glory proclaim;
With gold of obedience and incense of
    lowliness,
Kneel and adore Him; the Lord is His name.

**458** Author unknown.

**PEACE IS FLOWING LIKE A RIVER,**
Flowing out through you and me,
Spreading out into the desert,
Setting all the captives free.

*Let it flow through me,*
*Let it flow through me,*
*Let the mighty peace of God*
*Flow out through me.*
*Let it flow through me,*
*Let it flow through me,*
*Let the mighty peace of God*
*Flow out through me.*

Love is flowing...*(etc.)*

Joy is flowing...*(etc.)*

Faith is flowing...*(etc.)*

Hope is flowing...*(etc.)*

 **459** John Watson.
Copyright © Ampelos Music (UK)/
Kingsway's Thankyou Music 1989.

**PEACE LIKE A RIVER,**
Love like a mountain,
The wind of Your Spirit
Is blowing everywhere.
Joy like a fountain,
Healing spring of life;
Come, Holy Spirit,
Let Your fire fall.

 **460** Graham Kendrick.
Copyright © Make Way Music 1988.

**PEACE TO YOU.**
We bless you now in the name of the Lord.
Peace to you.
We bless you now in the name of the Prince of
    Peace.
Peace to you.

**461** Anne Ortlund.
Copyright © Singspiration Music Inc/
U.N. Music Publishing Ltd/CopyCare Ltd 1970.

**PRAISE GOD FOR THE BODY,**
Praise God for the Son;
Praise God for the life
That binds our hearts in one.

*Joy is the food we share;*
*Love is our home, brothers.*
*Praise God for the body;*
*Shalom, Shalom.*

Guard your circle, brothers,
Clasp your hand in hand;
Satan cannot break
The bond in which we stand.

Shed your extra clothing,
Keep your baggage light;
Rough will be the battle,
Long will be the fight, but

Praise God for the body,
Praise God for the Son;
Praise God for the life
That binds our hearts in one.
Praise God for the life
That binds our hearts in one.

 **462** Ken Thomas.
Copyright © Lexicon Music Inc/
U.N. Music Publishing Ltd/CopyCare Ltd 1972

**PRAISE GOD FROM WHOM ALL BLESSINGS**
    **FLOW,**
Praise Him, all creatures here below,
Praise Him above, ye heavenly host;
Praise Father, Son and Holy Ghost.

**463** Twila Paris.
Copyright © Singspiration Music/
U.N. Music Publishing Ltd.

**PRAISE HIM,** praise Him,
Praise Him with your song.
Praise Him, praise Him,
Praise Him all day long!

*For the Lord is worthy,*
*Worthy to receive our praise.*
*For the Lord is worthy,*
*Worthy to receive our praise.*

Praise Him, praise Him,
Praise Him with your heart.
Praise Him, praise Him,
Give Him all you are.

Praise Him, praise Him,
Praise Him with your life.
Praise Him, praise Him,
Lift His name up high.

**464** John Kennett.
Copyright © Kingsway's
Thankyou Music 1981.

**PRAISE HIM ON THE TRUMPET,**
The psaltery and harp,
Praise Him on the timbrel and the dance,
Praise Him with stringed instruments too.
Praise Him on the loud cymbals,
Praise Him on the loud cymbals,
Let everything that has breath praise the Lord.

Hallelujah, praise the Lord,
Hallelujah, praise the Lord,
Let everything that has breath praise the Lord.
Hallelujah, praise the Lord,
Hallelujah, praise the Lord,
Let everything that has breath praise the Lord.

**465**  Fanny J. Crosby.

## PRAISE HIM, PRAISE HIM! JESUS, OUR BLESSED REDEEMER;
Sing, O earth, His wonderful love proclaim!
Hail Him, hail Him! highest archangels in glory,
Strength and honour give to His holy name.
Like a shepherd, Jesus will guard His children,
In His arms He carries them all day long;
O ye saints that dwell in the mountains of Zion,
Praise Him! praise Him! ever in joyful song.

Praise Him, praise Him! Jesus, our blessed
   Redeemer;
For our sins He suffered and bled and died.
He, our Rock, our hope of eternal salvation,
Hail Him, hail Him! Jesus the Crucified.
Loving Saviour, meekly enduring sorrow,
Crowned with thorns that cruelly pierced His
   brow;
Once for us rejected, despised, and forsaken,
Prince of glory, ever triumphant now.

Praise Him, praise Him! Jesus, our blessed
   Redeemer;
Heavenly portals loud with hosannas ring!
Jesus, Saviour, reigneth for ever and ever,
Crown Him, crown Him! Prophet and Priest and
   King!
Death is vanquished, tell it with joy, ye faithful!
Where is now thy victory, boasting grave?
Jesus lives, no longer thy portals are cheerless;
Jesus lives, the mighty and strong to save.

**466**  Henry Francis Lyte.

## PRAISE, MY SOUL, THE KING OF HEAVEN;
To His feet thy tribute bring.
Ransomed, healed, restored, forgiven,
Who like thee His praise should sing?
Praise Him! Praise Him!
Praise Him! Praise Him!
Praise the everlasting King!

Praise Him for His grace and favour
To our fathers in distress;
Praise Him, still the same for ever,
Slow to chide, and swift to bless.
Praise Him! Praise Him!
Praise Him! Praise Him!
Glorious in His faithfulness.

Father-like, He tends and spares us;
Well our feeble frame He knows;
In His hands He gently bears us,
Rescues us from all our foes.
Praise Him! Praise Him!
Praise Him! Praise Him!
Widely as His mercy flows.

Angels in the height, adore Him;
Ye behold Him face to face;
Sun and moon, bow down before Him,
Dwellers all in time and space.
Praise Him! Praise Him!
Praise Him! Praise Him!
Praise with us the God of grace!

**467**  David Fellingham.
Copyright © Kingsway's
Thankyou Music 1986.

## PRAISE THE LORD, praise Him in His temple,
Praise Him in the sanctuary of His power.
Lift your voices with great rejoicing,
For God is great in all the earth.

Praise Him for His excellence,
Praise Him for His love;
Praise Him for His mercy,
Giving us new life.

**468**  Roy Hicks.
Copyright © Latter Rain Music/
U.N. Music Pub./CopyCare Ltd 1975.

## PRAISE THE NAME OF JESUS,
Praise the name of Jesus,
He's my rock, He's my fortress,
He's my deliverer, in Him will I trust.
Praise the name of Jesus.

**469**  John H. Newman.

## PRAISE TO THE HOLIEST IN THE HEIGHT,
And in the depth be praise;
In all His words most wonderful,
Most sure in all His ways.

O loving wisdom of our God!
When all was sin and shame,
A second Adam to the fight
And to the rescue came.

O wisest love! that flesh and blood,
Which did in Adam fail,
Should strive afresh against the foe,
Should strive and should prevail;

And that a higher gift than grace
Should flesh and blood refine
God's presence and His very self,
And essence all-divine.

O generous love! that He, who smote
In Man for man the foe,
The double agony in Man
For man should undergo;

And in the garden secretly,
And on the cross on high,
Should teach His brethren, and inspire
To suffer and to die.

Praise to the Holiest in the height,
And to the depth be praise;
In all His words most wonderful,
Most sure in all His ways.

**470**
Joachim Neander.
Tr. Catherine Winkworth 1863,
and P. Dearmer 1906.

**PRAISE TO THE LORD, THE ALMIGHTY,** the
King of creation!
O my soul, praise Him, for He is thy health and
salvation!
All ye who hear,
Brothers and sisters, draw near,
Praise Him in glad adoration.

Praise to the Lord, who doth prosper thy work
and defend thee;
Surely His goodness and mercy here daily
attend thee:
Ponder anew
What the Almighty can do,
Who with His love doth befriend thee.

Praise to the Lord, who doth nourish thy life
and restore thee,
Fitting thee well for the tasks that are ever
before thee,
Then to thy need
He like a mother doth speed,
Spreading the wings of grace o'er thee.

Praise to the Lord, who when tempests their
warfare are waging,
Who, when the elements madly around thee
are raging,
Biddeth them cease,
Turneth their fury to peace,
Whirlwinds and waters assuaging.

Praise to the Lord, who, when darkness of sin
is abounding,
Who, when the godless do triumph, all virtue
confounding,
Sheddeth His light,
Chaseth the horrors of night,
Saints with His mercy surrounding.

Praise to the Lord! O let all that is in me adore
Him!
All that hath life and breath, come now with
praises before Him!
Let the Amen
Sound from His people again:
Gladly for aye we adore Him.

**471**
Chris Bowater.
Copyright © Sovereign Lifestyle Music Ltd 1980.

**PRAISE YE THE LORD,** praise ye the Lord,
For He has done
Marvellous things whereof we are glad,
We are glad,
Praise ye the Lord, praise ye the Lord.

**472**
Nettie Rose.
Copyright © Kingsway's
Thankyou Music 1977.

**PRAISE YOU, LORD,**
For the wonder of Your healing,
Praise You, Lord,
For Your love so freely given;
Outpouring, anointing,
Flowing in to heal our wounds,
Praise You, Lord, for Your love for me.

Praise You, Lord,
For Your gift of liberation,
Praise You, Lord,
You have set the captives free;
The chains that bind are broken
By the sharpness of Your sword,
Praise You, Lord, You gave Your life for me.

Praise You, Lord,
You have borne the depths of sorrow,
Praise You, Lord,
For Your anguish on the tree;
The nails that tore Your body
And the pain that tore Your soul,
Praise You, Lord, Your tears they fell for me.

Praise You, Lord,
You have turned our thorns to roses,
Glory, Lord,
As they bloom upon Your brow;
The path of pain is hallowed,
For Your love has made it sweet,
Praise You, Lord, and may I love You now.

**473**
Mary Smail.
Copyright © Mary Smail.

**PREPARE THE WAY** of the Lord,
Make His paths straight,
Open the gates,
That He may enter freely into our life.
'Hosanna!' we cry to the Lord.

*And we will fill the earth with the sound of
His praise.
Jesus is Lord!
Let Him be adored!
Yes, we will have this Man to reign over us.
Hosanna! We follow the Lord!*

And He will come to us as He came before,
Clothed in His grace,
To stand in our place.
And we behold Him now our Priest and King.
Hosanna! We sing to the Lord.

His kingdom shall increase,
To fill all the earth
And show forth His worth.
Then every knee shall bow and every tongue
confess
That Jesus Christ is Lord.

**474**

**PRINCE OF PEACE YOU ARE,**
You're bright and morning star;
Wondrous royal King,
You have made my heart to sing.
I worship You in spirit and in truth;
Lifting my praise, Your name in song I raise.
I give to You my life,
I offer up my sacrifice,
I pledge my love to You,
My God and King.


**475**

**PURIFY MY HEART,**
Let me be as gold
And precious silver.
Purify my heart,
Let me be as gold,
Pure gold.

*Refiner's fire,*
*My heart's one desire*
*Is to be holy,*
*Set apart for You, Lord.*
*I choose to be holy,*
*Set apart for You, my Master,*
*Ready to do Your will.*

Purify my heart,
Cleanse me from within
And make me holy.
Purify my heart,
Cleanse me from my sin,
Deep within.


**476**

**RAISE UP AN ARMY,** *O God,*
*Awake Your people throughout the earth.*
*Raise up an army, O God,*
*To proclaim Your kingdom,*
*To declare Your word,*
*To declare Your glory, O God.*

Our hope, our heart, our vision,
To see in every land
Your chosen people coming forth.
Fulfilling Your holy mission,
United as we stand,
Pledging our lives unto You, Lord.

O God, our glorious Maker,
We marvel at Your grace,
That You would use us in Your plan.
Rejoicing at Your favour,
Delighting in Your ways,
We'll gladly follow Your command!


**477**

**RECONCILED,** I'm reconciled,
I'm reconciled to God for ever,
Know He took away my sin,
I know His love will leave me never.
Reconciled, I am His child,
I know it was on me He smiled,
I'm reconciled, I'm reconciled to God.

Hallelujah I'm

Justified, I'm justified,
It's just as if I'd never sinned,
And once I knew such guilty fear,
But now I know His peace within me.
Justified, I'm justified,
It's all because my Jesus died,
I'm justified, I'm justified by God.

Hallelujah I'll

Magnify, I'll magnify,
I'll magnify His name for ever,
Wear the robe of righteousness
And bless the name of Jesus, Saviour,
Magnify the One who died,
The One who reigns for me on high.
I'll magnify, I'll magnify my God.


**478**

**REIGN IN ME,** sovereign Lord,
Reign in me.
Reign in me, sovereign Lord,
Reign in me.
Captivate my heart,
Let Your kingdom come,
Establish there Your throne,
Let Your will be done.


**479**

**REIGNING IN ALL SPLENDOUR,**
Victorious love,
Christ Jesus the Saviour,
Transcendent above.
All earthly dominions
And kingdoms shall fall,
For His name is Jesus
And He is the Lord.

He is Lord,
He is Lord,
He is Lord,
He is Lord.

**REJOICE!** *Rejoice!*
*Christ is in you,*
*The hope of glory*
*In our hearts.*
*He lives! He lives!*
*His breath is in you,*
*Arise a mighty army,*
*We arise.*

Now is the time for us
To march upon the land,
Into our hands
He will give the ground we claim.
He rides in majesty
To lead us into victory,
The world shall see
That Christ is Lord!

God is at work in us
His purpose to perform,
Building a kingdom
Of power not of words,
Where things impossible,
By faith shall be made possible;
Let's give the glory
To Him now.

Though we are weak, His grace
Is everything we need;
We're made of clay
But this treasure is within.
He turns our weaknesses
Into His opportunities,
So that the glory
Goes to Him.

**REJOICE, REJOICE, REJOICE!**
Rejoice, rejoice, rejoice
My soul rejoices in the Lord.
(Repeat)

My soul magnifies the Lord,
And my spirit rejoices in God my Saviour;
My soul magnifies the Lord,
And my spirit rejoices in my God.

**REJOICE, THE LORD IS KING!**
Your Lord and King adore;
Mortals, give thanks, and sing,
And triumph evermore:

*Lift up your heart, lift up your voice;*
*Rejoice! Again I say: rejoice!*

Jesus the Saviour reigns,
The God of truth and love;
When He had purged our stains,
He took His seat above:

His kingdom cannot fail,
He rules o'er earth and heaven;
The keys of death and hell
Are to our Jesus given:

He sits at God's right hand
Till all His foes submit,
And bow to His command,
And fall beneath His feet:

Rejoice in glorious hope;
Jesus the Judge shall come,
And take His servants up
To their eternal home:

*We soon shall hear the archangel's voice;*
*The trump of God shall sound: rejoice!*

**RESTORE, O LORD,**
The honour of Your name,
In works of sovereign power
Come shake the earth again.
That men may see
And come with reverent fear
To the living God
Whose kingdom shall outlast the years.

Restore, O Lord,
In all the earth Your fame,
And in our time revive
The church that bears Your name.
And in Your anger
Lord remember mercy,
O living God,
Whose mercy shall outlast the years.

Bend us, O Lord,
Where we are hard and cold,
In Your refiner's fire
Come purify the gold.
Though suffering comes
And evil crouches near,
Still our living God
Is reigning, He is reigning here.

Restore, O Lord,
The honour of Your name,
In works of sovereign power
Come shake the earth again.
That men may see
And come with reverent fear
To the living God
Whose kingdom shall outlast the years.

**REVIVAL!** *We're praying for revival,*
*That Your kingdom may come,*
*Your will may be done*
*Throughout this land.*
*(Repeat)*

Send now Your Spirit, Lord, may He come;
Cause us to glorify Jesus Your Son,
That all in this nation might know
He is the Lord.
Send now Your Spirit, let truth arise;
Where darkness has blinded, open closed eyes,
Bring spiritual health to this nation
As we cry to You:
Come heal our land.
Come heal our land.
Come heal our land.
Come heal our land.

 **485**   H. H. Milman.

## RIDE ON, RIDE ON IN MAJESTY!
In lowly pomp ride on to die!
O Christ, Thy triumphs now begin
O'er captive death and conquered sin.

Ride on, ride on in majesty!
Hark all the tribes 'hosanna' cry;
Thine humble beast pursues his road
With palms and scattered garments strowed.

Ride on, ride on in majesty!
Thy last and fiercest strife is nigh;
The Father on His sapphire throne
Expects His own anointed Son.

Ride on, ride on in majesty!
In lowly pomp ride on to die!
Bow Thy meek head to mortal pain,
Then take, O God, Thy power, and reign!

**486**   Mark Altrogge.
Copyright © People of Destiny/
CopyCare Ltd 1982.

**RISE UP**, you champions of God,
Rise up, you royal nation;
Rise up, and bear His light abroad,
We'll reach this generation.
We've got our marching orders,
We've got our marching orders;
Now is the time to carry them forth.

  *Go forth! Jesus loves them.*
  *Go forth! Take the gospel.*
  *Go forth! The time is now.*
  *The harvest is ripening;*
  *Go forth!*

Feel now the burden of the Lord,
Feel how He longs to save them;
Feel now for those who never heard
About the Son He gave them.
We've got our marching orders,
We've got our marching orders;
Now is the time to carry them forth.

 **487**   Dougie Brown.
Copyright © Kingsway's
Thankyou Music 1980.

## RIVER WASH OVER ME,
Cleanse me and make me new.
Bathe me, refresh me and fill me anew,
River wash over me.

Spirit watch over me,
Lead me to Jesus' feet.
Cause me to worship and fill me anew,
Spirit watch over me.

Jesus rule over me,
Reign over all my heart.
Teach me to praise You and fill me anew,
Jesus rule over me.

**488**   Augustus Montague Toplady.

## ROCK OF AGES, cleft for me,
Let me hide myself in Thee;
Let the water and the blood,
From Thy riven side which flowed,
Be of sin the double cure,
Cleanse me from its guilt and power.

Not the labour of my hands
Can fulfil Thy law's demands;
Could my zeal no respite know,
Could my tears for ever flow,
All for sin could not atone:
Thou must save, and Thou alone.

Nothing in my hand I bring,
Simply to Thy cross I cling;
Naked, come to Thee for dress;
Helpless, look to Thee for grace;
Foul, I to the fountain fly:
Wash me, Saviour, or I die.

While I draw this fleeting breath,
When mine eyes shall close in death,
When I soar to worlds unknown,
See Thee on Thy judgement throne,
Rock of ages, cleft for me,
Let me hide myself in Thee.

**489**   Edward Caswall.

## SEE, AMID THE WINTER'S SNOW,
Born for us on earth below,
See, the Lamb of God appears,
Promised from eternal years.

  *Hail, thou ever-blessèd morn!*
  *Hail, redemption's happy dawn!*
  *Sing through all Jerusalem,*
  *Christ is born in Bethlehem!*

Lo, within a manger lies
He who built the starry skies,
He who throned in height sublime
Sits amid the cherubim.

Say, ye holy shepherds, say,
What your joyful news today;
Wherefore have ye left your sheep
On the lonely mountain steep?

'As we watched at dead of night,
Lo, we saw a wondrous light:
Angels singing, "Peace on earth"
Told us of the Saviour's birth.'

Sacred Infant, all divine,
What a tender love was Thine,
Thus to come from highest bliss
Down to such a world as this!

Teach, O teach us, holy Child,
By Thy face so meek and mild,
Teach us to resemble Thee
In Thy sweet humility.

**490**
Hilary Davies.
Copyright © Samsongs/Coronation Music/
Kingsway's Thankyou Music 1988.

**SEE HIM COME,** the King upon a donkey.
Where is all His majesty and power?
He who was glorious, yet for my sake
Put away glory to die upon the cross.
His body was broken,
His heart was torn apart for me upon the cross.

See the people line His path with palm leaves;
Hear the children shouting out His name.
He who was glorious, yet for my sake
Put away power to die upon the cross.
His body was broken,
His heart was torn apart for me upon the cross.

**491**
Michael Perry.
Copyright © Michael Perry/
Jubilate Hymns.

**SEE HIM LYING ON A BED OF STRAW,**
A draughty stable with an open door;
Mary cradling the babe she bore;
The Prince of glory is His name.

*O now carry me to Bethlehem,*
*To see the Lord appear to men;*
*Just as poor as was the stable then,*
*The Prince of glory when He came.*

Star of silver, sweep across the skies,
Show where Jesus in the manger lies;
Shepherds, swiftly from your stupor rise
To see the Saviour of the world.

Angels, sing again the song you sang,
Bring God's glory to the heart of man;
Sing that Bethlehem's little baby can
Be salvation to the soul.

Mine are riches, from Thy poverty,
From Thine innocence, eternity;
Mine, forgiveness by Thy death for me,
Child of sorrow for my joy.

**492**
Chris Bowater.
Copyright © Sovereign Lifestyle Music Ltd 1986.

**SEE HIS GLORY,** see His glory,
See His glory now appear.
See His glory, see His glory,
See His glory now appear.
God of light,
Holiness and truth, power and might,
See His glory, see it now appear.

Now we declare our God is good
And His mercies endure forever.
Now we declare our God is good,
And His mercies endure forever.

**493**
Karen Lafferty.
Copyright © Maranatha! Music USA/
CopyCare Ltd 1972.

**SEEK YE FIRST** the kingdom of God
And His righteousness,
And all these things shall be added unto you,
Hallelu, Hallelujah!

*Hallelujah! Hallelujah!*
*Hallelujah! Hallelu, Hallelujah!*

Man shall not live by bread alone,
But by every word
That proceeds from the mouth of God,
Hallelu, Hallelujah!

Ask and it shall be given unto you,
Seek and ye shall find.
Knock and it shall be opened unto you,
Hallelu, Hallelujah!

If the Son shall set you free,
Ye shall be free indeed.
Ye shall know the truth and the truth shall set
    you free,
Hallelu, Hallelujah!

Let your light so shine before men
That they may see your good works
And glorify your Father in heaven,
Hallelu, Hallelujah!

Trust in the Lord with all thine heart,
He shall direct thy paths,
In all thy ways acknowledge Him,
Hallelu, Hallelujah!

**494**
Author unknown.

**SET MY SPIRIT FREE** that I might worship
    Thee,
Set my spirit free that I might praise Thy name.
Let all bondage go and let deliverance flow,
Set my spirit free to worship Thee.

**SHOUT FOR JOY** and sing,
Let your praises ring;
See that God is building
A kingdom for a King.
His dwelling place with men,
The new Jerusalem;
Where Jesus is Lord over all.

*And we will worship, worship,*
*We will worship Jesus the Lord.*
*We will worship, worship,*
*We will worship Jesus the Lord.*

A work so long concealed,
In time will be revealed,
As the sons of God shall rise and take their
  stand.
Clothed in His righteousness,
The church made manifest,
Where Jesus is Lord over all.

Sovereign over all,
Hail Him risen Lord.
He alone is worthy of our praise.
Reigning in majesty,
Ruling in victory,
Jesus is Lord over all.

**SHOUT FOR JOY AND SING** your praises to the
  King,
Lift your voice and let your hallelujahs ring;
Come before His throne to worship and adore,
Enter joyfully now the presence of the Lord.

You are my Creator, You are my Deliverer,
You are my Redeemer, You are Lord,
And You are my Healer.
You are my Provider,
You are now my Shepherd and my Guide,
Jesus, Lord and King, I worship You.

**SHOW YOUR POWER, O LORD,**
Demonstrate the justice of Your kingdom.
Prove Your mighty word.
Vindicate Your name
Before a watching world.
Awesome are Your deeds, O Lord;
Renew them for this hour.
Show Your power, O Lord,
Among the people now.

Show Your power, O Lord,
Cause Your church to rise and take action.
Let all fear be gone,
Powers of the age to come
Are breaking through.
We Your people are ready to serve,
To arise and to obey.
Show Your power, O Lord,
And set the people free.
    *(Ending last time)*
Show Your power, O Lord,
And set the people—
Show Your power, O Lord,
And set the people—
Show Your power, O Lord,
And set the people free.

**SILENT NIGHT,** holy night!
Sleeps the world; hid from sight,
Mary and Joseph in stable bare
Watched o'er the Child beloved and fair,
Sleeping in heavenly rest,
Sleeping in heavenly rest.

Silent night, holy night!
Shepherds first saw the light,
Heard resounding clear and long,
Far and near, the angel-song:
'Christ the Redeemer is here,
Christ the Redeemer is here.'

Silent night, holy night!
Son of God, O how bright
Love is smiling from Thy face!
Strikes for us now the hour of grace,
Saviour, since Thou art born,
Saviour, since Thou art born.

*(Men)*
**SING HALLELUJAH TO THE LORD,**
Sing Hallelujah to the Lord,
Sing Hallelujah, sing Hallelujah,
Sing Hallelujah to the Lord.

*(Women)*
Sing Hallelujah to the Lord,
Sing Hallelujah,
Hallelujah,
Sing Hallelujah to the Lord.

Jesus is risen from the dead... *(etc.)*

Jesus is Lord of heaven and earth... *(etc.)*

Jesus is living in His church... *(etc.)*

Jesus is coming for His own... *(etc.)*

**500**  Melva Lea.
Copyright © Larry Lea Ministries.

**SING PRAISES UNTO GOD,** *sing praises,*
*Sing praises unto God, sing praises,*
*Sing praises unto God, sing praises,*
*Hallelujah!*
  (Repeat)

For God is the King over all the earth,
Sing praises unto Him with understanding.
O clap your hands and shout, all ye people,
For He is to be greatly praised.

**501**  Noel & Tricia Richards.
Copyright © Kingsway's
Thankyou Music 1990.

**SING TO THE LORD,** be joyful in praise,
Exalt his magnificent ways.
Sing to the Lord, again and again,
For ever his glory proclaim.
Let anthems of worship ascend to the King,
Giving all honour to Him.
Great is his name throughout all the earth,
With all of our strength let us sing,
Let us sing.

  *Glory to the Lord!*
  *Glory to the Lord!*
  *With our voices we shall give*
  *Glory to the Lord.*

**502**  Mick Ray.
Copyright © Kingsway's
Thankyou Music 1977.

**SING UNTO THE LORD A NEW SONG,**
*Sing unto the Lord, all the earth,*
*Sing to the Lord, bless His name,*
*He is greatly to be praised,*
*Sing unto the Lord a new song.*
  (Last time only)
*Sing unto the Lord a new song.*

Tell among the nations the Lord reigns,
The world shall never be moved,
Let the heavens be glad
And the earth rejoice,
Sing unto the Lord a new song.

Then shall all the trees sing for joy
Before the Lord, for He comes,
He will judge the world
With His righteousness,
Sing unto the Lord a new song.

**503**  Dave Bilbrough.
Copyright © Kingsway's
Thankyou Music 1983.

**SO FREELY,**
Flows the endless love You give to me;
So freely,
Not dependent on my part.
As I am reaching out
Reveal the love within Your heart,
As I am reaching out
Reveal the love within Your heart.

Completely,
That's the way You give Your love to me.
Completely,
Not dependent on my part.
As I am reaching out
Reveal the love within Your heart,
As I am reaching out
Reveal the love within Your heart.

So easy,
I receive the love You give to me.
So easy,
Not dependent on my part.
Flowing out to me
The love within Your heart,
Flowing out to me
The love within Your heart.

**504**  Cindy Gough.
Copyright © Mercy Publishing/
Kingsway's Thankyou Music 1989.

**SOFTEN MY HEART** Lord, I want to meet You
  here.
Soften my heart Lord, tender me with tears,
For Your presence is beyond anything I could
  desire;
Soften my heart Lord, consume me with Your
  holy fire.

Soften my heart Lord, I have made a choice.
Soften my heart Lord, I want to hear Your
  voice,
For Your presence is beyond anything I could
  desire;
Soften my heart Lord, consume me with Your
  holy fire.

**505**  Graham Kendrick.
Copyright © Make Way Music 1988.

**SOFTEN MY HEART, LORD,**
Soften my heart,
From all indifference
Set me apart.
To feel Your compassion,
To weep with Your tears;
Come soften my heart, O Lord,
Soften my heart.

**506**  Charles Wesley.

**SOLDIERS OF CHRIST, ARISE,**
And put your armour on;
Strong in the strength which God supplies,
Through His eternal Son;

Strong in the Lord of hosts,
And in His mighty power;
Who in the strength of Jesus trusts
Is more than conqueror.

Stand, then, in His great might,
With all His strength endued;
And take, to arm you for the fight,
The panoply of God.

Leave no unguarded place,
No weakness of the soul;
Take every virtue, every grace,
And fortify the whole.

From strength to strength go on,
Wrestle and fight and pray;
Tread all the powers of darkness down,
And win the well-fought day.

That having all things done,
And all your conflicts past,
Ye may o'ercome, through Christ alone,
And stand complete at last.

 **507**
John Wimber.
Copyright © Mercy Publishing/
Kingsway's Thankyou Music 1979.

**SON OF GOD**, this is our praise song.
Jesus, my Lord, I sing to You.
Come now, Spirit of God,
Breathe life into these words of love;
Angels join from above
As we sing our praise song.

*We praise You, we praise You,*
*We praise You, we worship You.*
*We praise You, we worship You.*

Son of God, this is our love song.
Jesus, my Lord, I sing to You.
Come now, Spirit of God,
Breathe life into these words of love;
Angels join from above
As we sing our love song.

*We love You, we love You,*
*We love You, we worship You.*
*We love You, we worship You.*

 **508**
Noel & Tricia Richards.
Copyright © Kingsway's
Thankyou Music 1990.

**SOVEREIGN LORD** I am Yours,
Now and evermore.
You're my King, You're the One
I am living for.
I choose to do what pleases You,
Lord, may my life forever be
A living sacrifice.

**509**
Graham Kendrick & Dave Bilbrough.
Copyright © Kingsway's Thankyou Music/
Make Way Music 1990.

**SPIRIT BREATHE ON US**, fall afresh on us,
As we gather in Your name.
Bring Your healing touch, do Your work in us,
As we gather in Your holy name.
Join us together, one to another,
As we surrender to You,
To You, O Lord.

 **510**
Daniel Iverson.
Copyright © Birdwing Music/
BMG Songs 1935, 1963.

**SPIRIT OF THE LIVING GOD,**
Fall afresh on me;
Spirit of the living God,
Fall afresh on me.
Break me, melt me, mould me, fill me.
Spirit of the living God,
Fall afresh on me.

**511**
Paul Armstrong.
Copyright © Restoration Music Ltd/
Sovereign Lifestyle Music Ltd 1984.

**SPIRIT OF THE LIVING GOD**
Fall afresh on me,
Spirit of the living God
Fall afresh on me.
Fill me anew,
Fill me anew.
Spirit of the Lord
Fall afresh on me.

**512**  James Montgomery.

**STAND UP, AND BLESS THE LORD,**
Ye people of His choice;
Stand up, and bless the Lord your God
With heart, and soul, and voice.

Through high above all praise,
Above all blessing high,
Who would not fear His holy name,
And laud and magnify?

O for the living flame
From His own altar brought,
To touch our lips, our minds inspire,
And wing to heaven our thought!

God is our strength and song,
And His salvation ours;
Then be His love in Christ proclaimed
With all our ransomed powers.

Stand up, and bless the Lord,
The Lord your God adore;
Stand up, and bless His glorious name
Henceforth for evermore.

**513**  George Duffield.

**STAND UP! STAND UP FOR JESUS,**
Ye soldiers of the cross!
Lift high His royal banner,
It must not suffer loss.
From victory unto victory
His army He shall lead,
Till every foe is vanquished,
And Christ is Lord indeed.

Stand up, stand up for Jesus!
The trumpet-call obey;
Forth to the mighty conflict
In this His glorious day!
Ye that are His, now serve Him
Against unnumbered foes;
Let courage rise with danger,
And strength to strength oppose.

Stand up, stand up for Jesus!
Stand in His strength alone;
The arm of flesh will fail you,
Ye dare not trust your own.
Put on the gospel armour,
Each piece put on with prayer;
Where duty calls, or danger,
Be never wanting there.

Stand up, stand up for Jesus!
The strife will not be long;
This day the noise of battle,
The next the victor's song.
To him that overcometh
A crown of life shall be;
He with the King of glory
Shall reign eternally.

**514** Graham Kendrick.
Copyright © Make Way Music 1988.

**SUCH LOVE,** pure as the whitest snow;
Such love, weeps for the shame I know;
Such love, paying the debt I owe;
O Jesus, such love.

Such love, stilling my restlessness;
Such love, filling my emptiness;
Such love, showing me holiness;
O Jesus, such love.

Such love, springs from eternity;
Such love, streaming through history;
Such love, fountain of life to me;
O Jesus, such love.

**515** Dave Bryant.
Copyright © Kingsway's
Thankyou Music 1982.

**SUCH LOVE!** Such grace!
Makes the pieces come falling into place,
Breaks through the darkness,
Turns on the light,
Making blindness give way to sight.
Your love has conquered,
Has set us free
To become all You've called us to be.
Healing the wounded, making us stand,
Bringing peace and a sword in our hand.

And no power in the universe
Can separate us from the love of God.
We're Yours for ever
With nothing to fear,
Willing slaves to the love that brought us here.

**516** Ronnie Wilson.
Copyright © Kingsway's
Thankyou Music 1978.

**SWEET FELLOWSHIP,** Jesus in the midst,
Life blossoms in the Church,
Men by men are blessed
When Jesus is in the midst.

Peace and harmony—Jesus reigning here;
The Church moves at His command,
No room for doubt or fear,
For Jesus is reigning here.

I've never known a time like this,
Feel the spirit within me rise.
Come and see what God is doing.
Lord, we love You.

Sweet fellowship, Jesus in the midst,
Life blossoms in the Church,
Men by men are blessed
When Jesus is in the midst.

**517** Chris Bowater.
Copyright © Sovereign Lifestyle Music Ltd 1986.

**SWING WIDE THE GATES,**
Let the King come in;
Swing wide the gates,
Make a way for Him.
Here He comes, the King of Glory,
Here He comes, mighty in victory,
Here He comes, in splendour and majesty.
Swing wide the gates,
Swing wide the gates,
Let the King come in.

**518** Paul Simmons.
Copyright © Kingsway's
Thankyou Music 1985.

**TAKE, EAT, THIS IS MY BODY,**
*Broken for you,*
*For I am come that you might have life,*
*Eat of My flesh and live,*
*Eat of My flesh and live.*

My blood was shed for many,
Taking away your sin,
And if I shall make you free
Then you shall be free indeed,
You shall be free indeed.

Though your sins be as scarlet
They shall be white as snow,
Though they be red like crimson
They shall be as wool,
They shall be as wool.

For God so loved the world
He gave His only Son,
That whosoever believeth on Him
Might have everlasting life,
Might have everlasting life.

**519**   Frances Ridley Havergal.

## TAKE MY LIFE, AND LET IT BE
Consecrated, Lord, to Thee;
Take my moments and my days,
Let them flow in ceaseless praise.

Take my hands, and let them move
At the impulse of Thy love;
Take my feet, and let them be
Swift and beautiful for Thee.

Take my voice, and let me sing
Always, only, for my King;
Take my lips, and let them be
Filled with messages from Thee.

Take my silver and my gold,
Not a mite would I withhold;
Take my intellect, and use
Every power as Thou shalt choose.

Take my will, and make it Thine;
It shall be no longer mine:
Take my heart, it is Thine own;
It shall be Thy royal throne.

Take my love; my Lord, I pour
At Thy feet its treasure store:
Take myself, and I will be
Ever, only, all for Thee.

**520**   Timothy Dudley-Smith.
          Copyright © Timothy Dudley-Smith.

## TELL OUT, MY SOUL, the greatness of the
    Lord!
Unnumbered blessings give my spirit voice;
Tender to me the promise of His word;
In God my Saviour shall my heart rejoice.

Tell out, my soul, the greatness of His name!
Make known His might, the deeds His arm has
    done;
His mercy sure, from age to age the same;
His holy name– the Lord, the mighty One.

Tell out, my soul, the greatness of His might!
Powers and dominions lay their glory by;
Proud hearts and stubborn wills are put to
    flight,
The hungry fed, the humble lifted high.

Tell out, my soul, the glories of His word!
Firm is His promise, and His mercy sure:
Tell out, my soul, the greatness of the Lord
To children's children and for evermore!

**521**   Robert Stoodley.
          Copyright © Mustard Seed Music 1978.

## THANKS BE TO GOD
Who gives us the victory,
Gives us the victory,
Through our Lord Jesus Christ.

He is able to keep us from falling
And to set us free from sin
So let us each live up to our calling
And commit our way to Him.

> *Thanks be to God*
> *Who gives us the victory,*
> *Gives us the victory*
> *Through our Lord Jesus Christ,*
> *Our Lord Jesus Christ.*

Jesus knows all about our temptations,
He has had to bear them too.
He will show us how to escape them,
If we trust Him he will lead us through.

He has led us from the power of darkness
To the kingdom of His blessed Son.
So let us join in praise together
And rejoice in what the Lord has done.

**522**   Graham Kendrick.
          Copyright © Kingsway's
          Thankyou Music 1985.

## THANK YOU FOR THE CROSS,
The price You paid for us,
How You gave Yourself,
So completely,
Precious Lord, (precious Lord).
Now our sins are gone,
All forgiven,
Covered by Your blood,
All forgotten,
Thank You Lord, (thank You Lord).

> *Oh I love You, Lord,*
> *Really love You, Lord.*
> *I will never understand*
> *Why You love me.*
> *You're my deepest joy,*
> *You're my heart's desire,*
> *And the greatest thing of all, O Lord, I see:*
> *You delight in me!*

For our healing there
Lord, You suffered,
And to take our fear
You poured out Your love,
Precious Lord, (precious Lord).
Calvary's work is done,
You have conquered,
Able now to save
So completely,
Thank You, Lord, (thank You, Lord).

**523**   Alison Huntley
          Copyright © Kingsway's
          Thankyou Music 1978.

## THANK YOU, JESUS, *thank You, Jesus,*
*Thank You, Lord, for loving me.*
*Thank You, Jesus, thank You, Jesus,*
*Thank You, Lord, for loving me.*

You went to Calvary,
And there You died for me,
Thank You, Lord, for loving me.
You went to Calvary,
And there You died for me,
Thank You, Lord, for loving me.

You rose up from the grave,
To me new life You gave,
Thank You, Lord, for loving me.
You rose up from the grave,
To me new life You gave,
Thank You, Lord, for loving me.

**524** Diane Davis Andrew.
Copyright © Celebration/
Kingsway's Thankyou Music 1971, 1975.

**THANK YOU, LORD, FOR THIS FINE DAY,**
Thank you, Lord, for this fine day,
Thank you, Lord, for this fine day,
Right where we are.

> *Alleluia, praise the Lord!*
> *Alleluia, praise the Lord!*
> *Alleluia, praise the Lord!*
> *Right where we are.*

Thank you, Lord, for loving us…*(etc.)*

Thank you, Lord, for giving us peace…*(etc.)*

Thank you, Lord, for setting us free…*(etc.)*

**525** Samuel John Stone.

**THE CHURCH'S ONE FOUNDATION**
Is Jesus Christ, her Lord;
She is His new creation
By water and the word;
From heaven He came and sought her
To be His holy bride,
With His own blood He bought her,
And for her life He died.

Elect from every nation,
Yet one o'er all the earth,
Her charter of salvation
One Lord, one faith, one birth;
One holy name she blesses,
Partakes one holy food,
And to one hope she presses
With every grace endued.

Though with a scornful wonder
Men see her sore oppressed,
By schisms rent asunder,
By heresies distressed,
Yet saints their watch are keeping,
Their cry goes up, 'How long?'
And soon the night of weeping
Shall be the morn of song.

'Mid toil, and tribulation,
And tumult of her war,
She waits the consummation
Of peace for evermore;
Till with the vision glorious
Her longing eyes are blessed,
And the great church victorious
Shall be the church at rest.

Yet she on earth hath union
With God the Three in One,
And mystic sweet communion
With those whose rest is won:
O happy ones and holy!
Lord, give us grace that we,
Like them, the meek and lowly,
On high may dwell with Thee.

**526**  Dave Bilbrough.
Copyright © Kingsway's
Thankyou Music 1986.

**THE CHURCH'S ONE FOUNDATION**
Is Jesus Christ the Lord,
And on that revelation,
Each one of us is called
To taste His full salvation,
To know His life within;
A pure and holy nation
To glorify the King.

> *Hallelujah, how great You are,*
> *Reigning in glory, enthroned in power;*
> *Bright Morning Star, how great You are;*
> *Reigning in glory, enthroned in power.*

This time of preparation
Eventually will yield
The fruit of all His labours;
His heart will be fulfilled.
From every tribe and nation
His people shall be known;
Drawn to be His kingdom,
Made out of living stones.

See Him and be radiant,
Taste the Lord and know
He wants to take us deeper,
For what we are we sow;
With streams of living water
He longs to overflow,
That out to all creation
His glory He will show.

**527** John Ellerton.

**THE DAY THOU GAVEST, LORD, IS ENDED,**
The darkness falls at Thy behest;
To Thee our morning hymns ascended,
Thy praise shall sanctify our rest.

We thank Thee that Thy church unsleeping,
While earth rolls onward into light,
Through all the world her watch is keeping,
And rests not now by day or night.

As o'er each continent and island
The dawn leads on another day,
The voice of prayer is never silent,
Nor dies the strain of praise away.

The sun that bids us rest is waking
Our brethren 'neath the western sky,
And hour by hour fresh lips are making
Thy wondrous doings heard on high.

So be it, Lord! Thy throne shall never,
Like earth's proud empires, pass away;
Thy kingdom stands, and grows for ever,
Till all Thy creatures own Thy sway.

**528** Graham Kendrick.
Copyright © Kingsway's
Thankyou Music 1986.

**THE EARTH IS THE LORD'S**  (Men)
*And ev'rything in it,*  (Women)
*The earth is the Lord's*  (Men)
*The work of His hands,*  (Women)
*The earth is the Lord's*  (Men)
*And ev'rything in it;*  (Women)
*And all things were made*
*For His glory.*  (All)

(Last time)
*And all things were made,*
*Yes, all things were made,*
*And all things were made*
*For His glory.*

The mountains are His,
The seas and the islands,
The cities and towns,
The houses and streets.
Let rebels bow down
And worship before Him,
For all things were made
For His glory.

**529**  Author unknown.

**THE FIRST NOWELL** the angel did say
Was to certain poor shepherds in fields as they
    lay;
In fields where they lay keeping their sheep,
On a cold winter's night that was so deep.

*Nowell, nowell, nowell, nowell,*
*Born is the King of Israel!*

They lookèd up and saw a star
Shine in the east, beyond them far,
And to the earth it gave great light,
And so it continued both day and night.

And by the light of that same star
Three wise men came from country far;
To seek for a King was their intent,
And to follow the star wherever it went.

This star drew nigh to the north-west;
Over Bethlehem it took its rest,
And there it did both stop and stay
Right over the place where Jesus lay.

Then entered in those wise men three
Full reverently upon their knee,
And offered there in His presence
Their gold, and myrrh, and frankincense.

Then let us all with one accord
Sing praises to our heavenly Lord,
That hath made heaven and earth of nought,
And with His blood mankind hath bought.

**530**  Thomas Olivers.

**THE GOD OF ABRAHAM PRAISE,**
Who reigns enthroned above,
Ancient of everlasting days,
And God of love.
Jehovah! Great I AM!
By earth and heaven confessed;
I bow and bless the sacred name
For ever blessed.

The God of Abraham praise,
At whose supreme command
From earth I rise, and seek the joys
At His right hand.
I all on earth forsake—
Its wisdom, fame, and power—
And Him my only portion make,
My shield and tower.

The God of Abraham praise,
Whose all-sufficient grace
Shall guide me all my happy days
In all my ways.
He calls a worm His friend,
He calls Himself my God;
And He shall save me to the end
Through Jesu's blood.

He by Himself hath sworn,
I on His oath depend:
I shall, on eagles' wings upborne,
To heaven ascend;
I shall behold His face,
I shall His power adore,
And sing the wonders of His grace
For evermore.

There dwells the Lord our King,
The Lord our Righteousness,
Triumphant o'er the world and sin,
The Prince of Peace;
On Zion's sacred height
His kingdom still maintains,
And glorious with His saints in light
For ever reigns.

The God who reigns on high
The great archangels sing;
And, holy, holy, holy, cry,
Almighty King.
Who was and is the same,
And evermore shall be;
Jehovah, Father, Great I AM,
We worship Thee.

Before the Saviour's face
The ransomed nations bow;
O'erwhelmed at His almighty grace,
For ever new:
He shows His prints of love,
They kindle to a flame,
And sound through all the worlds above
The slaughtered Lamb.

The whole triumphant host
Give thanks to God on high;
Hail, Father, Son, and Holy Ghost!
They ever cry.
Hail, Abraham's God, and mine!
I join the heavenly lays;
All might and majesty are Thine,
And endless praise.

# 531 Thomas Kelly.

**THE HEAD THAT ONCE WAS CROWNED WITH
    THORNS**
Is crowned with glory now;
A royal diadem adorns
The mighty Victor's brow.

The highest place that heaven affords
Is His by sovereign right,
The King of kings, the Lord of lords,
And heaven's eternal light.

The joy of all who dwell above,
The joy of all below,
To whom He manifests His love,
And grants His name to know.

To them the cross, with all its shame,
With all its grace, is given;
Their name an everlasting name,
Their joy the joy of heaven.

They suffer with their Lord below,
They reign with Him above;
Their profit and their joy to know
The mystery of His love.

The cross He bore is life and health,
Though shame and death to Him;
His people's hope, His people's wealth,
Their everlasting theme.

# 532
Graham Kendrick.
Copyright © Kingsway's
Thankyou Music 1981.

**THE KING IS AMONG US,**
His Spirit is here,
Let's draw near and worship,
Let songs fill the air.

He looks down upon us,
Delight in His face,
Enjoying His children's love,
Enthralled by our praise.

For each child is special,
Accepted and loved,
A love gift from Jesus
To His Father above.

And now He is giving
His gifts to us all,
For no one is worthless
And each one is called.

The Spirit's anointing
On all flesh comes down,
And we shall be channels
For works like His own.

We come now believing
Your promise of power,
For we are Your people
And this is Your hour.

The King is among us,
His Spirit is here,
Let's draw near and worship,
Let songs fill the air.

# 533 Henry Williams Baker.

**THE KING OF LOVE** my Shepherd is,
Whose goodness faileth never;
I nothing lack if I am His
And He is mine for ever.

Where streams of living water flow
My ransomed soul He leadeth,
And where the verdant pastures grow
With food celestial feedeth.

Perverse and foolish oft I strayed,
But yet in love He sought me,
And on His shoulder gently laid,
And home rejoicing brought me.

In death's dark vale I fear no ill
With Thee, dear Lord, beside me;
Thy rod and staff my comfort still,
Thy cross before to guide me.

Thou spread'st a table in my sight;
Thy unction grace bestoweth:
And O what transport of delight
From Thy pure chalice floweth!

And so through all the length of days
Thy goodness faileth never;
Good Shepherd, may I sing Thy praise
Within Thy house for ever.

## 534

Author unknown.

**THE LORD HAS GIVEN** a land of good things,
I will press in and make them mine.
I'll know His power, I'll know His glory,
And in His kingdom I will shine.

*With the high praises of God in our mouth*
*And a two-edged sword in our hand*
*We'll march right on to the victory side,*
*Right into Canaan's land.*

Gird up your armour, ye sons of Zion,
Gird up your armour, let's go to war.
We'll win the battle with great rejoicing,
And so we'll praise Him more and more.

We'll bind their kings in chains and fetters,
We'll bind their nobles tight in iron,
To execute God's written judgement;
March on to glory, sons of Zion!

## 535

Chris Bowater.
Copyright © Sovereign Lifestyle Music Ltd 1982.

**THE LORD HAS LED FORTH** *His people with*
*joy,*
*And His chosen ones with singing, singing.*
*The Lord has led forth His people with joy,*
*And His chosen ones with singing.*

He has given to them the lands of the nations,
To possess the fruit and keep His laws,
And praise, praise His name.

## 536

Graham Kendrick.
Copyright © Kingsway's
Thankyou Music 1986.

**THE LORD IS MARCHING OUT** in splendour,
In awesome majesty He rides,
For truth, humility and justice,
His mighty army fills the skies.

*O give thanks to the Lord for His love*
*endures,*
*O give thanks to the Lord for His love*
*endures,*
*O give thanks to the Lord for His love*
*endures,*
*For ever, for ever.*

His army marches out with dancing
For He has filled our hearts with joy.
Be glad the kingdom is advancing,
The love of God our battle cry!

## 537

Scottish Psalter.

**THE LORD'S MY SHEPHERD,** I'll not want;
He makes me down to lie
In pastures green; He leadeth me
The quiet waters by.

My soul He doth restore again;
And me to walk doth make
Within the paths of righteousness,
E'en for His own name's sake.

Yea, though I walk in death's dark vale,
Yet will I fear no ill;
For Thou art with me; and Thy rod
And staff me comfort still.

My table Thou hast furnishèd
In presence of my foes;
My head Thou dost with oil anoint,
And my cup overflows.

Goodness and mercy all my life
Shall surely follow me;
And in God's house for evermore
My dwelling place shall be.

## 538

Author unknown.

**THE LORD YOUR GOD IS IN YOUR MIDST**
The Lord of lords His name;
He will exult over you with joy,
He will renew you in His love,
He will rejoice over you
With shouts of joy, shouts of joy.
Shouts of joy, shouts of joy,
Shouts of joy.

## 539

Mark Altrogge.
Copyright © People of Destiny/
CopyCare Ltd 1986.

**THE NATIONS ARE WAITING** for us,
They're dying to hear the song we sing.
The nations are waiting for us,
Waiting for the gospel we will bring,
That in each nation men might come to know
the King.

Jesus, you lead us,
Calling us onward,
A glorious army
With banners unfurled.
It's our decision
To follow Your vision,
We're on a mission,
A mission to the world.
And the nations are waiting,
The nations are waiting,
Waiting.

## 540

Graham Kendrick.
Copyright © Kingsway's
Thankyou Music 1983.

**THE PRICE IS PAID,**
Come let us enter in
To all that Jesus died
To make our own.
For every sin
More than enough He gave,
And bought our freedom
From each guilty stain.

*The price is paid,*
*Alleluia,*
*Amazing grace*
*So strong and sure;*
*And so with all my heart,*
*My life in every part,*
*I live to thank You for*
*The price You paid.*

The price is paid,
See Satan flee away;
For Jesus crucified
Destroys his power.
No more to pay,
Let accusation cease,
In Christ there is
No condemnation now.

The price is paid,
And by that scourging cruel
He took our sicknesses
As if His own.
And by His wounds,
His body broken there,
His healing touch may now
By faith be known.

The price is paid,
'Worthy the Lamb' we cry,
Eternity shall never
Cease His praise.
The church of Christ
Shall rule upon the earth,
In Jesus' name we have
Authority.

 **541** Ruth Lake.
Copyright © Scripture in Song/
CopyCare Ltd 1972.

**THEREFORE THE REDEEMED** of the Lord shall
   return
And come with singing unto Zion,
And everlasting joy shall be upon their head.

Therefore the redeemed of the Lord shall
   return
And come with singing unto Zion,
And everlasting joy shall be upon their head.

They shall obtain gladness and joy,
And sorrow and mourning shall flee away.

Therefore the redeemed of the Lord shall
   return
And come with singing unto Zion,
And everlasting joy shall be upon their head.

**542** Cecil Frances Alexander.

**THERE IS A GREEN HILL FAR AWAY,**
Outside a city wall,
Where the dear Lord was crucified,
Who died to save us all.

We may not know, we cannot tell,
What pains He had to bear;
But we believe it was for us
He hung and suffered there.

He died that we might be forgiven,
He died to make us good,
That we might go at last to heaven,
Saved by His precious blood.

There was no other good enough
To pay the price of sin;
He only could unlock the gate
Of heaven, and let us in.

O dearly, dearly has He loved!
And we must love Him too,
And trust in His redeeming blood,
And try His works to do.

**543** Frederick Whitfield.

**THERE IS A NAME I LOVE TO HEAR,**
I love to speak its worth;
It sounds like music in my ear,
The sweetest name on earth.

   *O, how I love the Saviour's name,*
   *O, how I love the Saviour's name,*
   *O, how I love the Saviour's name,*
   *The sweetest name on earth.*

It tells me of a Saviour's love,
Who died to set me free;
It tells me of His precious blood,
The sinner's perfect plea.

It tells of One whose loving heart
Can feel my deepest woe;
Who in my sorrow bears a part
That none can bear below.

It bids my trembling heart rejoice,
It dries each rising tear;
It tells me in a still, small voice
To trust and never fear.

Jesus, the name I love so well,
The name I love to hear!
No saint on earth its worth can tell,
No heart conceive how dear!

**544** Melody Green.
Copyright © Cherry Lane Music 1982.

**THERE IS A REDEEMER,**
Jesus, God's own Son,
Precious Lamb of God, Messiah,
Holy One.

   *Thank You, O my Father,*
   *For giving us Your Son,*
   *And leaving Your Spirit—*
   *Till the work on earth is done.*

Jesus my Redeemer,
Name above all names,
Precious Lamb of God, Messiah,
O for sinners slain.

When I stand in glory
I will see His face.
And there I'll serve my King for ever
In that Holy Place.

**545** Noel Richards.
Copyright © Kingsway's
Thankyou Music 1989.

**THERE IS POWER IN THE NAME OF JESUS;**
We believe in His name.
We have called on the name of Jesus;
We are saved! We are saved!
At His name the demons flee.
At His name captives are freed.
For there is no other name that is higher
Than Jesus.

There is power in the name of Jesus,
Like a sword in our hands.
We declare in the name of Jesus,
We shall stand! We shall stand!
At His name God's enemies
Shall be crushed beneath our feet.
For there is no other name that is higher
Than Jesus.

**546** Tedd Smith.
Copyright © Hope Publishing Co 1973.

**THERE'S A QUIET UNDERSTANDING**
When we're gathered in the Spirit,
It's a promise that He gives us
When we gather in His name.
There's love we feel in Jesus,
There's a manna that He feeds us,
It's a promise that He gives us
When we gather in His name.

And we know when we're together,
Sharing love and understanding,
That our brothers and our sisters
Feel the oneness that He brings.
Thank You, thank You, thank You, Jesus,
For the way You love and feed us,
For the many ways You lead us;
Thank You, thank You, Lord.

**547** Graham Kendrick.
Copyright © Kingsway's
Thankyou Music 1978.

**THERE'S A SOUND ON THE WIND** like a victory
    song,
Listen now, let it rest on your soul.
It's a song that I learned from a heavenly King,
It's a song of a battle royal.

There's a loud shout of victory that leaps from
    our hearts
As we wait for our conquering King.
There's a triumph resounding from dark ages
    past
To the victory song we now sing.

Come on heaven's children,
The city is in sight.
There will be no sadness
On the other side.

There'll be crowns for the conquerors and
    white robes to wear,
There will be no more sorrow or pain.
And the battles of earth shall be lost in the
    sight
Of the glorious Lamb that was slain.

Now the King of the ages approaches the earth,
He will burst through the gates of the sky,
And all men shall bow down to His beautiful
    name,
We shall rise with a shout, we shall fly!

Come on, heaven's children,
The city is in sight.
There will be no sadness
On the other side.

Now the King of the ages approaches the earth,
He will burst through the gates of the sky,
And all men shall bow down to His beautiful
    name,
We shall rise with a shout, we shall fly!

**548** Chris Bowater.
Copyright © Sovereign Lifestyle Music Ltd 1985.

**THE SPIRIT OF THE LORD,**
The sovereign Lord, is on me,
Because he has anointed me
To preach good news to the poor:

> *Proclaiming Jesus, only Jesus—*
> *It is Jesus, Saviour, healer and baptiser,*
> *And the mighty King,*
> *The victor and deliverer—*
> *He is Lord, He is Lord, He is Lord!*

And he has called on me
To bind up all the broken hearts,
To minister release
To every captivated soul:

Let righteousness arise
And blossom as a garden;
Let praise begin to spring
In every tongue and nation:

**549** Edith McNeil.
Copyright © Celebration/
Kingsway's Thankyou Music 1974, 1975.

**THE STEADFAST LOVE OF THE LORD** never
    ceases,
His mercies never come to an end,
They are new every morning,
New every morning.
Great is Thy faithfulness, O Lord,
Great is Thy faithfulness.

**550**

**THE TRUMPETS SOUND,** the angels sing,
The feast is ready to begin;
The gates of heaven are open wide,
And Jesus welcomes you inside.

Tables are laden with good things,
O taste the peace and joy He brings;
He'll fill you up with love divine,
He'll turn your water into wine.

> *Sing with thankfulness songs of pure
>     delight.
> Come and revel in heaven's love and light;
> Take your place at the table of the King.
> The feast is ready to begin.
> The feast is ready to begin.*

The hungry heart He satisfies,
Offers the poor His paradise;
Now hear all heaven and earth applaud
The amazing goodness of the Lord.

*Ldr:* Jesus,        *(All echo each line)*
    We thank You
    For Your love,
    For Your joy.
    Jesus,
    We thank You
    For the good things
    You give to us.

**551**

**THINE BE THE GLORY,**
Risen, conquering Son,
Endless is the victory
Thou o'er death hast won.
Angels in bright raiment
Rolled the stone away,
Kept the folded grave-clothes
Where Thy body lay.

> *Thine be the glory,
> Risen, conquering Son,
> Endless is the victory
> Thou o'er death hast won!*

Lo, Jesus meet us,
Risen from the tomb!
Lovingly He greets us,
Scatters fear and gloom.
Let the Church with gladness
Hymns of triumph sing,
For her Lord now liveth,
Death hath lost its sting.

No more we doubt Thee
Glorious Prince of life;
Life is naught without Thee:
Aid us in our strife;
Make us more than conquerors,
Through Thy deathless love;
Lead us in Thy triumph
To Thy home above.

**552**

**THINE, O LORD IS THE GREATNESS,**
*And the power and the glory.*
*Thine, O Lord, is the victory,*
*And majesty, and majesty.*

All that is in heaven and earth is Thine,
Thou art exalted as head over all!

In Thy hand is power and might to make great,
In Thy hand is power to give strength to all!

Now is come salvation and power and might
For the kingdom of our God has been given to
    His Christ!

**553**

**THIS IS THE DAY,** this is the day
That the Lord has made, that the Lord has
    made;
We shall rejoice, we shall rejoice
And be glad in it, and be glad in it.
This is the day that the Lord has made,
We shall rejoice and be glad in it;
This is the day, this is the day
That the Lord has made.

**554**

**THOU ART WORTHY,** Thou art worthy,
Thou art worthy, O Lord.
To receive glory, glory and honour,
Glory and honour and power.
For Thou hast created, hast all things created,
Thou hast created all things;
And for Thy pleasure they are created,
Thou art worthy, O Lord.

**555**

**THOU DIDST LEAVE THY THRONE** and Thy
    kingly crown,
When Thou camest to earth for me;
But in Bethlehem's home there was found no
    room
For Thy holy nativity:
O come to my heart, Lord Jesus!
There is room in my heart for Thee.

Heaven's arches rang when the angels sang,
Proclaiming Thy royal degree;
But of lowly birth cam'st Thou, Lord, on earth,
And in great humility,
O come to my heart, Lord Jesus!
There is room in my heart for Thee.

The foxes found rest, and the birds had their
    nest,
In the shade of the cedar tree;
But Thy couch was the sod, O Thou Son of
    God,
In the deserts of Galilee.
O come to my heart, Lord Jesus!
There is room in my heart for Thee.

Thou camest, O Lord, with the living word
That should set Thy children free;
But with mocking scorn, and with crown of
    thorn,
They bore Thee to Calvary.
O come to my heart, Lord Jesus!
Thy cross is my only plea.

When heaven's arches shall ring, and her
    choirs shall sing,
At Thy coming to victory,
Let Thy voice call me home, saying, 'Yet there
    is room,
There is room at My side for thee.'
And my heart shall rejoice, Lord Jesus,
When Thou comest and callest for me.

**556** Don Thomas & Charles Williams.
Copyright © Word Music/Spoone Music/
Word Music (UK)/CopyCare Ltd 1980.

**THOU, O LORD, ART A SHIELD ABOUT ME,**
You're my glory,
You're the lifter of my head.
Thou, O Lord, art a shield about me,
You're my glory,
You're the lifter of my head.

Hallelujah,
Hallelujah.
Hallelujah,
You're the lifter of my head.

**557** John Marriott.

**THOU, WHOSE ALMIGHTY WORD**
Chaos and darkness heard,
And took their flight;
Hear us, we humbly pray,
And where the gospel-day
Sheds not its glorious ray,
Let there be light!

Thou who didst come to bring,
On Thy redeeming wing,
Healing and sight,
Health to the sick in mind,
Sight to the inly blind,
O now to all mankind
Let there be light!

Spirit of truth and love,
Life-giving, holy Dove,
Speed forth Thy flight;
Move on the waters' face,
Bearing the lamp of grace,
And in earth's darkest place
Let there be light!

Blessèd and holy Three,
Glorious Trinity,
Wisdom, love, might;
Boundless as ocean's tide
Rolling in fullest pride,
Through the world far and wide
Let there be light!

**558** Dale Garratt.
Copyright © Scripture in Song/
CopyCare Ltd 1979.

**THROUGH OUR GOD** *we shall do valiantly,*
*It is He who will tread down our enemies.*
*We'll sing and shout His victory,*
*Christ is King!*
    *(Last time only)*
*Christ is King! Christ is King!*

For God has won the victory
And set His people free,
His word has slain the enemy,
The earth shall stand and see that—

**559** Fanny J. Crosby.

**TO GOD BE THE GLORY!** great things He hath
    done!
So loved He the world that He gave us His Son,
Who yielded His life an atonement for sin,
And opened the life-gate that all may go in.

    *Praise the Lord! Praise the Lord!*
    *Let the earth hear His voice!*
    *Praise the Lord! Praise the Lord!*
    *Let the people rejoice!*
    *O come to the Father through Jesus the*
       *Son;*
    *And give Him the glory, great things He*
       *hath done!*

O perfect redemption, the purchase of blood!
To every believer the promise of God;
The vilest offender who truly believes,
That moment from Jesus a pardon receives.

Great things He hath taught us, great things He
    hath done,
And great our rejoicing through Jesus the Son:
But purer and higher and greater will be
Our wonder, our worship, when Jesus we see!

**560** Debbye Graafsma.
Copyright © Integrity's Hosanna! Music.
Adm. Kingsway's Thankyou Music 1985.

**TO HIM WHO SITS ON THE THRONE** and unto
    the Lamb,
To Him who sits on the throne and unto the
    Lamb
Be blessing and glory and honour and power
    for ever,
Be blessing and glory and honour and power
    for ever.

**561**

**UNTO THEE, O LORD,** do I lift up my soul,
Unto Thee, O Lord, do I lift up my soul.

*O my God, I trust in Thee,*
*Let me not be ashamed,*
*Let not mine enemies triumph over me.*

Yea, let none that wait on Thee be ashamed,
Yea, let none that wait on Thee be ashamed.

Show me Thy ways, Thy ways, O Lord,
Teach me Thy paths, Thy paths, O Lord.

Remember not the sins of my youth,
Remember not the sins of my youth.

The secret of the Lord is with them that fear
    Him,
The secret of the Lord is with them that fear
    Him.

Unto Thee, O Lord, do I lift up my soul,
Unto Thee, O Lord, do I lift up my soul.

**562**

**UNTO YOU, O LORD**
Do I open up my heart.
Unto You, O Lord
Do I lift my voice.
Unto You, O Lord
Do I raise my hands,
Unto You, O Lord of hosts.

**563**

**WE ARE A CHOSEN PEOPLE,** *a royal*
    *priesthood,*
*A holy nation, belonging to God.*
*We are a chosen people, a royal priesthood,*
*A holy nation, belonging to God.*

You have called us out of darkness
To declare Your praise.
We exalt You and enthrone You,
Glorify Your name.

You have placed us into Zion
In the new Jerusalem.
Thousand thousand are their voices,
Singing to the Lamb.

**564**

**WE ARE ALL TOGETHER**
To call upon Your name;
There is nothing we like better,
Than to sing and give You praise.

Lord, we welcome You,
We welcome You,
We welcome You,
Come fill this place.

Bring healing and salvation,
Let Your kingdom come
Right here just like in heaven,
Lord, may Your will be done.

Father, come fill this place,
We welcome You;
Jesus, we seek Your face,
'Cause all we want to do
Is give our love to You.

**565**

**WE ARE A PEOPLE OF POWER,**
We are a people of praise;
We are a people of promise,
Jesus has risen, He's conquered the grave!
Risen, yes, born again,
We walk in the power of His name;
Power to be the sons of God,
The sons of God! The sons of God!
We are the sons, sons of God!

**566**

**WE ARE BEING BUILT INTO A TEMPLE,**
Fit for God's own dwelling place;
Into the house of God which is the Church,
The pillar and the ground of truth,
As precious stones that Jesus owns,
Fashioned by His wondrous grace.
And as we love and trust each other
So the building grows and grows.

**567**

**WE ARE HERE TO PRAISE YOU,**
Lift our hearts and sing.
We are here to give You
The best that we can bring.
And it is our love
Rising from our hearts,
Everything within us cries:
'Abba Father.'
Help us now to give You
Pleasure and delight,
Heart and mind and will that say:
'I love You Lord.'

**568**
Ian Smale.
Copyright © Kingsway's
Thankyou Music 1987.

**WE ARE IN GOD'S ARMY,**
*We are in the army of the Lord, yeah, yeah,
yeah.
We are in God's army,
We're in the Glorie, Glorie, Glorie, the Glorie
Company.*

The enemy's attacking, convinced he's gaining
ground,
But the only voice that he can hear is the one
he shouts around;
But we're not fooled by his lies, we know that
he is wrong—
We may be weak as soldiers, but as an army
we are strong.

The enemy's regrouping, as he tries another
plan,
He can't pick off an army but he can pick out a
man;
So we'll stay close together, and sing this
battle-song—
We may be weak as soldiers, but as an army
we are strong.

The enemy's realising that his future's looking
poor,
Though he loves single combat, he's already
lost the war;
United, not divided, together we belong—
We may be weak as soldiers, but as an army
we are strong.

**569**
Geron Davis.
Copyright © Meadowgreen Music Co/
U.N. Publishing/CopyCare Ltd 1983.

**WE ARE STANDING** on holy ground,
And I know that there are angels all around.
Let us praise Jesus now.
We are standing in His presence on holy
ground.

**570**
John Pantry.
Copyright © Kingsway's
Thankyou Music 1990.

**WE ARE THE HANDS OF GOD,**
Our task to do His will,
Lay our hands upon this world,
And by His Spirit see it healed.

*We are the Church invincible,
The flesh and blood of Christ.
We are the Gospel visible,
Our lives the Saviour's light to the world.*

We are the word of God,
And by the things we say
This world will judge the Prince of life
And be drawn in or turn away.

We are the feet of God,
Who walk the narrow way,
And every step we take is watched
By those for whom we fast and pray.

Though persecution comes,
And governments oppose,
Beneath the crushing weight of law
The church of Jesus grows and grows.

**571**
David Fellingham.
Copyright © Kingsway's
Thankyou Music 1986.

**WE ARE YOUR PEOPLE** who are called by Your
name.
We call upon You now to declare Your fame.
In this nation of darkness You've called us to
be light.
As we seek Your face, Lord, stir up Your might.
Build Your church and heal this land,
Let Your kingdom come.
Build Your church and heal this land,
Let Your will be done.

**572**
Graham Kendrick.
Copyright © Kingsway's
Thankyou Music 1986.

**WE BELIEVE** in God the Father,
Maker of the universe,
And in Christ His Son our Saviour,
Come to us by virgin birth.
We believe He died to save us,
Bore our sins, was crucified.
Then from death He rose victorious,
Ascended to the Father's side.

*Jesus, Lord of all, Lord of all,
Jesus, Lord of all, Lord of all,
Jesus, Lord of all, Lord of all,
Jesus, Lord of all, Lord of all.
Name above all names,
Name above all names.
(Last time only)
Name above all names.*

We believe He sends His Spirit,
On His church with gifts of power.
God His word of truth affirming,
Sends us to the nations now.
He will come again in glory,
Judge the living and the dead.
Every knee shall bow before Him,
Then must every tongue confess.

**573**
Chris Rolinson.
Copyright © The Central Board of
Finance of the C of E 1980/1988.

**WE BREAK THIS BREAD** to share in the body of
Christ: *(Men)*
We break this bread to share in the body of
Christ. *(Women)*

*Though we are many, we are one body,*
*Because we all share, we all share in one*
*bread.*
(Repeat)

We drink this cup to share in the body of
Christ: *(Men)*
We drink this cup to share in the body of
Christ. *(Women)*

**574** Kirk Dearman.
Copyright © Stamps-Baxter Music/
U.N. Music Publishing Ltd/CopyCare Ltd 1981.

## WE BRING THE SACRIFICE OF PRAISE
Into the house of the Lord,
We bring the sacrifice of praise
Into the house of the Lord.
We bring the sacrifice of praise
Into the house of the Lord,
We bring the sacrifice of praise
Into the house of the Lord.
And we offer up to You
The sacrifices of thanksgiving,
And we offer up to You
The sacrifices of joy.

**575** Graham Kendrick.
Copyright © Kingsway's
Thankyou Music 1986.

(Men and women in canon)
## WE DECLARE THAT THE KINGDOM OF GOD
## IS HERE,
*We declare that the kingdom of God is here,*
*Among you, among you.*

(Last time)
*We declare that the kingdom of God is*
*here* (Men)
*We declare that the kingdom of God is*
*here* (Women)
*We declare that the* (Men)
*Kingdom of God is here.* (All)

The blind see, the deaf hear,
The lame men are walking;
Sicknesses flee at His voice.
The dead live again,
And the poor hear the good news:
Jesus is King, so rejoice!

 Pete Roe.
Copyright © Kingsway's
Thankyou Music 1985.

## WE DECLARE THERE'S ONLY ONE LORD,
And the earth belongs to Him,
We proclaim the day of salvation,
It's His kingdom and He's the King.

There is none like our mighty King,
He gave His life to free us.
There is none more worthy of
Our lives and our allegiance.

**577** Malcolm du Plessis.
Copyright © Kingsway's
Thankyou Music 1984.

## WE DECLARE YOUR MAJESTY,
We proclaim that Your name is exalted;
For You reign magnificently,
Rule victoriously
And Your power is shown throughout the
earth.
And we exclaim our God is mighty,
Lift up Your name, for You are holy.
Sing it again, all honour and glory,
In adoration we bow before Your throne.

**578** David Fellingham.
Copyright © Kingsway's
Thankyou Music 1987.

## WE EXTOL YOU, our God and King.
We bless Your name
For ever and for ever,
For You open up Your hand
And shower us with goodness,
Your mercy and Your grace
Are freely lavished on us.

*So we sing Your praise, (Jesus is Lord)*
*We extol Your name, (Jesus is Lord)*
*Tell the glory of Your kingdom and Your*
*mighty power;*
*Clothed in majesty, (Jesus is Lord)*
*Reigning sovereignly, (Jesus is Lord)*
*Your greatness is unsearchable, O God.*

 Bruce Ballinger.
Copyright © Sound III Inc./
Word Music (UK)/CopyCare Ltd 1976.

## WE HAVE COME INTO THIS PLACE
And gathered in His Name to worship Him,
We have come into this place
And gathered in His Name to worship Him,
We have come into this place
And gathered in His Name
To worship Christ the Lord,
Worship Him, Christ the Lord.

So forget about yourself
And concentrate on Him and worship Him,
So forget about yourself
And concentrate on Him and worship Him,
So forget about yourself
And concentrate on Him
And worship Christ the Lord,
Worship Him, Christ the Lord.

He is all my righteousness,
I stand complete in Him and worship Him,
He is all my righteousness,
I stand complete in Him and worship Him,
He is all my righteousness,
I stand complete in Him
And worship Christ the Lord,
Worship Him, Christ the Lord.

Let us lift up holy hands
And magnify His Name and worship Him,
Let us lift up holy hands
And magnify His Name and worship Him,
Let us lift up holy hands
And magnify His Name
And worship Christ the Lord,
Worship Him, Christ the Lord.

**580**

## WE HAVE COME TO MOUNT ZION,
To the city of the living God,
To Jesus our Redeemer,
And the sprinkling of His blood.
We're part of a kingdom that cannot be shaken,
We've got a foundation that cannot be moved;
So let us praise Him,
Hallelujah,
Let us praise the living God.

Now we draw near to Him by faith,
Come through the veil,
For Jesus brings us by His new and living way
   into His holy place.
So let us come with boldness to the very
   throne of God the Father,
Enter in with confidence to meet Him face to
   face.

**581**

## WE KNOW THAT ALL THINGS work together
   for our good
For good to those who love the Lord;
For God has called us to be just like His Son,
To live and walk according to His word.

*We are more than conquerors,*
*We are more than conquerors,*
*Through Christ, through Christ.*

I am persuaded that neither death nor life,
Nor angels, principalities, nor powers,
Nor things that are now, nor things that are to
   come,
Can separate us from the love of Christ.

If God is for us, who against us can prevail?
No one can bring a charge against His chosen
   ones;
And there will be no separation from our Lord,
He has justified us through His precious blood.

**582**

## WE'LL SING A NEW SONG of glorious triumph,
For we see the government of God in our lives.
We'll sing a new song of glorious triumph,
For we see the government of God in our lives.
He is crowned, God of the whole world
   crowned,
King of creation crowned,
Ruling the nations now.
Yes, He is crowned, God of the whole world
   crowned,
King of creation crowned,
Ruling the nations now.

**583**

## WE'LL WALK THE LAND,
With hearts on fire,
And every step
Will be a prayer.
Hope is rising,
New day dawning,
Sound of singing
Fills the air.

Two thousand years
And still the flame
Is burning bright
Across the land.
Hearts are waiting,
Longing, aching,
For awakening
Once again.

   *Let the flame burn brighter*
   *In the heart of the darkness,*
   *Turning night to glorious day.*
   *Let the song grow louder*
   *As our love grows stronger,*
   *Let it shine, let it shine.*
      *(Last time)*
   *Let it shine, let it shine.*

We'll walk for truth,
Speak out for love.
In Jesus' name
We shall be strong.
To lift the fallen,
To save the children,
To fill the nation
With Your song.

**584**

## WE PLACE YOU ON THE HIGHEST PLACE,
For You are the Great High Priest,
We place You high above all else;
And we come to You and worship at Your feet.

**585** Matthias Claudius.
Tr. Jane M. Campbell.

**WE PLOUGH THE FIELDS** and scatter
The good seed on the land,
But it is fed and watered
By God's almighty hand;
He sends the snow in winter,
The warmth to swell the grain,
The breezes and the sunshine,
And soft refreshing rain.

*All good gifts around us*
*Are sent from heaven above;*
*Then thank the Lord, O thank the Lord,*
*For all His love.*

He only is the Maker
Of all things near and far;
He paints the wayside flower,
He lights the evening star;
The winds and waves obey Him,
By Him the birds are fed;
Much more to us, His children,
He gives our daily bread.

We thank Thee, then, O Father,
For all things bright and good;
The seed-time and the harvest,
Our life, our health, our food.
No gifts have we to offer
For all Thy love imparts,
But that which Thou desirest,
Our humble, thankful hearts.

**586** Ed Baggett.
Copyright © Celebration/
Kingsway's Thankyou Music 1974, 1975.

**WE REALLY WANT TO THANK YOU LORD,**
*We really want to bless Your name,*
*Hallelujah! Jesus is our King!*
*We really want to thank You Lord,*
*We really want to bless Your name,*
*Hallelujah! Jesus is our King!*

We thank You Lord, for Your gift to us,
Your life so rich beyond compare,
The gift of Your body here on earth
Of which we sing and share.

We thank You Lord for our life together,
To live and move in the love of Christ,
Tenderness which sets us free
To serve You with our lives.

**587** E. G. Cherry.

**WE REST ON THEE, OUR SHIELD AND OUR
DEFENDER!**
We go not forth alone against the foe;
Strong in Thy strength, safe in Thy keeping
tender,
We rest on Thee, and in Thy name we go.
Strong in Thy strength, safe in Thy keeping
tender,
We rest on Thee, and in Thy name we go.

Yes, in Thy name, O Captain of salvation!
In Thy dear name, all other names above,
Jesus our Righteousness, our sure Foundation,
Our Prince of glory and our King of love.
Jesus our Righteousness, our sure Foundation,
Our Prince of glory and our King of love.

We go in faith, our own great weakness feeling,
And needing more each day Thy grace to
know:
Yet from our hearts a song of triumph pealing;
We rest on Thee, and in Thy name we go.
Yet from our hearts a song of triumph pealing;
We rest on Thee, and in Thy name we go.

We rest on Thee, our Shield and our Defender!
Thine is the battle, Thine shall be the praise;
When passing through the gates of pearly
splendour,
Victors, we rest with Thee, through endless
days.
When passing through the gates of pearly
splendour,
Victors, we rest with Thee, through endless
days.

**588** Joan Parsons.
Copyright © Kingsway's
Thankyou Music 1978.

**WE SHALL BE AS ONE,**
We shall be as one,
He the Father of us all,
We His chosen sons;
And by His command
Take each other's hand,
Live our lives in unity.
We shall be as one.

We shall be as one,
We shall be as one;
And by this shall all men know
Of the work He has done.
Love will take us on
Through His precious Son;
Love of Him who first loved us.
We shall be as one.

**589** Graham Kendrick.
Copyright © Make Way Music 1988.

**WE SHALL STAND**
*With our feet on the Rock.*
*Whatever men may say,*
*We'll lift Your name up high.*
*And we shall walk*
*Through the darkest night.*
*Setting our faces like flint,*
*We'll walk into the light.*

Lord, You have chosen me
For fruitfulness,
To be transformed into
Your likeness.
I'm gonna fight on through
'Till I see You, face to face.

Lord, as Your witnesses
You've appointed us.
And with Your Holy Spirit
Anointed us.
And so I'll fight on through,
'Till I see You, face to face.

**590** Twila Paris.
Copyright © Singspiration Music Inc/
U.N. Music Publishing Ltd/CopyCare Ltd 1982.

**WE WILL GLORIFY** the King of kings,
We will glorify the Lamb;
We will glorify the Lord of lords,
Who is the great 'I Am'.

Lord Jehovah reigns in majesty,
We will bow before His throne;
We will worship Him in righteousness,
We worship Him alone.

He is Lord of heaven, Lord of earth,
He is Lord of all who live;
He is Lord above the universe,
All praise to Him we give.

Hallelujah to the King of kings,
Hallelujah to the Lamb;
Hallelujah to the Lord of lords,
Who is the great 'I Am'.

**591** Phil Lawson Johnston.
Copyright © Kingsway's
Thankyou Music 1987.

**WE WILL HONOUR YOU,** *we will honour*
*You,*
*We will exalt the Holy One of Israel.*
*We will honour You, yes, we will honour*
*You,*
*We will enthrone You in our praise.*

You are the Alpha and Omega;
You are the beginning and the end.
There is no other we can turn to,
No other rock on which we can depend.

You will not share Your praise with idols;
All glory belongs to You alone.
Who in the skies can be compared with
The Lord Almighty Father God and King?

All of the earth will bow before You;
They will be left no place to hide.
No longer Satan's rule of darkness,
But the name of Jesus ever glorified.

**592** Ge Baas.
Copyright © Kingsway's
Thankyou Music 1983.

**WE WORSHIP AND ADORE YOU,**
Christ our King. (Christ our King.)
We worship and adore You,
Christ our King. (Christ our King.)
And we follow You together,
We follow You together,
And we follow You together
Christ our King. (Christ our King.)

**593**  Joseph M. Scriven.

**WHAT A FRIEND WE HAVE IN JESUS,**
All our sins and griefs to bear!
What a privilege to carry
Everything to God in prayer!
O what peace we often forfeit!
O what needless pain we bear!
All because we do not carry
Everything to God in prayer.

Have we trials and temptations?
Is there trouble anywhere?
We should never be discouraged;
Take it to the Lord in prayer.
Can we find a friend so faithful
Who will all our sorrows share?
Jesus knows our every weakness;
Take it to the Lord in prayer.

Are we weak and heavy-laden,
Cumbered with a load of care?
Precious Saviour, still our refuge,
Take it to the Lord in prayer.
Do thy friends despise, forsake thee?
Take it to the Lord in prayer;
In His arms He'll take and shield thee,
Thou wilt find a solace there.

**594** Keri Jones & David Matthews.
Copyright © Springtide/
Word Music (UK)/CopyCare Ltd 1978.

**WHEN I FEEL THE TOUCH**
Of Your hand upon my life,
It causes me to sing a song
That I love You, Lord.
So from deep within
My spirit singeth unto Thee,
You are my King, You are my God,
And I love You, Lord.

**595** Wayne & Cathy Perrin.
Copyright © Integrity's Hosanna! Music.
Adm. Kingsway's Thankyou Music 1980.

**WHEN I LOOK INTO YOUR HOLINESS,**
When I gaze into Your loveliness,
When all things that surround
Become shadows in the light of You;
When I've found the joy of reaching Your heart,
When my will becomes enthralled in Your love,
When all things that surround
Become shadows in the light of You:

I worship You, I worship You,
The reason I live is to worship You.
I worship You, I worship You,
The reason I live is to worship You.

**596**  Isaac Watts.

**WHEN I SURVEY THE WONDROUS CROSS**
On which the Prince of glory died,
My richest gain I count but loss,
And pour contempt on all my pride.

Forbid it, Lord, that I should boast,
Save in the death of Christ my God:
All the vain things that charm me most,
I sacrifice them to His blood.

See from His head, His hands, His feet,
Sorrow and love flow mingled down:
Did e'er such love and sorrow meet,
Or thorns compose so rich a crown?

Were the whole realm of Nature mine,
That were an offering far too small;
Love so amazing, so divine,
Demands my soul, my life, my all!

## 597 Tr. Edward Caswall.

### WHEN MORNING GILDS THE SKIES
My heart awaking cries:
'May Jesus Christ be praised!'
Alike at work and prayer
To Jesus I repair:
'May Jesus Christ be praised!'

Does sadness fill my mind?
A solace here I find:
'May Jesus Christ be praised!'
When evil thoughts molest,
With this I shield my breast:
'May Jesus Christ be praised!'

To God, the Word, on high
The hosts of angels cry:
'May Jesus Christ be praised!'
Let mortals, too, upraise
Their voice in hymns of praise:
'May Jesus Christ be praised!'

Let earth's wide circle round
In joyful notes resound:
'May Jesus Christ be praised!'
Let air, and sea, and sky,
From depth to height, reply:
'May Jesus Christ be praised!'

Be this while life is mine
My canticle divine:
'May Jesus Christ be praised!'
Be this the eternal song,
Through all the ages long:
'May Jesus Christ be praised!'

## 598 Author unknown.

### WHEN THE SPIRIT OF THE LORD is within my heart
I will sing as David sang.
When the Spirit of the Lord is within my heart
I will sing as David sang.
I will sing, I will sing,
I will sing as David sang.
I will sing, I will sing,
I will sing as David sang.

When the Spirit of the Lord is within my heart,
I will clap...dance...praise...(etc.)

## 599 John Henry Sammis.

### WHEN WE WALK WITH THE LORD
In the light of His Word,
What a glory He sheds on our way!
While we do His good will,
He abides with us still,
And with all who will trust and obey!

*Trust and obey!*
*For there's no other way*
*To be happy in Jesus,*
*But to trust and obey.*

Not a shadow can rise,
Not a cloud in the skies,
But His smile quickly drives it away;
Not a doubt nor a fear,
Not a sigh nor a tear,
Can abide while we trust and obey!

Not a burden we bear,
Not a sorrow we share,
But our toil He doth richly repay:
Not a grief nor a loss,
Not a frown nor a cross,
But is blessed if we trust and obey!

But we never can prove
The delights of His love
Until all on the altar we lay;
For the favour He shows,
And the joy He bestows,
Are for those who will trust and obey.

Then in fellowship sweet
We will sit at His feet,
Or we'll walk by His side in the way;
What He says we will do,
Where He sends we will go;
Never fear, only trust and obey!

## 600 Author unknown.

### WHERE YOU GO I WILL GO,
Where you lodge I will lodge,
Do not ask me to turn away,
For I will follow you.
We'll serve the Lord together
And praise Him day to day,
For He brought us together
To love Him and serve Him always.

**WHETHER YOU'RE ONE** or whether you're two
Or three or four or five,
Six or seven or eight or nine it's good to be
  alive.
It really doesn't matter how old you are,
Jesus loves you whoever you are.

*La, la, la, la, la, la, la, la, la,
Jesus loves us all.*

Whether you're big or whether you're small
Or somewhere in-between,
First in the class or middle or last,
We're all the same to Him.
It really doesn't matter how clever you are,
Jesus loves you whoever you are.

**602**

**WHILE SHEPHERDS WATCHED** their flocks by
  night,
All seated on the ground,
The angel of the Lord came down
And glory shone around.

'Fear not' said he, for mighty dread
Had seized their troubled mind;
'Glad tidings of great joy I bring
To you and all mankind.'

'To you in David's town this day
Is born of David's line
A Saviour, who is Christ the Lord,
And this shall be the sign.'

'The heavenly babe you there shall find
To human view displayed,
All meanly wrapped in swaddling bands,
And in a manger laid.'

Thus spoke the seraph; and forthwith
Appeared a shining throng
Of angels, praising God, who thus
Addressed their joyful song:

'All glory be to God on high
And on the earth be peace;
Goodwill henceforth from heaven to men
Begin and never cease.'

**603**

**WHO CAN EVER SAY THEY UNDERSTAND**
All the wonders of His master plan?
Christ came down and gave Himself to man
For evermore.

He was Lord before all time began,
Yet made Himself the sacrificial lamb,
Perfect love now reconciled to man
For evermore.

*For evermore we'll sing the story
Of love come down
For evermore the King of glory
We will crown.*

He is coming back to earth again,
Every knee shall bow before His name,
'Christ is Lord', let thankful hearts proclaim
For evermore.

**604**

**WHO CAN SOUND THE DEPTHS OF SORROW**
In the Father heart of God,
For the children we've rejected,
For the lives so deeply scarred?
And each light that we've extinguished
Has brought darkness to our land,
Upon our nation, upon our nation,
Have mercy Lord.

We have scorned the truth You gave us,
We have bowed to other lords.
We have sacrificed the children
On the altars of our gods.
O let truth again shine on us,
Let Your holy fear descend.
Upon our nation, upon our nation,
Have mercy, Lord.

*(Men only)*
Who can stand before Your anger?
Who can face Your piercing eyes?
For You love the weak and helpless,
And You hear the victims' cries.
  *(All)*
Yes, You are a God of justice,
And Your judgement surely comes.
Upon our nation, upon our nation,
Have mercy, Lord.

*(Women only)*
Who will stand against the violence?
Who will comfort those who mourn?
In an age of cruel rejection,
Who will build for love a home?
  *(All)*
Come and shake us into action,
Come and melt our hearts of stone.
Upon Your people, upon Your people,
Have mercy, Lord.

Who can sound the depths of mercy
In the Father heart of God?
For there is a Man of sorrows
Who for sinners shed His blood.
He can heal the wounds of nations,
He can wash the guilty clean.
Because of Jesus, because of Jesus,
Have mercy, Lord.

**605** Benjamin R. Hanby.

**WHO IS HE IN YONDER STALL,**
At whose feet the shepherds fall?

*'Tis the Lord!*
*O wondrous story!*
*'Tis the Lord, the King of glory!*
*At His feet we humbly fall.*
*Crown Him! Crown Him, Lord of all!*

Who is He to whom they bring
All the sick and sorrowing?

Who is He that stands and weeps
At the grave where Lazarus sleeps?

Who is He on yonder tree
Dies in pain and agony?

Who is He who from the grave
Comes to rescue, help, and save?

Who is He who from His throne
Sends the Spirit to His own?

Who is He who comes again,
Judge of angels and of men?

**606** Judy Horner-Montemayor.
Copyright © Integrity's Hosanna! Music.
Adm. Kingsway's Thankyou Music 1975.

**WHO IS LIKE UNTO THEE,**
O Lord amongst gods?
Who is like unto Thee, glorious in holiness,
Fearful in praises, doing wonders?
Who is like unto Thee?

**607** Frances R. Havergal.

**WHO IS ON THE LORD'S SIDE?**
Who will serve the King?
Who will be His helpers
Other lives to bring?
Who will leave the world's side?
Who will face the foe?
Who is on the Lord's side?
Who for Him will go?
By Thy call of mercy,
By Thy grace divine,
We are on the Lord's side,
Saviour, we are Thine.

Jesus, Thou hast bought us
Not with gold or gem,
But with Thine own life-blood,
For Thy diadem.
With Thy blessing filling
Each who comes to Thee
Thou hast made us willing,
Thou hast made us free.
By Thy grand redemption,
By Thy grace divine,
We are on the Lord's side
Saviour, we are Thine.

Fierce may be the conflict,
Strong may be the foe,
But the King's own army
None can overthrow;
Round His standard ranging
Victory is secure;
For His truth unchanging
Makes the triumph sure.
Joyfully enlisting,
By Thy grace divine,
We are on the Lord's side,
Saviour, we are Thine.

Chosen to be soldiers
In an alien land,
Chosen, called, and faithful,
For our Captain's band;
In the service royal
Let us not grow cold,
Let us be right loyal
Noble, true, and bold.
Master, Thou wilt keep us,
By Thy grace divine,
Always on the Lord's side,
Saviour, always Thine.

**608** Phil Rogers.
Copyright © Kingsway's
Thankyou Music 1984.

**WHO IS THIS** that grows like the dawn,
As bright as the sun, as fair as the moon?
Who is this that grows like the dawn,
As awesome as an army, as an army with
banners?

*It is the church in the eyes of the Lord,*
*The bride of Christ preparing for her King.*

Washed in His blood and clothed in
righteousness,
Anointed with the Spirit and waiting for her
Lord.
Who is this that grows like the dawn,
As awesome as an army, as an army with
banners?

**609** Jane & Betsy Clowe.
Copyright © Celebration/
Kingsway's Thankyou Music 1974, 1975.

**WIND, WIND, BLOW ON ME,**
*Wind, wind, set me free,*
*Wind, wind, my Father sent*
*The blessed Holy Spirit.*

Jesus told us all about You,
How we could not live without You,
With His blood the power bought,
To help us live the life He taught.

When we're weary, You console us;
When we're lonely You enfold us;
When in danger You uphold us,
Blessed Holy Spirit.

When unto the Church You came
It was not Your own but Jesus' name.
Jesus Christ is still the same,
He sends the Holy Spirit.

Set us free to love our brothers;
Set us free to live for others,
That the world the Son might see,
And Jesus' name exalted be.

**610**

**WITH ALL MY HEART** I thank You Lord.
With all my heart I thank You Lord,
For this bread and wine we break,
For this sacrament we take,
For the forgiveness that You make,
I thank You Lord.

With all my soul I thank You Lord.
With all my soul I thank You Lord,
For this victory that You've won,
For this taste of things to come,
For this love that makes us one,
I thank You Lord.

With all my voice I thank You Lord.
With all my voice I thank You Lord,
For the sacrifice of pain,
For the Spirit and the flame,
For the power of Your name,
I thank You Lord.

**611**

**WITH MY WHOLE HEART** I will praise You,
Holding nothing back, Hallelujah!
You have made me glad and now
I come with open arms to thank You,
With my heart embrace, Hallelujah!
I can see Your face is smiling.
With my whole life I will serve You
Captured by Your love, Hallelujah!
Oh amazing love, Oh amazing love!

Lord Your heart is overflowing
With a love divine, Hallelujah!
And this love is mine for ever.
Now Your joy has set You laughing
As You join the song, Hallelujah!
Heaven sings along, I hear the
Voices swell to great crescendos
Praising Your great love, Hallelujah!
Oh amazing love, Oh amazing love!

Come O Bridegroom, clothed in splendour,
My Beloved One, Hallelujah!
How I long to run and meet You.
You're the fairest of ten thousand,
You're my life and breath, Hallelujah!
Love as strong as death has won me.
All the rivers, all the oceans
Cannot quench this love, Hallelujah!
Oh amazing love, Oh amazing love!

**612**

**WONDERFUL LOVE** coming to me,
Wonderful grace, freedom and mercy;
Bought with a price, death on a cross,
Wonderful love, Jesus, You've given to me.

You are Christ, Son of God,
Suffering Lamb, pouring out Your life;
You've conquered death,
And You're reigning supreme in my life.

**613**

**WORSHIP THE LORD!** In His presence we
    stand;
He cares for you and He understands.
Come Holy Spirit, reaching us now;
Grace, joy and peace, love abound.

*Holy, holy, holy is the Lord.*

(Additional choruses)
*Worthy…*
*Mighty…*

**614**

**WORTHY ART THOU,** O Lord our God,
Of honour and power,
For You are reigning now on high, Hallelujah!
Jesus is Lord of all the earth,
Hallelujah, Hallelujah, Hallelujah!

**615**

**WORTHY IS THE LAMB SEATED ON THE
    THRONE,**
Worthy is the Lamb who was slain,
To receive power and riches
And wisdom and strength,
Honour and glory, glory and praise,
For ever and evermore.

**616**

**WORTHY IS THE LAMB WHO WAS SLAIN.**
Worthy is the Lamb who was slain,
Who was slain.
Worthy is the Lamb who was slain,
Who was slain.

*To receive power and wealth,*
*To receive wisdom and strength.*
*To receive honour and glory.*
*To receive glory and praise.*

Now to Him who sits on the throne
And to the Lamb who was slain,
Now be praise and honour and glory,
And power for ever,
And power for ever.

*Worthy of power and wealth,*
*Worthy of wisdom and strength.*
*Worthy of honour and glory,*
*Worthy of glory and praise.*

(Final Chorus)
*Unto the Lamb be power and wealth,*
*Unto the Lamb be wisdom and strength.*
*Unto the Lamb be honour and glory,*
*Unto the Lamb be glory and praise.*

**617**

**WORTHY, O WORTHY ARE YOU LORD,**
Worthy to be thanked and praised
And worshipped and adored.
Worthy, O worthy are You Lord,
Worthy to be thanked and praised
And worshipped and adored.

Singing Hallelujah, Lamb upon the throne,
We worship and adore You, make Your glory
known.
Hallelujah, glory to the King:
You're more than a conqueror,
You're Lord of everything.

**618**

**WORTHY, THE LORD IS WORTHY,**
And no one understands the greatness of His
name.
Gracious, so kind and gracious,
And slow to anger, and rich, so rich in love.

*My mouth will speak in praise of my Lord,*
*Let every creature praise His holy name.*
*For ever, and evermore.*
*For ever, and evermore.*
*For ever, and evermore.*
*For ever, and evermore.*

Faithful, the Lord is faithful
To all His promises, and loves all He has made.
Righteous, in all ways righteous,
And He is near to all who call on Him in truth.

**619**

**YE HOLY ANGELS BRIGHT,**
Who wait at God's right hand,
Or through the realms of light
Fly at your Lord's command,
Assist our song,
Or else the theme too high
Doth seem for mortal tongue.

Ye blessèd souls at rest,
Who see your Saviour's face,
Whose glory, e'en the least
Is far above our grace,
God's praises sound,
As in His sight
With sweet delight
Ye do abound.

Ye saints who toil below,
Adore your heavenly King,
And onward as ye go,
Some joyful anthem sing;
Take what He gives,
And praise Him still
Through good and ill,
Who ever lives.

My soul, bear thou thy part,
Triumph in God above,
And with a well-tuned heart
Sing thou the songs of love.
Let all thy days
Till life shall end,
Whate'er He send,
Be filled with praise.

**620**

**YE SERVANTS OF GOD,**
Your Master proclaim,
And publish abroad
His wonderful name;
The name all-victorious
Of Jesus extol;
His kingdom is glorious
And rules over all.

God ruleth on high,
Almighty to save;
And still He is nigh,
His presence we have;
The great congregation
His triumph shall sing,
Ascribing salvation
To Jesus our King.

Salvation to God,
Who sits on the throne!
Let all cry aloud,
And honour the Son;
The praises of Jesus
The angels proclaim,
Fall down on their faces,
And worship the Lamb.

Then let us adore,
And give Him His right,
All glory and power,
All wisdom and might,
All honour and blessing,
With angels above,
And thanks never ceasing,
And infinite love.

**621**

YOU ARE BEAUTIFUL beyond description,
Too marvellous for words,
Too wonderful for comprehension
Like nothing ever seen or heard.
Who can grasp Your infinite wisdom?
Who can fathom the depth of Your love?
You are beautiful beyond description,
Majesty, enthroned above.

And I stand, I stand in awe of You.
I stand, I stand in awe of You.
Holy God, to whom all praise is due,
I stand in awe of You.

**622**

YOU ARE COMPASSIONATE and gracious,
Patient and abounding in love;
As far as the East is from the West
You took the sins we were guilty of.
And You deal tenderly with us,
And You deal tenderly with us.

And higher than the heavens,
So great is Your love;
Yes, higher than the heavens
Is Your love for us.

**623**

YOU ARE CROWNED WITH MANY CROWNS,
And rule all things in righteousness,
You are crowned with many crowns,
Upholding all things by Your word.
You rule in power and reign in glory!
You are Lord of heaven and earth!
You are Lord of all,
You are Lord of all.

**624**

YOU ARE HERE and I behold Your beauty,
Your glory fills this place.
Calm my heart to hear You,
Cause my eyes to see You.
Your presence here is the answer
To the longing of my heart.

I lift my voice to worship and exalt You,
For You alone are worthy.
A captive now set free
Your kingdom's come to me.
Glory in the highest,
My heart cries unto You.

**625**

YOU ARE MY HIDING PLACE,
You always fill my heart with songs of
    deliverance,
Whenever I am afraid
I will trust in You.
I will trust in You;
Let the weak say I am strong
In the strength of my God.

**626**

YOU ARE THE HOLY ONE,
The Lord Most High,
You reign in majesty,
You reign on high.

You are the Worthy One
Lamb that was slain,
You bought us with Your blood,
And with You we'll reign.

*We exalt Your name,*
*High and Mighty One of Israel,*
*We exalt Your name.*
*Lead us on to war,*
*In the power of Your name,*
*We exalt Your name*
*The Name above all names,*
*Our victorious King,*
*We exalt Your name.*

You are the King of kings
The Lord of lords;
All men will bow to You,
Before Your throne.

**627**

YOU ARE THE KING OF GLORY,
You are the Prince of Peace,
You are the Lord of heaven and earth,
You're the Sun of righteousness.
Angels bow down before You,
Worship and adore, for
You have the words of eternal life,
You are Jesus Christ the Lord.

Hosanna to the Son of David!
Hosanna to the King of kings!
Glory in the highest heaven,
For Jesus the Messiah reigns.

**628**

YOU ARE THE MIGHTY KING,
The living Word;
Master of everything,
You are the Lord.

And I praise Your name,
And I praise Your name.

You are Almighty God,
Saviour and Lord;
Wonderful Counsellor,
You are the Lord.

And I praise Your name,
And I praise Your name.

You are the Prince of Peace,
Emmanuel;
Everlasting Father,
You are the Lord.

And I love Your name,
And I love Your name.

You are the Mighty King,
The living Word;
Master of everything,
You are the Lord.

**629** Danny Daniels & Randy Rigby
Copyright © Mercy Publishing/
Kingsway's Thankyou Music 1982.

**YOU ARE THE VINE,**
*We are the branches,*
*Keep us abiding in You.*
*You are the Vine,*
*We are the branches,*
*Keep us abiding in You.*

Then we'll grow in Your love,
Then we'll go in Your name,
That the world will surely know
That You have power to heal and to save.

**630** John Daniel Lawtum.
Copyright © Jaydee Music/
Sovereign Lifestyle Music Ltd 1982.

**YOU ARE WORTHY,**
Lord, You're worthy,
So I lift my heart, I lift my voice and cry 'Holy'.
You have saved me, and I love You,
Jesus ever more I live to praise Your name.

**631** Mark Altrogge.
Copyright © People of Destiny/
CopyCare Ltd 1985.

**YOU DID NOT WAIT FOR ME** to draw near to
    You,
But You clothed Yourself in frail humanity.
You did not wait for me to cry out to You,
But You let me hear Your voice calling me.

And I'm for ever grateful to You,
I'm for ever grateful for the cross;
I'm for ever grateful to You
That You came to seek and save the lost.

**632** Bob Kauflin.
Copyright © People of Destiny/
CopyCare Ltd 1988.

**YOU HAVE BEEN GIVEN** the Name above all
    names,
And we worship You, yes we worship You.
You have been given the Name above all
    names,
And we worship You,
Yes we worship You.

We are Your people, made for Your glory,
And we worship You, yes we worship You.
We are Your people, made for Your glory,
And we worship You,
And we worship You.

You have redeemed us from every nation,
And we worship You, yes we worship You.
You have redeemed us from every nation,
And we worship You,
And we worship You.

**633** Noel Richards.
Copyright © Kingsway's
Thankyou Music 1985.

**YOU LAID ASIDE YOUR MAJESTY,**
Gave up everything for me,
Suffered at the hands of those You had
    created.
You took all my guilt and shame,
When You died and rose again;
Now today You reign,
In heaven and earth exalted.

I really want to worship You, my Lord,
You have won my heart
And I am Yours for ever and ever;
I will love You.
You are the only one who died for me,
Gave Your life to set me free,
So I lift my voice to You in adoration.

**634** Patricia Morgan & Sue Rinaldi.
Copyright © Kingsway's Thankyou Music 1990.

**YOU MAKE MY HEART FEEL GLAD.**
*You make my heart feel glad.*
*Jesus, You bring me joy;*
*You make my heart feel glad.*

Lord, Your love brings healing and a peace into
    my heart,
I want to give myself in praise to You.
Though I've been through heartache
You have understood my tears,
O Lord, I will give thanks to You.

When I look around me, and I see the life You
    made,
All creation shouts aloud in praise;
I realise Your greatness, how majestic is Your
    name,
O Lord, I love You more each day.

**635**
Mark Veary & Paul Oakley.
Copyright © Kingsway's
Thankyou Music 1986.

**YOU, O LORD,** rich in mercy,
Because of Your great love.
You, O Lord, so loved us,
Even when we were dead in our sins.

*(Men)*
You made us alive together with Christ,
And raised us up together with Him,
And seated us with Him in heavenly places,
And raised us up together with Him,
And seated us with Him in heavenly places in
Christ.

*(Women)*
You made us alive together with Christ,
And raised us up,
And seated us,
And raised us up,
And seated us in Christ.

**636**
John G. Elliot.
Copyright © LCS Songs & Charlie Monk Music/
U.N. Music Publishing Ltd/CopyCare Ltd 1987.

**YOU PURCHASED MEN** with precious blood,
From every nation, tribe and tongue;
Brought from slavery, freed from prison
chains;
Brought through death so they might rise
again,
Born to serve and to reign:

> *Worthy is the Lamb that was slain, to*
> *receive*
> *Highest honour, and glory, and power, and*
> *praise!*
> *Worthy is the Lamb that was slain, to*
> *receive*
> *Highest honour, and glory, and praise!*

Holy, holy to our God,
Who was, and is, and is to come;
Let us join the throng who see His face,
Bowing down to Him both night and day,
Lost in wonder and praise.

**637**
Wes Sutton.
Copyright © Springtide/
Word Music (UK)/CopyCare Ltd 1988.

**YOUR MERCY FLOWS** upon us like a river.
Your mercy stands unshakeable and true.
Most holy God, of all good things the Giver,
We turn and lift our fervent prayer to You.

> *Hear our cry,*   (echo)
> *O Lord,*   (echo)
> *Be merciful*   (echo)
> *Once more;*   (echo)
> *Let Your love*   (echo)
> *Your anger stem,*   (echo)
> *Remember mercy, O Lord, again.*

Your church once great, though standing
clothed in sorrow,
Is even still the bride that You adore;
Revive Your church, that we again may honour
Our God and King, our Master and our Lord.

As we have slept, this nation has been taken
By every sin ever known to man;
So at its gates, though burnt by fire and
broken,
In Jesus' name we come to take our stand.

**638**
Andy Park.
Copyright © Mercy Publishing/
Kingsway's Thankyou Music 1987.

**YOUR WORKS LORD,** (Your works Lord)
Are awesome, (are awesome)
Your power, (Your power)
Is great.
*(Repeat)*

> *Great are Your works Lord,*
> *Great are Your deeds,*
> *Awesome in power,*
> *So awesome to me.*

You will reign, (You will reign)
For ever, (for ever)
In power, (in power)
You will reign.
*(Repeat)*

Because of, (because of)
Your greatness, (Your greatness)
All the earth, (all the earth)
Will sing.
*(Repeat)*

**639**
Mark Altrogge.
Copyright © People of Destiny/
CopyCare Ltd 1984.

**YOU SAT DOWN** at the right hand of the Father
in majesty,
You sat down at the right hand of the Father in
majesty.
You are crowned Lord of all,
You are faithful and righteous and true,
You're my Master, You're my Owner,
And I love serving You.

**640**
Steffi Geiser Rubin & Stuart Dauermann.
Copyright © Lillenas Publishing Co/
Kingsway's Thankyou Music 1975.

**YOU SHALL GO OUT WITH JOY**
And be led forth with peace,
And the mountains and the hills
Shall break forth before you.
There'll be shouts of joy,
And the trees of the field
Shall clap, shall clap their hands.
And the trees of the field shall clap their hands,
And the trees of the field shall clap their hands,
And the trees of the field shall clap their hands,
And you'll go out with joy.

# INDEXES

In *Songs of Fellowship* the songs appear in alphabetical order by first line (letter by letter), for easy use in praise and worship meetings. Indexes of Titles and First Lines and Scriptures both appear in this book.
The music edition features a full complement of indexes, including: Index of Titles and First Lines, showing the key in which each song is played, in bold; Index of Scriptures; Index of Themes; Index of Tunes and Index of Copyright Addresses.

## Index of titles and first lines
Author's titles, where different from first lines, are shown in *italics*.

# Scripture index

This index lists the *key* Bible passages quoted or echoed in the songs, and not every *passing* reference. In many cases the whole Bible passage will repay further exploration, beyond the verses given here.